GLOBALIZATION OF UNEQUAL NATIONAL ECONOMIES

Books by Adam Zwass
published by *M.E. Sharpe*, INC.

Globalization of Unequal National Economies
Players and Controversies

Incomplete Revolutions
The Successes and Failures of Capitalist
Transition Strategies in Post-Communist Economies

From Failed Communism to Underdeveloped Capitalism
Transformation of Eastern Europe, the Post-Soviet Union, and China

The Council for Mutual Economic Assistance
The Thorny Path from Political to Economic Integration

Market, Plan, and State
The Two World Economic Systems

The Economies of Eastern Europe in a Time of Change

Money, Banking, and Credit in the Soviet Union and Eastern Europe

Monetary Cooperation Between East and West

GLOBALIZATION OF UNEQUAL NATIONAL ECONOMIES

PLAYERS AND CONTROVERSIES

ADAM ZWASS

M.E. Sharpe
Armonk, New York
London, England

Translated by Michel Vale.

Library of Congress Cataloging-in-Publication Data

Zwass, Adam
Globalization of unequal national economies : players and controversies / Adam Zwass
p. cm.
Includes bibliographical references and index.
ISBN 0-7656-0731-X (alk. paper)
1. Comparative economics. 2. Economic history—20th century. 3. Post-communism.
4. Postcolonialism. 5. Globalization—Economic aspects—Case studies. I. Title.

HB90.Z89 2002
337—dc21 2001034197

Printed in the United States of America

The paper used in this publication meets the minimum requirements of
American National Standard for Information Sciences
Permanence of Paper for Printed Library Materials,
ANSI Z 39.48-1984.

∞

BM (c) 10 9 8 7 6 5 4 3 2 1

Remembering Adam Zwass: 1913–2001

One of the most extraordinary events of Adam Zwass's life took place when he was barely twenty. His family had moved from Cisna to Lvov. Poland was then beset by the disabling world economic crisis and its own ineffectual military dictatorship. The ancient tradition of anti-Semitism repeatedly erupted in violence. Many enlightened young people had no recourse but to join the organized opposition. Adam Zwass became district leader of the Communist Party. He led a street demonstration and was shot in the stomach and left for dead. Of course, a person does not survive by willpower alone. But anyone who knew Adam Zwass knows that willpower had a lot to do with it.

He spent six years in Sieradz political prison, turned into a university by its earnest occupants. That was the beginning of his higher education. This episode ended in 1939, when Soviet and German armies advanced from east and west. The Russians arrived first, but the prisoners had already liberated themselves. Characteristically, Soviet ideologues sent Zwass to the Urals as an untrustworthy individual, but then they regarded most foreign Communists as untrustworthy. There he became commissar of a construction battalion and by choice starved more than the others.

In the upheaval after World War II, Adam Zwass became an executive of the central bank in Lvov and then in Warsaw. He went to Moscow in 1964 to head the financial department of the Council of Mutual Economic Assistance, Comecon, the Eastern Bloc counterpart to the European Common Market. Everyone who knew Zwass will without hesitation attribute these accomplishments to the force of his lifelong decisiveness and prodigious intellect. But with fame, privilege, travel, access, and relative wealth, he still could not endure the repression and resurgent anti-Semitism, even though they passed him by. In 1969 he and his wife Friederika crossed the border into Austria as immigrants.

At the age of fifty-six, again in a foreign land speaking a foreign language, he started all over. But not quite all over. With his intimate knowledge of Comecon, he soon became advisor to the board of the Austrian National Bank on Soviet and Eastern European foreign trade and finance. Here again, in a democratic country, he earned fame, privilege, and access, and finally felt at ease.

Meanwhile, he was writing, writing, writing. I had already published two of his books before I met him in a hotel lobby in Vienna in 1983. I asked my friend Vladimir Zwass how I would recognize his parents. "They will be the two shortest people there," was the answer. Indeed, they were.

But in every other respect, Adam Zwass was exceedingly tall—and so was Friederika. I found that out about Adam when he moved to Saddle River in 1996 to be with his family after Friederika had died. Thereafter we met several times a year at social gatherings and had intense discussions, perhaps being rude to others by our mutual concentration. At last I found the man who knew everything. And seemingly more than everything from first-hand knowledge of events and people in Central Europe and the former Soviet Union. And a man of self-command who wrote, walked, swam, and socialized precisely the hours he chose to, making most of the rest of us with similar aspirations feel like abject failures.

I dare say that a mutual admiration society sprang up. Our views were identical on everything: Communism (a disaster); capitalism (a successful failure); the transitions in Russia (terrible) and China (possibilities, but question mark); Gorbachev (good man, tried hard); Yeltsin (besotted poseur); Putin (black belt in politics, question mark); Jiang Zemin (ruthless, question mark); Clinton (talked the talk, didn't walk the walk).

Here is the essence of Adam Zwass. He started as a communist idealist. He hated what developed. He retained a belief in democratic socialism. He was humane. He was fair. He understood.

I am amazed when I look back and find that *Globalization of Unequal National Economies: Players and Controversies* is the eighth book by Adam Zwass that I have published. He has gotten in a last kick at the worldwide injustice he abhorred. He died while reading the page proofs.

M.E. Sharpe

Note: I am grateful to Vladimir Zwass for much of the information in this remembrance.

Contents

List of Tables

Acknowledgments

Thanks are due to several individuals who have helped me generously with this project. I owe a debt of gratitude to Myron E. Sharpe, who is now the publisher of eight of my books, for his continuing support. Many thanks go to Dr. Robert Schediwy of the Austrian Chamber of Commerce for his efforts in improving the manuscript at various stages of its emergence. I am especially grateful to my son, Professor Vladimir Zwass, for his help in many ways, as well as to Mrs. Miriam Karr, retired vice president of Chase Manhattan Bank, for the many interesting ideas that emerged in our discussions. Mrs. Charlotte Mally is to be thanked for transcribing the partly illegible German manuscript and Mr. Michel Vale for his careful translation.

Introduction

The striving for a world-encompassing globalization is not an exclusive hallmark of the dawn of the third millennium. The greatest impetus toward the internationalization of societal relationships appeared in fact in the fourth century as the Christianity radiating from Europe. Yet the hope that a single religion would put an end to the separation of peoples and bring about a free movement of people, goods, and cultural values has not been fulfilled. The means adopted by the church of Saint Peter led to further polarization of the world. The European wars, some lasting thirty or a hundred years and including the empire-building Napoleonic struggles, fractured that continent.

The next great attempt at the globalization of relationships among nation-states took place in the mid–nineteenth century, when Great Britain lifted the corn laws that limited world trade. Trade, if not becoming entirely free, blossomed. Tensions among nations were, however, greater than prospects of peaceful coexistence and collaboration in a global economy. World War I and the global economic depression extinguished the hopes for a common planetary home. In the aftermath of the war, the Russian October Revolution of 1917 brought forward a destructive alternative to the traditional economic and political relationships.

An enunciated goal of the Soviet Union was to foment world revolution that would bring about an internationalization of the Soviet system. The exclusion of a significant part of the world's land mass from the market system greatly limited the opportunities for market-based globalization. Indeed, recently opened secret Soviet archives clearly confirm the fact. Six years after the October Revolution, the Communist International (Comintern) saw in the devastated Germany its first opportunity. The minutes of the Politburo meeting of October 4, 1923, include the following: "On November 9, 1923, German revolution will bring to power a Communist government as a prelude to world revolution." A commitment was made to send the Soviet army in aid of the revolutionaries. History was not made by these decisions, as we know full well. Stalin had to back off and proclaim the strategy of "socialism in one country."

After the victory in World War II, Stalin effectively cut off Central and Eastern Europe from the world polity, acting on the principle of the Westphalian Peace of three centuries prior: *cuius regio eius religio* (religion is supplied by him who reigns). Following Mao's victory in China in 1949 the autarkic economic system and the authoritarian political system calling itself communism encompassed almost a third of the world population. The Communist globalization alternative was a miscalculation. The bureaucratically managed state economy was no match for the market-driven ones and was drained by military expenditures. The military-industrial complex absorbed 70 percent of the gross domestic product (GDP). "Proletarian internationalism" was no match for market-oriented and democratic societies as a paradigm for globalization. The Soviet empire imploded under its own weight. The alternative world system has ceased to exist. Earlier, in 1978, Deng Xiaoping had declared the establishment of a socialist market economy, with private property and an opening to the external world, as a means to reform the inefficient state economy of China. Ten years later, Vietnam chose to take this road as well.

The computer and Internet revolutions and the development of an information society, as well as capitalism as the universal steering system, have given a strong impetus to globalization. As the third of the world's population has started its return to the framework of Western civilization, the success or failure of that effort holds the fate of the globalization movement in the balance. The outcome in countries with high population such as China and Russia will be of great importance for the progress of globalization. The reforms undertaken by these two countries are, however, vastly different. China has elected to take an evolutionary road. Privatization has been enabled and capital markets have been created, yet the commanding heights are occupied by the state and the Communist Party is the only governing force. So far, this road has proven successful in developing the national economy. The average annual growth rate in recent years has been 7 percent; in the first half of 2000 industrial production grew by 11 percent, to $132.8 billion. According to Bill Clinton, during the twenty years of the reform, 200 million people have been liberated from poverty. Foreign trade and foreign investment have grown significantly; the number of Internet users has quadrupled in recent years and has reached 9 million, and the number was expected to grow to 20 million by the year 2000. In Clinton's words, "By agreeing to work with us on its terms of entry into [the] World Trade Organization, China has chosen to work within the international system."[1]

Russia has chosen a wrong transformation path, however, with dire consequences for the living standard of its citizens and the development of its economy. Through shock therapy, prices and the exchange rate were thrown abruptly into the play rules of the market economy, and state enterprises came into the possession of the "red directors" at symbolic prices. A major part of the industry is in the hands of twenty oligarchs, who recognize no business code. Half of the economy and banking system is ruled by Mafia methods, taxes remain in large part unpaid, exports are negligible, and industrial production has fallen almost by half. Of particular interest are recent attempts by President Vladimir Putin to limit the power of the oligarchs, to place the media under state control, and to limit the power of regional governors.

The transformation of Central Europe has been more successful. Poland, the Czech Republic, and Hungary are already NATO members. Growth rates in Poland, Hungary, and Estonia exceed those in Western Europe. Nevertheless, entry into the European Union (EU), so desired by all the reforming countries, will take time. None of the candidates has come close to the industrialization levels of the present EU members. Slovenia comes the closest with a GDP per capita of $10,981. The other candidates are, according to International Monetary Fund (IMF) data, far behind the EU average of $22,672: the Czech Republic with $5,170, Hungary with $4,801, Poland with $3,984, and Estonia with $3,565. At the other end of the spectrum are Bulgaria ($1,540) and Romania ($1,523). A particular obstacle is the condition of agriculture. If the EU were to be expanded to encompass the ten Central European candidates, the number of consumers would grow by 28 percent, but the number of people employed in agriculture would grow by 50 percent. Addressing an East–West conference in Vienna on November 8, 2000, the director of the IMF, Horst Kohler, stated: "Between 1987 and 1998, the Eastern European population with no more than $2 in daily income rose from 16 million to 93 million."[2]

This book presents in some detail the development and the role of the big players in the present phase of globalization. No country can substitute for the leading role of the United States, the only superpower left in the world after the collapse of the Soviet Union. The robust U.S. economy has been unceasingly growing for the last fifty years. The United States is a beneficiary of globalization. Japan, the second most powerful economy of the world, is still in the throes of a recession and unable to jump-start its industry. Attempts to polish its image by strengthening its military are worrisome, above all to Japan's neighbors. The EU has a chance to play a greater role if it can deepen integration and reverse the fall of its common currency.

The main obstacle to the successful progress of globalization is the widening chasm between the ever-richer North and the sinking-into-poverty South. With 11.6 percent of the world's population, the seven leading industrial economies produce 45.8 percent of world GDP and 48.9 percent of world exports. At the same time, the 128 least developed countries, with 77.7 percent of the world's population, produce 36.8 percent of world GDP and 18 percent of world exports.[3] The book analyzes development in the world's poorest countries, in the highly populated India in particular.

The chasm between the rich and poor is now tenfold greater than thirty years ago. The average annual income in 1999 was $25,480 in the twenty richest countries and $520 in the twenty poorest. The gap has created opposition to globalization and its institutions. The demands of the opposition presented themselves particularly starkly in Seattle in November 1999, when some forty thousand demonstrators blocked the meeting of the World Trade Organization. Demonstrations against the Bretton Woods institutions in Washington, D.C., in April 2000 and in Prague in September of that year were quite violent. Discussions held in Prague among the leading personalities of these institutions and the opposition were highly noticeable and called highly productive. Stanley Fischer, the deputy head of the IMF, expressed the opinion that the vast majority of demonstrators were opposed not to globalization, but to the way the process has been carried out. The leading proponent of a constructive dialogue was the host of the conference, Czech president Václav Havel, who noted that "We often hear about the need to restructure the economies of the poorer countries. . . . But I deem even more important that we should begin also to think about another restructuring—a restructuring of the entire system of values that forms the basis of our civilization today."[4] At the Prague meeting several strategically important reforms surfaced for the Bretton Woods institutions, such as a more effective division of functions between the World Bank, which should orient itself more toward alleviating the poverty of the Third World, and the IMF, which should concentrate more on securing economic stability and less on bailing out bankrupt banking systems. A prompter write-off of debts for the poorest countries of the world, as well as a fairer and more generally useful financial system, is to be worked out.

The 500 largest multinationals, created through transatlantic mergers, have in their hands 70 percent of world trade. One hundred of these have a collective turnover of $2 trillion. This extraordinary concentration is the hallmark of the present form of globalization. These enterprises escape control by nation-states or by international bodies. Asea Brown Boveri, with annual revenues of $36 billion and 1,300 divisions in 140 countries, is an example of a firm under the control only of its global management. IBM, General Motors, and others proceed likewise.

Another feature of globalization is the spread of speculative capital (or "casino capital") around the world. It is not directed at production or at banking, but at capital markets. Its volume is now much greater and it moves much more quickly than productive capital. It moves from continent to continent with the push of a button and with the speed of light, causing financial disasters, such as those in Southeast Asia and Russia.

Experience shows that any ideas of a functional world order are utopian. Nevertheless, improved coordination of the presently existing international institutions is a worthwhile objective. The coordinating organs of the global economy have much to offer in narrowing the gap between the rich and the poor. Mega-multinationals, with their immense productive capacities, if properly steered, have an important role to play. Speculative capital needs to be channeled into productive uses. Globalization cannot be stopped. But this process will succeed in its civilizing mission and free us from global conflicts only if it can help poor countries come closer to the rich.

GLOBALIZATION OF UNEQUAL NATIONAL ECONOMIES

1

Genesis, Evolution, and Critique

At the beginning of the twenty-first century, the globalization of national economies is being hailed as a civilizing revolution, the leitmotif of the century, and the logical consequence of the three industrial revolutions. It is viewed above all as a consequence of the last of the three revolutions, the computer revolution, which promises entirely new possibilities and prospects for human civilization. It arouses hopes, especially in developing countries, for a palpable improvement in the miserable standard of living. It arouses hopes for (among other things) greater social equality, a reduction in the huge gap between widespread poverty and wealth (which is concentrated in the hands of a few), closer cooperation among states and nations in the economic and cultural domains, the elimination of conflicts among states, and the dismantling of the nuclear arsenal, which threatens the very survival of the human race.

Yet people are aware of a certain risk. Globalization is not an international institution under the control of an international executive board, but rather a mode of exchange brought about by the evolution of the steering mechanisms of the division of labor among nations that furthers and perfects the latter. It allows for a free, steadily growing transfer of goods and capital, as well as entire areas of production. With the mere press of a button, huge sums, running into the billions, can be transferred by an investment fund from one part of the planet to another at the speed of light. The financial crisis in Southeast Asia in 1997 and 1998, which was triggered by (among other factors) the influx and later by the panicked flight of massive sums of money, made clear to the world the danger of an uncontrolled, unregulated transfer of "casino capital," which by far exceeds the capital engaged in industrial production.

The globalization of the world economy in its present form, coupled with the current constellation of nations, is coming increasingly under the influence of the world's economically strongest countries, as well as the inordinate power of the fifty to sixty super-multinationals, which are on the verge of bringing the most important national and world wide economic branches under their control. These multis are shifting a major portion of their production to low-wage countries, but in doing so, they imperil the employment situation in their own homelands. In order to expand their sphere of influence, these multis use national and worldwide megamergers to bring entire economic sectors under their domination. To name just a few examples, there is the merger of two U.S. giants in the entertainment industry, the online service AOL and Time-Warner, with an unprecedented volume of $465 billion, and there are the transatlantic mergers of Daimler-Benz and Chrysler; Ford and Volvo; and the Deutsche Bank AG and Bankers' Trust. Such megamergers reduce competition and thus competition's quite salubrious effect on efficiency. The furious progress of technology and economic efficiency is increasingly excluding the employed, causing a dramatic increase in unemployment, the rates of which in many countries, although in the midst of an economic boom, threaten to exceed the unemployment rates reached during the world economic crisis.

Nor should one forget that the beginning of the twentieth century, like that of the twenty-first, was also celebrated with hopeful wishes. On January 1, 1901, the *Chicago Tribune* wrote of the peaceful coexistence and brotherhood of the nations that the new century would bring. However, things turned out otherwise. The twentieth century was, according to the prominent historian of ideas Isaiah Berlin, the most terrible in human history. Two world wars and innumerable conflicts among states cost the lives of tens of millions of human beings. The Cold War, a conflict with roots in ideology, also did immeasurable harm to world civilization, although it fortunately did not degenerate into a third world war. This was only due, however, to the extremely costly "balance of horror"—that is, thousands of missiles with nuclear warheads, only a few of which would be enough to wipe civilization from the face of the earth in an instant.

The Collapse of Soviet Communism Promotes Capitalism to a Universal System

In this context, the question must be raised whether the great historical turning point of the last decade of the previous millennium—namely, the implosion of the Soviet empire—will contribute to a globalization leading to peaceful cooperation among the nations of the world—in other words, whether Russia, now professing its allegiance to the market and democracy, may be seen as a friend of Western civilization. Harvard professor and former government adviser Richard Pipes answers this question affirmatively.[1] Nevertheless, in order to answer it properly, a brief retrospective is necessary.

The origins of the Cold War and other hostilities are to be found in the Communist utopia, which Marx and Engels elevated to the rank of a science and which Russia's revolutionaries tried in vain to realize. After three-quarters of a century of this failed attempt, Russia now has another project—namely, rejoining Western civilization—which has not—or not yet—occurred. Such utopia is an ancient, ingenious, enticing, and by definition unrealizable perfect and just society. It was of this utopia that Thomas More long ago dreamed. In the sixteenth century, More's ruler, Henry VIII, sentenced him to death for heresy. More dreamed of a Communist society in which gold, once highly valued, would henceforth be used only to produce chamber pots. In the nineteenth century, Charles Fourier dreamed of communal settlements (*phalanstères*) in which equality and brotherhood would reign. Robert Owen founded production cooperatives to achieve much the same effect: equal wages for equal work and efficient economies without owners. Karl Marx and Friedrich Engels were the worthy successors of these great visionaries. They believed, and led their followers to believe, that they had found the way to transform the visions of their predecessors into a science. This belief was based on the thesis they promulgated that the proletariat, the producers of the goods of this world, had a historical role and hence the right to rise up from the exploited stratum to become the Demiurge of human civilization. Proletarians were to expropriate the exploiters, the capitalists, and to take the factories under their control. In this society, "paltry" money would be abolished. Simple coupons would circulate for the procurement of mass consumer goods, according to the motto "To everyone according to his needs and from everyone according to his abilities." Marx and Engels's *Communist Manifesto* of 1848 made a tremendous impression on millions of people, who hoped that the realization of this manifesto would free them from misery and oppression. As zealous pupils of the great German philosopher Georg Hegel, the authors of the manifesto combined Hegel's dialectic and Ludwig Feuerbach's materialism in a socialist ideology that was to change the world. At the same time, Marx and Engels were also among the leaders of a powerful movement intent on helping these visions to become a reality, the Socialist International. After a failed attempt in the mid-1860s to form a mass organization via the first Socialist International, which fell apart as a result of internal controversies, the second Socialist International was founded in 1889, just after Marx's death and on the one hundredth anniversary of the French Revolution. This "Second International" was to have a tremendous influence on world events. In the context of this study, however, it is important to stress that Marx's ideology led to the division of the world. As bad luck would have it, Russia's revolutionaries made this ideology into an instrument to overthrow the hated tsarist regime and violently establish a socialist system in semifeudal Russia, the most backward and uncivilized country in Europe. Karl Marx attempted in vain to make clear to the Russian radical revolutionary Vera Zasulich that his ideology was not meant for tsarist Russia, a country of peasants in which 80 percent of the population at that time lived on the land and only 5 percent were factory workers. Rather it was meant for the industrial developed countries of Europe, which were in the process of creating a vast stratum of factory workers who would be able to demand the establishment of a "dictatorship of the proletariat," Marx's proclaimed revolutionary objective. Russia, on the contrary, was only at the beginning of this development.

But Russia's ultrarevolutionaries were not to be persuaded. Marx was so impressed with their energy that toward the end of his life he even began to learn Russian. In 1903, Vladimir Ilyich Lenin split the Russian social democracy and organized his Bolshevik faction into a party of cadres primed to seize power in a proletarian revolution. In the confusion of World War I, which was a catastrophe for the untrained Russian army, the German general staff succeeded in sneaking Lenin and his comrades-in-arms into St. Petersburg to overthrow the bourgeois government of Alexander Kerensky. Kerensky's time in office marked the first and only democratic regime in the history of Russia; it lasted only eight months. In October 1917, it was overthrown by Lenin and his consorts. Bolshevik power was established.

The consequences are well known: the necessary preconditions for realizing Marx's utopia were totally absent in Russia, which had been devastated by the war. The proletariat did not participate in the revolution. At first glance, it was more of a "velvet" seizure of power, which was carried out by Leon Trotsky with a minimal number of victims.

There were no more casualties to mourn in the October uprising than at the fall of the Bastille in the French Revolution of 1789. The civil war unleashed by the "white generals," which lasted for three years, did not begin until later. The Bolsheviks had won because of the general devastation of the country and the exhaustion of the other European powers as a result of World War I (England and France intervened halfheartedly on the side of the whites but soon withdrew). Trotsky's army, however, also fought against the rebellious Kronstadt sailors, the soldiers of the revolution who clamored for the fulfillment of the proclaimed socialist objectives, and the Volga peasants and rebels in the Ukraine and Central Asia. Peace did not come again to the country until 1920. Moreover, "full power" was not handed over to the worker and peasant soviets, as was initially announced, but to the arrogant, power-craving, bribe-hungry bureaucracy, which stifled any initiative from below. To save the country from starvation, the ailing leader of the revolution, Lenin, tried to shift course in 1921 and introduced a New Economic Policy (NEP), which allowed private entrepreneurs to develop production activities. The NEP and American grain alleviated the acute starvation of the Russian people, and Lenin came to view this transitional period as a longer-term development. Despite their outstanding achievements, the so-called NEP men were not given their political due; on the contrary, many viewed them as a "relapse into capitalism." Stalin, who had the backing of several like-minded ideologues, put a sudden end to the NEP, which Lenin had drafted with the first of his five-year plans for accelerated industrialization in 1928. Despite the fact that they had simply fulfilled their assigned tasks, the NEP men were once again expropriated; most of them were shipped to Siberia. This marked the definitive embarkation on the path of state socialism. The Russian state did not wither away, as Marx and Lenin had once dreamed, but expanded into a surveillance state that watched over the slightest movement of every citizen. Later came the collectivization of agriculture, forcibly implemented with terror and violence, and the great purges that cost the lives of millions of innocent people.

The best Russian poets and writers, such as Boris Pilniak, Isaak Babel, and Osip Mandelstam, who with Dante's *Inferno* in hand wandered into the inferno of the Gulag, lost their lives. Forty thousand officers were not afforded the chance to fight in the war against Hitler. They died in their homeland shortly before, including field marshals such as the civil war hero Mikhail N. Tukhachevsky and Vasily K. Blukher, who had brought the Japanese to their knees at Khalkhin-Gol. Elected the journalist of the century in 1999 for his probity, Rudolf Augstein attempted to answer the question of why so much horror had occurred in this country. His answer was a reference to a tradition lasting over hundreds of years: Ivan the Terrible split the nobility and conquered Kazan, where much blood was shed. In a rage, he killed his son, the crown prince, with his scepter. Peter the Great instigated an "orgy of blood" in Moscow that lasted for months, until even the bishop begged for an end. He prayed on his deathbed in 1725: "Lord, when you sit in judgement over me, do not forget what country it was with which I had to deal." The successor to the throne, Alexei, was killed at the command of his father, Peter the Great. Almost one hundred thousand soldiers had to die, writes Rudolf Augstein, because Field Marshal Georgi Zhukov received the order from Stalin to conquer Berlin by May 1, 1945.[2]

Soviet policy was also cruel in the outlying areas of the empire, in Eastern and Central Europe as well as in the Baltic states, which Stalin, as a consequence of the victorious world war, annexed to the Soviet empire. The slightest impulse to shake off Soviet rule was put down with tanks. This use of force was evident, for instance, in the Soviet crushing of the East German workers' uprising in June 1953 and 1956 Hungarian revolution (whose leaders, Imre Nagy and General Pal Maleter, were sentenced to death), as well as in the move against the vanguard of the "Prague Spring" in 1968. The Soviet Union's economic policy was also cruel. It concentrated the best forces and technological equipment in the military-industrial complex. An economic structure hostile to human beings was created in which about 70 percent of the GNP was fed into the huge military-industrial complex, and the rest went to provide for the needs of the citizens. The shopping bag, *avos'ka*, which a citizen always had with him or her (because there just might be something to get a hold of), became the symbol of the scarcity that prevailed throughout the entire Soviet period.

Perestroika, spontaneous, ill-considered, and overly hasty, was indeed the Soviet Union's last effort to revive the failing economy. As President Vladimir Putin said, Gorbachev's perestroika marked "years of unreflected attempts to swiftly reorganize and accelerate everything." Gorbachev's successor, Boris Yeltsin, who attempted to transform Russia into a democracy and market economy, transferred the bulk of industrial enterprises into the hands of the former "red directors," who had administered the enterprises on behalf of the party and government.

He thereby finished the job of ruining Russia's economy completely. Production decreased by 50 percent. An unprecedented gap between the rich and poor arose, unlike anywhere else in the world. Yeltsin's successor, however, is sticking with the course of his predecessor. That is the course that Mikhail Gorbachev described as, "that infernal course which has driven 80 percent of Russians into misery and poverty." He went on to say that the country was humiliated and torn to bits by corruption. Gorbachev added: "If the Putin variant was merely devised to maintain the old regime, then God have mercy on us."[3]

The regime had always turned to the state security service for support in times of great danger. Thus right after the October Revolution in 1917, the "iron man," Feliks Dzerzhinsky, founded the "Extraordinary Commission," the all-powerful Cheka, which purged the country of its former political elite with an iron hand. It should be noted in passing that on the night of the Duma elections on December 19, 1999, Vladimir Putin visited the notorious Lubyanka headquarters of the KGB to celebrate the anniversary of the founding of the Cheka. And a few days before, at the silver anniversary of a KGB comrade, Yevgeny Primakov, Putin's predecessor as head of the FSB (the current name of the KGB successor), invited all the Cheka members present to rise. Vladimir Putin, who had been invited to the celebration, also rose. After all, both the present FSB staff and the president are proud that they are upholding the Cheka spirit. In the 1930s, Stalin, whose power position was being attacked by the party leadership, also relied on the powerful secret police to protect himself from the Communist Party. In the last month of his presidency, Boris Yeltsin also sought salvation from the security service, first with Yevgeny Primakov and then with the police general Sergey Stepashin. The multibillionaire Boris Berezovsky, the true kingmaker and financier of the political in-crowd, the Yeltsin extended "family," said that these personalities had proved to be weak willed. It took Putin, who had the requisite will power, to carry out the reform policy.

Why such will power was necessary became evident shortly after Putin was appointed head of government in August 1999. The prime minister was called upon to defeat the Chechens, which he proceeded to do with the brutal deployment of tanks and airplanes against a small group of rebels, but mainly against a civilian population who was forced to abandon Grozny, the capital of the country. The democratic countries of Europe and America protested only faintly against this unparalleled cruelty. They understood Russia's effort to try to keep its disintegrating federation together. Mikhail Gorbachev called the possible fall of Chechnya a dangerous precedent. Many politicians of the West were of the same opinion. However, this war of revenge for the shameful defeat in the first war in 1996 is extremely popular among the Russian people. In fact, because of this popularity the government party, Unity, though it had been founded just prior to the Duma elections in December 1999, acquired seventy-six deputies, compared with sixty-two mandates for Primakov's and Yuri Luzhkov's (the mayor of Moscow) party, which had been so certain of victory. Together with other right-wing parties, Putin's party would now be able to break the dominance of the Communists, who still had around six hundred thousand members and were the strongest party in the Duma, with 113 deputies. A more important factor, however, is that Putin, this hitherto unknown member of the secret service, was able to achieve a popularity in just a few months that enabled him to play the second role for which he was intended—namely, to take over the presidential scepter from Boris Yeltsin. Yeltsin had become a "senile, seldom sober monarch," a degenerate human being steered via remote control by those around him (in the words of Zbigniew Brzezinski, former U.S. national security adviser). Brzezinski commented: "No shot was fired, but it was still a coup, even without violence."[4]

Yeltsin's resignation was forced by a small group who represented the interests of institutions and financial circles. Nonetheless, the army and the security service, whose loyal servant Vladimir Putin was and remains, were also participants. There is also evidence to back up the thesis that it was a putsch against Yeltsin: just the day before his resignation, Yeltsin had signed a law concerning the presidential election setting the election date for June 4. Yeltsin's resignation and Putin's appointment to interim president moved the election date forward to March 26, 2000. On the evening before his resignation, Yeltsin taped a New Year's speech of five minutes. However, the next day in a new, and of course amended, speech of twenty minutes Yeltsin announced his resignation and asked to be forgiven for having not been able to keep his promise to raise the standard of living.

The answer to the question posed by Richard Pipes—namely, whether Russia has remained an enemy of the West after the Cold War—is of major importance. Indications to this effect are not lacking: the new security model in Putin's Decree No. 24 differs substantially from Yeltsin's "multipolar world order" doctrine, which had been in force since 1997. Putin's decree envisions a conflict situation with the West, which, led by the United States, is trying to settle the world's key problems through its military might. Whereas previously the danger of aggression had been put aside, now the level and scope of danger in military matters were increasing. Moreover, according to Putin's decree, the use of nuclear weapons against an attack with conventional arms would be acceptable "if all other means are ineffective." For this reason, the impoverished country retains its gigantic nuclear arsenal of ten thousand warheads. But under the pressure of the growing budget deficit Putin decided on November 10, 2000, to reduce the enormous army by six hundred thousand soldiers.

Those who pulled the strings behind Yeltsin's resignation had sufficient evidence that he was not totally innocent of charges that he had stashed bribe money abroad. Thus they were able to pressure him to resign. The Moscow newspaper *Versiia* published a fax from the Gotthard Bank in Switzerland, account number 182605, which was purported to have been signed by Yeltsin. Theo Paccioli, head of the Swiss firm Mabatex, admitted that Yeltsin's family had taken money from the Mabatex account. According to sources, there were several such accounts, with a total of over $15 million. Thanks to the generous help of Boris Berezovsky and other oligarchs who had supported Yeltsin, his family was well taken care of. One of Yeltsin's son-in-law, Valery Okulov, rose to the position of general director of the profitable Aeroflot. Another son-in-law, Alexei Dyachenko, became coproprietor of the powerful oil giant Rosneft, and his wife, Tatyana Dyachenko, became the official adviser to her father, the president. Yeltsin's forced resignation was sweetened by the fact that he would avoid prosecution. This was ensured by Vladimir Putin, who signed a decree of immunity that became effective on the day of Yeltsin's historic resignation. On the following day, however, his daughter, the adviser, was removed from office.

Putin's colleagues say that he is a talented specialist but only in security matters. In an interview in *Der Spiegel*, Gorbachev said, "in order to lead Russia in such difficult times, one needs experience, especially in economics. In this area [Putin] is very limited. . . . If he proves to be only a puppet in the hands of those familiar, cunning puppeteers, then things do not look good for Russia." [5] But Putin, the security man, has been lucky: the price of crude oil has doubled within a short time, and oil is Russia's principal export item. Earnings in 1999 increased by $20 billion, and industrial production rose at a record 8.1 percent; in contrast, the previous year, 1998, saw a decline of 5.2 percent. The 1999 figure is the greatest annual increase since the collapse of the Soviet Union.

Nonetheless, the necessary prerequisites for a permanent upswing still do not exist. Economic structures, of which the military-industrial complex still accounts for a preponderant share, cannot be converted so rapidly to mass-consumption-oriented industrial production. Russia still does not have an entrepreneurial middle class that could enable its backward economy to meet the challenge of the world market in the foreseeable future. The managerial stratum still relies on the former red directors, whose duty it was to fulfill the planning directives handed down by higher-level administrators. Russia lacks an effective entrepreneurial code that could motivate those involved to build honest relations with both the state and economic partners. Half of industrial production functions clandestinely, and tax evasion is still a generally acceptable practice. The attempt to train a functional political class appears to be proceeding just as poorly. No party in Russia has a mass base infused with a democratic ideology. The only way to inspire the people to "action" is through a belief in Russia's position as a superpower, a belief for which there are no longer any convincing arguments. The last secretary general of the Communist Party, Mikhail Gorbachev, speaks of a Social Democratic alternative. Reaching this alternative would be possible: "if the new Kremlin bosses break with the old regime, opt for reforms that place priority on freedom, turn to a welfare-oriented economy, battle corruption, and emphasize openness and an active role of the state in defending people's interests."[6] But in this regard, the Kremlin's present boss and those in his immediate entourage are quite remote.

Globalization as a Consequence of the Three Industrial Revolutions That Restructured Society

The first half of the twentieth century was one of the greatest catastrophes in more than five thousand years of human history. The two world wars cost the lives of millions of people and ruined the material livelihood of many. Whereas World War I resulted in the ideological division of the world, World War II, the most brutal of all wars, threatened to eradicate human civilization. Adolf Hitler, Germany's Führer in a period of unprecedented decadence, had thoroughly undermined, over for a considerable period of time, man's basic trust in civilization, a trust that had sustained human beings right up to the present. The world crisis of the 1930s had already caused doubt as to whether the capitalist market was capable of steering the fate of the economy without destructive disruptions. The second half of the twentieth century, however, fundamentally altered the world. Europe, shaken from centuries of internal struggles, found its way to unity and to the creation of a "common home." In this regard, Germany, which had started two world wars, played a leading role in the transformation of society, the economy, and social life. Thanks to its growing productivity and high standard of living, the West's social system, based on a welfare market economy, had demonstrated to the Soviet public its superiority over the encrusted, centrally planned economy that throttled any initiative from below. The October Revolution, though it had been initiated under counterfeit, often unrealizable objectives, had promised that the state would wither away. Instead it created an all-powerful surveillance state with a tremendous bureaucracy and state police, which brought neither freedom nor prosperity to the people. All of this has disappeared from the picture. The three industrial revolutions carried out by Western civilization have brought about a qualitative transformation in economic and social structures throughout the world. They have carried human civilization forward throughout the past century.

A comparison presented by *The Economist* confirms this thesis entirely: in 1913, agriculture, forestry, and the fishing industry accounted for 28 percent of total employment in the United States, 41 percent in France, 60 percent in Japan, but only 12 percent in Great Britain. [7] Thanks to mechanization and modern technology, the proportion of the population of these countries working in these sectors has declined to 6 percent. The technological revolution has fundamentally altered the structure of the economy and employment. In the nineteenth century and early in the first half of the twentieth century, industrial production was the leading sector in developed industrial countries. In the last few decades of the twentieth century, however, it has yielded to the service sector. Yet the content and character of this sector are different from what they were in the nineteenth century. Whereas earlier services were mainly from person to person, they have now expanded to include information, education, accounting, communication, and the media (among other areas). In other areas, however, the role of services has diminished tangibly. For instance, housekeeping has been largely mechanized thanks to electric washing machines, vacuum cleaners, dishwashers, and the like.

It was an extensive revolution that liberated women from the most burdensome parts of housework. Moreover, thanks to the dynamic expansion of food production and the fact that it is now possible to store foods over longer periods, women have been largely freed from the kitchen and can devote themselves to a professional career.

Even before World War I, in some developed countries the service sector accounted for a greater proportion of economic activity than agricultural production. In 1913, for example, this figure was 43 percent in America and 44 percent in Great Britain, but only 27 percent in France and 22 percent in Japan. At present this figure has risen to 60 percent in Japan and about 75 percent in America. In every sector, working conditions, as well as the relations between the sectors, have changed substantially. Mass employment in agriculture was replaced by mass employment in industrial production. This allowed, as a result of progressive urbanization, huge concerns to form. The mode of production is changing continuously. As a result, many workers have been replaced by a growing mechanization and automation. The proportion of white-collar workers, as well as the number of workers in nonprofit organizations (hospitals, for example), has risen considerably. The latter account for 8 percent of all employed people in America (1995), 6 percent in Great Britain, and more than 12 percent in Holland. Trade unions, which grew appreciably during the course of industrialization, have lost ground recently. In 1930 the proportion of trade union members among all the employed was no more than 6.8 percent in America and 25.3 percent in Great Britain, but in 1950, those figures had risen to 22.3 percent and 39.9 percent respectively. By 1996–97 the figures had declined to 14 percent and 30.1 percent. The proportion of government spending in GNP has increased considerably. In 1930 it was 1.8 percent in the United States, 6.3 percent in Sweden, 8.3 percent in Japan, 12.7 percent in Great Britain, 14.8 percent in Germany, and 17 percent in France; present figures are 34 percent in America, 54 percent in France, and 65 percent in Sweden. As a consequence, taxes have risen. Spending for holidays, moreover, has also increased from around 2–3 percent of America's GNP in the first years of the twentieth century to its present figure of 10 percent. The number of working hours has diminished palpably, from 2,700 per year at the beginning of the twentieth century to 1,400–1,800 at the end of the century. In January 2000, the French government reduced the work week from 38 to 35 hours. The length of paid vacations has increased considerably: from 2–3 weeks every year in

America and Japan to 6 weeks in Germany. In the era of globalization, one of the greatest achievements of capitalism is the successful control of recessions and the lengthening of the business cycle.

The uninterrupted boom of the U.S. economy in the last decade of the twentieth century and almost full employment are unprecedented in economic history. However, whether the government has truly drawn a lesson from the mistakes of its inglorious past is dubious. Conservatives still heavily attack deficit spending, a reduction in the work week, training, etc. Nevertheless, it is almost inconceivable that the government will repeat the mistakes it made in the depressions of the 1930s—for instance, when the Federal Reserve Board increased interest rates in the midst of an acute crisis; cut back on loans when liquidity was diminishing; repeatedly increased interest rates in 1931–32, after Great Britain had abandoned the gold standard, which came precisely at a time when an intensification of foreign trade was urgently necessary to revive the economy; and the government radically increased in customs duties as a result of the Smoot-Hawley Tariff Act, which caused the already shrinking foreign trade in 1929 to diminish by two-thirds in 1933. All of the above conditions would be difficult to imagine today. In the spirit of Milton Friedman, *The Economist*, from which the above figures were taken, stated its conviction that the government's measures at that time transformed a rather negligible recession into the most devastating decline of the century.[8] This might seem a bit exaggerated, but there is no doubt that the governments involved made some serious mistakes.

This does not mean that capitalism in the era of globalization will be free from abrupt crises. For example, the financial crisis in Southeast Asia in 1997–98, with its tendency to expand to Russia or Brazil, has proved that this danger has not been eliminated. Although capitalism is rising to the rank of a universal governing system for the world economy—and after the disintegration of the Soviet empire is even on the verge of expanding to totalitarian China or Vietnam—the composition of capital has changed dramatically in the last decades. For example, there has been an incessant increase in the mass of free-floating capital, which is sent from continent to continent at the press of a button, or at the slightest suspicion of an imminent currency devaluation, and is capable of leading the affected countries to take panic-like action. The capitalism of the era of globalization is no longer the classical industrial capitalism of the nineteenth and first half of the twentieth centuries; rather, it is a capitalism of service and information. In any case, its structure has changed fundamentally. The proportion of casino capital, speculative money, already exceeds the capital active in the industrial sector and has a greater influence on the business cycle. This capital, which is beyond nation ties, eludes any governmental controls. U.S. sociologist Daniel Bell has claimed that we will live in a postindustrial society.[9] Progress in the economy and technology will be based on theoretical research. Bell further observes, "The role of universities and research institutions will be more important than in the preceding period. The development of an intellectual technology, which will be as important for human affairs as the technology of machinery, will be of paramount importance."[10] In comparison to the capitalism the preceding century, the capitalism of the twenty-first century will have a universal, more aggressively competitive form. "The international community," writes the former director of the IMF, Michel Camdessus, "faces, at the beginning of the new millennium, a different, urgent challenge that will require even more courage: the reduction of poverty in the poorer countries of the world."[11] If the tremendous gap between rich countries and developing countries is not reduced, globalization will encounter major obstacles. It will be extremely difficult to regulate relations among nations, a difficulty that was graphically demonstrated to the world public by the "battle of Seattle."

WTO Globalization and the Protests in Seattle

The unrest in Seattle has a good chance of going down in history. Even at its peak, the left-wing student movement of the 1970s never succeeded in taking the ministers and diplomats of 135 countries practically hostage—and all this in the United States, the center of "world capitalism." The protesters of Seattle kicked up a lot of dust, burned cars, broke many windows, and terrified conference participants. Nonetheless, to brand them as the cause of the failure of the WTO's conference in Seattle is quite certainly far removed from the truth. The true cause of the failure of the WTO conference, which was attended by so many luminaries and raised the hopes of many, was poor preparation.

New York Times columnist Thomas Friedman is right when he says the ecofundamentalists on Seattle's streets, with their concern for the environment, and the steelworkers and dockworkers who, fearing for their jobs, came to Seattle on AFL–CIO money, did not have much in common with the stone-throwing anarchists. They did not have a common platform.[12] People's Global Action (PGA), an antiglobalization group that had planned a worldwide day of action against the "global capitalist system" on November 13, 1999 (the opening day of the Seattle conference), and had marched through the streets with slogans such as "The WTO kills people, kill the WTO," was only one of a thousand groups prepared to fight the WTO. Finally, the director of the Viennese laborers' chamber (AK), Werner Muhm, expressed concerns similar to those put forth by the protesters in Seattle. Two weeks before the conference began, Muhm emphasized that the service negotiations on the agenda of the WTO conference, for example, could have far-reaching effects in Austria.[13] The service sector, which is divided into thirteen categories comprising branches such as transport, construction, health, and tourism, employs two-thirds of the total number employed in Austria. For the time being, there are still many barriers for a few "key" persons (as the definition is worded) from non-EU countries who can work for three months in Austria without special permission as accountants, artists, or stewards/stewardesses. Liberalization, Muhm continues, brings many advantages, especially to the industrial countries, but one must proceed circumspectly and make sure to open the labor market only under "clear, predefined conditions." We might note in passing that these statements from an influential politician imply that Austria had been very careful in allowing foreign workers to enter the country even before the formation of a coalition government with the right-wing radical party of Jörg Haider.

Since 1986, when the first trade talks were initiated on an international level in Punta del Este (Uruguay), everything proceeded without particularly attracting the attention of the world public. This situation continued during the seven subsequent negotiations of the General Agreement on Tariffs and Trade (GATT), the predecessor of the WTO, which was given greater powers and a broader area of influence. It should be borne in mind that the international negotiations in Uruguay included topics such as services, the agrarian economy, intellectual property, and health standards. This round of negotiations gave birth to the WTO, which has an even stronger mechanism for implementation at its disposal than GATT had. The WTO is the only international body that has a chance to develop into an institution with global control over trade and investments, working conditions, and environmental protection.

The millennium agenda of the Seattle conference was rather modest: unfinished problems from the Uruguay meetings; specifically further liberalization in the agrarian and service sectors, as well as a review of the provisions for intellectual property, were to be the main topics. The United States rejected themes proposed by the EU, such as investment and competition policy. Moreover, the developing countries spoke out against new provisions on working conditions and environmental protection. In view of this rather modest agenda, one may rightfully ask why this Seattle conference provoked such a vast protest movement. *The Economist* answers this question: "The WTO has become a magnet for resistance to globalization by both old fashioned protectionists and newer critics of free trade."[14]

The WTO had become the whipping boy for every sort of interest group worldwide. It is, nonetheless, indisputable that multilateral liberalization of foreign trade has contributed to a tremendous boom and hence economic growth. This positive aspect of WTO activity—namely, the adoption of transparent provisions that promote foreign trade—can hardly be overlooked. Between 1950 and 1998, foreign trade increased worldwide by almost twenty-fold, the proportion of exports in the GNP increased from 8 to 26.4 percent, and the world economy grew by more than five-fold.[15] Two ambitious agreements were indispensable for the success of the Seattle conference: a transatlantic agreement between America and the EU that would account for two-fifths of world trade and an agreement between the rich North and the poor South. However, there is still a long way to go before such agreements are reached. In fact, the only point of agreement was that the provisions of the Seattle negotiations should last only three years, not eight years, like those of the Uruguay negotiations. However, no agreement was reached on U.S. demands for the introduction of a far-reaching information technology, growing WTO transparency, or the gradual elimination of customs tariffs in eight categories (chemistry, energy and environment, forestry products, fish, gems, medicine, scientific equipment, and children's toys). This was a result of the opposition's argument that these agreements took only U.S. preferences into account. The developing countries, on the other hand, claimed that the Uruguay talks had provided them with too few advantages in regard to agrarian products and textiles, and they demanded concessions for their intellectual property, investment protections, and antidumping measures. They criticized the EU's Common Agricultural Policy (CAP), which in their opinion is all too protectionist, and also the U.S. slowdown of the liberalization of the textile sector, which will not come into force before 2005. Clinton's government was not prepared to make far-reaching concessions and thus did not have that much to offer in this regard.

The U.S. economy is prospering, and greater access to world markets does not seem to be absolutely necessary. Furthermore, the president has promised Congress to withdraw from the WTO if it should restrict the United States's sovereign right of decision. Congress has refused several times to grant the chief executive far-reaching negotiating powers. The developing countries—above all the populous ones such as China, India, and Mexico—did not come to Seattle to listen to florid speeches full of promises or to bring the WTO into disrepute. Instead, they came to gain concrete advantages for their foreign trade relations. Mexico's president, Ernesto Zedillo, sharply criticized the "globophobics," who, he said, are protesting to "bar the peoples of the developing countries from participating in development." Egypt's economic minister, Youssef Boutros-Ghali, said that most countries (i.e., the developing countries) came to Seattle to gain a bigger piece of the pie, not to destroy it. Growth is impossible without integration into the world economy, but trade conditions are unfair for developing countries. He closed his speech with the following words: "We open to you, but you don't open to us." It was not the protesters that condemned the WTO conference in Seattle to failure, but the still unbridgeable gap between the developed and developing countries.

Francis Fukuyama questions, perhaps somewhat sanctimoniously, why the Left is protesting so violently against globalization and against the WTO, which is supposed to help implement globalization successfully: "It is ironic," he writes, "that the Left should rebel against globalization, since globalization is one of the most progressive forces in the world today."[16] For every blue-collar job that an industrial country such as the United States exports to the Third World, several jobs are created in Malaysia, India, or China, thus offering these countries the possibility of entrance into the modern world. Fukuyama objects to the left-wing argument that globalization exerts downward pressure on wages in the poor countries as well as in the West and that it creates conditions enabling the international multis to exploit workers worldwide. The alternatives, he says, are even worse, for they keep the peasants streaming into the cities from building a better existence for themselves in an industrial enterprise. The foreign investments of the multis force local concerns about worldwide competition. Globalization is, according to Fukuyama, the vehicle of modernization, for it brings more transparency, education, and more perfect management, as well as a better overview of global media. By establishing the WTO, global capitalism has solved the collectivist problem of the Left. The WTO, according to Fukuyama, is the only international organization that sets down rules not only for foreign trade and foreign investment, but also for labor standards and environmental protection. Fukuyama says that by observing the Left's protest against the WTO, one gets the idea that it is not attempting to prevent the negative consequences of globalization but would rather like to return to protectionist nationalist markets. Law professors Jack L. Goldsmith and John C. Joo take this criticism of the protesters a step further. Under the pretext of defending U.S. sovereignty, they are not concerned with democratic institutions but are opposed to free trade and economic independence.[17]

The Left is not the only one rebelling against globalization and the WTO; right-wing radicals do so as well. For example, Horst Mahler, a German citizen and former member of the Red Army Faction (RAF) who distanced himself from the RAF while in prison and now appears as a guest speaker for the extreme right-wing National Democratic Party of Germany (a party with an affinity for Nazi ideas), stated in a speech in Vienna (at the invitation of the Association of Free Academics) that the Left has abandoned its criticism of capitalism and identifies with internationalization and the "American way of life." Mahler, the former socialist turned nationalist, demands in response that "globalism be abandoned and that money and the mechanism of the market be forced back into a subservient role." In reference to Germany's problem with foreigners, he continues more concretely: the fifty years of reeducation of the German people are responsible for the fact that "our people no longer dare to resist their own extinction through a deluge of foreigners." Mahler also sees the media as the enemy par excellence: "For me the media are a new hostile occupying force."[18]

Globalism, however, is not an ideology that a few incorrigible visionaries would like to see realized as the goal of their dreams. Rather, it is a logical process in the progress of human civilization, and no one can hold it back. The critics of great economic changes were incapable of resisting upheavals such as the evolution of agrarian society into an industrial society or the three industrial revolutions that led to the transformation of industrial society into a service and information society, with its computer and Internet revolutions. These changes were just as inexorable as the transition from a crude barter economy or the transformation of money from a primitive, material-value-based currency into the developed circulation of money and a gigantic banking system with branches spanning the world. Globalism is an inevitable consequence of these processes, which bring the nations of this planet closer together, in particular through the feverish development of the mechanisms of communication. Globalization, however, brings both unmistakable advantages and undeniable disadvantages. One need only look at the high price Russia and other nations have had to pay for trying to block globalization (not least because of Russia's dizzying arms expenditures). Surely a continuation of the traditional path of development would have been better.

However, William Greider correctly claims that today's world is not only reaching the end of traditional ideologies, but is at the same time witnessing the beginning of conflicts over the present character of capitalism.[19] Capitalism is indeed laying claim to an ever-greater proportion of national income, as well as a greater control over workers. The struggle for wealth and power has grown more bitter, and the gap between rich and poor, both within nation-states and between developed and developing countries, has not narrowed. A growing proportion of capital has become independent and reaps its profits not in the process of production, in factories, in coal mines, or in oil deposits, but on the capital market. The stock market speculator need not be concerned with the development of new products, a license, corresponding up-to-date technology, or a sales market, but rather learns the rules of the game of the capital market with the help of refined information technology. He moves vast sums of money from one continent to another with the push of a button. In this zero-sum game, the lucky speculator profits at the expense of the unlucky one. There is thus no increase in prosperity for all. Exploding capital markets, on which share prices seem to lose any relation with the real material assets of the issuer, at least in the short term, have nothing in common with the traditional rules of the price-determining game. In 1987, the U.S. capital market plunged from a peak of 2,700 on the Dow Jones index to 1,700. However, by 1995 it had reached a record high of 4,800, and one year later, 6,000.[20] On June 1, 2000, the Dow Jones index was at 10,652 (after soaring to over 11,000 during parts of 1999 and the first half of 2000).

Financial assets grew much more than the economy and in 1992 were at the level of $35 trillion in the OECD nations, which is double the value of their economic output.[21] Share trading increased by 17 percent annually from 1980 to 1995—that is, seven times as rapidly as the economic growth of the OECD countries.[22] A total of 766 investment funds invested their vastly inflated capital everywhere in the world from Bangkok to Buenos Aires and took the savings of the population with them. Americans have invested $250 billion in savings in such funds.[23] In 1997 the stock assets of Germans increased by 40 percent to DM 443 billion.[24] The capital markets elude any control by national governments. Nevertheless, their growth also has positive aspects. For instance, more and more citizens, dreaming of equality of opportunity for all, big and small, are participating as buyers or sellers of stocks and bonds in this unpredictable game. They consider themselves co-owners of the vast national assets of their nation. In the United States, 40 percent of the middle class is now participating in the stock market game. To become rich has become a national obsession; mammon evokes frenzied passion, and the Internet becomes the medium in its service. At the same time, 32 million Americans subsist below the minimum standard of living and 35 million have no health insurance.

The Seattle protesters declared war on globalism and the WTO because (among other things) a few industrial countries have not learned how to make use of the rapid progress of technology to raise the standard of living. Almost 75 million jobs have been lost because of technological progress, says the Canadian author John Ralston Saul. Jobs are also lost in the developed industrial countries because of the transfer of whole areas of production to low-wage countries. The following data are given as an example: 40 percent of IBM employees are foreigners, not Americans, and seventy-five thousand IBM workers have been dismissed in the 1990s to cut costs.[25] General Electric produces its most important electronic components in Singapore, where it employs one hundred thousand workers. Hence it has become the biggest private employer in Singapore. The electronics thus produced are then reexported to America. The Boeing 777 aircraft is produced in twelve countries, among them Japan, where the main body is produced by Mitsubishi. A fifth of the total output of U.S. firms is produced outside America. This means a loss of jobs for the United States. However, the transfer of production capacities helps the developing countries at least partially to decrease their lag behind the industrial countries of the West. In this way, the big concerns fulfill their promise to bring more equality to the planet.

Thanks to progress in the mechanisms of information and communication, globalism is gradually opening the way to free trade and investment in foreign countries. The following definition by Thomas Friedman is euphoric but somewhat inaccurate: "The driving idea behind globalization is free-market capitalism. The more you let market forces rule and the more you open your economy to free trade and competition, the more efficient and flourishing your economy will be. Globalization means the spread of free-market capitalism to virtually every country in the world."[26]

The United States leads all other countries in the transfer of production capacities. It has learned, however, how to use perfected technology without imperiling full employment. This would suggest that advanced technology need not conflict with the labor market. If the protesters at Seattle had used their energy, temperament, and willpower to see to it that globalization, which is inevitable, moves in the right direction, introduces more free foreign trade, and makes certain that the "world cake" is distributed more justly among the nations of the world, then they would have done a greater deed for the development of human civilization than by simply trying to run against the current. The only alternative to free trade is protectionism, which means trade quotas and customs barriers that impede the international division of labor and have caused incalculable damage in their time. In a sense, this struggle against the inexorable march of human civilization and its promotion of progress resembles the struggle of the British Luddites in 1810 against the mechanization of the textile industry, which was eliminating jobs. Like the Seattle protesters, Ned Lud, the leader of the machinery wreckers, also said that his movement was not against progress, but against being excluded from progress. The results are well known: the revolt was crushed with severe violence, and the British textile industry could continue its mechanization to the benefit of Great Britain. The process of globalization in the progress of human civilization cannot be stopped. The most praiseworthy task of all true democrats, including the Seattle protesters, is to organize globalization, as well as capitalism, more perfectly.

The Discrepancy Between Developing and Industrial Countries as the Principal Obstacle to Globalization

Wealth is increasing, but poverty is also increasing. There are now worldwide 160 multibillionaires and 2 million multimillionaires, yet, according to the former director of the IMF, Michel Camdessus, 1.3 billion people must survive on less than $1 per day.[27] In 1960, 20 percent of the most affluent citizens of this planet had an income that was thirty times that of the poorest 20 percent. In 1989 this discrepancy had increased to fifty-nine-fold and has remained at this level.[28] Burbach, Nunez, and Kagarlitsky write, "The economics of globalization has pushed them [the Third World] deeper in misery, violence, social decomposition, drug trafficking and ecological degradation."[29] Robert D. Kaplan is more blunt. He claims that scarcity, crime, overpopulation, clan mentality, and diseases in Africa and many other countries of the Third World are progressively destroying "the social fabric of our planet."[30] Africa, the most miserable continent on this planet, with 747.2 million inhabitants (1996), had an economic growth of 3.5 percent in 1999 (a decline from 5 percent in 1996); it was greater than the population growth only because the population is declining. This continent has the highest mortality rate: 2 million persons have died in the last few years from AIDS, and 220,000 have died in conflicts between countries. Two million persons disappeared in the Sudanese civil war, 5 million are without shelter and starving, and 800,000 inhabitants of Rwanda were mercilessly murdered in 100 days. No major steps were taken to prevent this genocide. Moreover, the continent is deeply in debt. Africa's debt was $300 billion at the end of 1999 and the per capita GNP was no more than $662. Furthermore, 44 percent of the adult population can neither read nor write. Mozambique, Botswana, and Angola, however, have economic growth rates that are far above the average—10, 8.9, and 8 percent respectively.[31]

The countries of the Third World were colonies of the industrial countries of the West before World War II. Whereas in 1947 there were 55 independent states, today there are almost 200, including 110 developing countries with over 4 billion persons, roughly four-fifths of the world's population. India was the largest colony and the first to gain its independence after World War II (on August 5, 1947). After it was liberated from British colonial rule, the country was divided into India, dominated by the Hindus, and Muslim Pakistan. However, following the independence, a population explosion occurred that has proceeded much more rapidly than economic growth: while in 1947 there were 300 million persons on the entire Indian subcontinent, at present there are 1.18 billion, almost as many as in China. According to the estimates of Indian statisticians, India alone would reach the 1 billion level in May 2000.

Portugal did not grant independence to its two biggest colonies, Angola and Mozambique, until after Marcello Caetano, the successor to the dictator Antonio Salazar was overthrown in 1974. Whereas Great Britain granted independence to its colonies successively from 1957 to 1965, France granted independence to all its colonies in Africa in a single year (1960). After independence, the main concern was what kind of social order would replace the regime of the colonial powers. On March 6, 1957, Ghana became independent, and by the mid-1960s, thirty African countries had freed themselves from colonial power. Kwame Nkrumah, the leader of Ghana's liberation movement, had proclaimed in 1955, that when Ghana achieved independence, it would be transformed into a paradise on earth within 10 years. "African socialism" was to be the new social order. Tanzania's Julius Nyerere; the charismatic leader of Kenya, Jomo Kenyatta; and Kenneth Kaunda of Zambia opted for the same path. In 1961, Nkrumah visited the Soviet Union and was impressed by the rapid rate of industrialization. He imposed a seven-year plan on his country under the slogan "Build as many factories as rapidly as possible." However, Nkrumah became increasingly remote from his people, and in 1964 he introduced a one-party regime and allowed himself to be celebrated as the "deliverer." He also built prestigious edifices such as the Volta Dam, which could not be fully utilized under given conditions. The people had benefited little from his efforts. On February 24, 1966, as Nkrumah was visiting Burma on his way to China, he learned that the army had carried out a coup against him and had seized power. He returned to Africa and traveled to Guinea, whose president, Sékou Touré, appointed him co-president. Nkrumah died in 1972 in exile. Other African leaders suffered much more terrible destinies. A further example is that of Tanzanian president Julius Nyerere, who was praised as the "father of the nation" (*mwalimu*). Nyerere never became a bloody dictator and remained highly respected in the West. His government, which lasted decades, ended in impoverishment and corruption under the aegis of real socialism (albeit a milder form). His life also ended in exile. By the time Nyerere died in a London hospital on October 15, 1999, at the age of seventy-seven, his experiment and the experiment of his successor, who continued to govern on socialist principles, had definitively failed. But the result of adapting real socialism was even worse in countries such as Angola, Mozambique, and Ethiopia, where it led to years of civil war and foreign interference.

African socialism, which failed to benefit the peoples of the continent, has had its day. In the meantime, globalism has accelerated Africa's transformation to traditional capitalism. Africa founders in poverty, starvation, and civil wars. It is the poorest continent on the planet. But other developing countries in Asia and South America must also endure hunger and deprivation. The discrepancy between the developing and developed countries, however, is much greater in regard to wages than productivity. Capitalism is just more aggressive in these countries than elsewhere. A few examples graphically demonstrate the scale of this disproportion: in the United States, 3.4 hours of labor are necessary to produce a ton of steel; in Brazil the figure is 5.8 hours. However, the wage ratio is 10:1 ($13 an hour versus $1.28). It takes fourteen minutes to produce a shirt in the U.S. textile industry; in Bangladesh it takes twenty-five minutes. But while the average hourly wage in the United States is $7.35, in Bangladesh it is only 25 cents.[32] A similar discrepancy is found between quite high levels of productivity and low wages in the Mexican car industry. In Mexico's manufacturing industry, labor productivity has risen by 40 percent since 1980, but wages have decreased by 40 percent. The inference is obvious: it is not so much low productivity that is to blame for the poverty in developing countries, but rather the unfair distribution of national income to the detriment of the workers and to the benefit of the employers. The proportion of workers in the value of production is declining, not only in the developing countries, but also in the highly developed countries of the West. Greider notes that in the last twenty years the proportion of wages in value creation has declined from 45 to 35 percent in the United States, and from 47 to 42 percent in Germany. An exception is South Korea, where, as a consequence of mass protests, the share of workers increased from 23 to 30 percent in a few years. In the United States, however, the discrepancy between the rich and the poor has also risen. While the income of the super rich (5 percent) has increased by 50 percent in the last fifteen years, the income of the lower 60 percent of the poor has scarcely changed.[33] As a result of its work ethic and remarkable frugality, Asia has a considerable potential for development. Nonetheless, because industrial control, political power, and finance capital are concentrated in only a few hands, Asia is handicapped. In Indonesia, 61.7 percent of the capital market is in the hands of just fifteen super-rich families. The figures are similar in the Philippines and Thailand—55.1 percent and 53.3 percent respectively.[34]

The consequences of globalization and (among other things) the growing discrepancy between the poor and rich were the center points of a debate in Florence (November 20–22, 1999) to which Massimo D'Alema, Italy's head of government at that time, invited U.S. president Bill

Clinton, the president of the EU Commission, Romano Prodi, and the Social Democratic prime ministers of Great Britain (Tony Blair), Germany (Gerhard Schröder), France (Lionel Jospin), and Portugal (Antonio Guterres). In 1999, the developing countries expected a growth rate of 1.5 percent, the lowest in the last seventeen years, lower even than the population growth. In response to this, Clinton urged the elimination of social injustices and proposed a "global economy with a human face." "My third way," said the president, "is to enable everyone to extract the greatest possible potential from technical development."[35] "Equality of opportunity must be promoted, he said. The world, however, is still far from this goal. Romano Prodi countered that while Europe could learn much from the United States on how to create jobs, America must also "recognize the success of the old continent in achieving a more just income distribution."[36] On the other hand, Gerhard Schröder voiced the opinion that it was necessary to restructure the welfare state and demanded an "activating role" for the state, which would only be possible at the expense of the workers. At that time, Schröder was about to put through a package of cost-cutting measures, which caused the Social Democratic Party (SPD) painful losses in five federal states in the autumn elections of 1999. Nonetheless, the chancellor said that the people must learn to stand on their own two feet again. Tony Blair also pleaded for a new social contract with citizens. Margaret Thatcher, who had implemented comprehensive frugality measures that proved painful for the citizens, had already prepared this path. D'Alema took the same tack: "We need a courageous reformism," he said. Lionel Jospin, who represents a more traditional course in a social democracy, was more critical and warned against a "clinical capitalism." In the debate on the role of the state in a world economy, he spoke up unequivocally for strengthening the nation-state. He pointed to the danger that nation-states would be "inundated" by the consolidating world economy and emphasized that "nation-states are still the place where democracy is born."[37]

Globalization Versus Nation-State?

It was no accident that in Florence, Clinton spoke of the "inequalities" that had to be eliminated if globalization were to succeed. The United States is a great power in the world economy and is capable of setting many things in motion. More far-sighted American politicians are aware of this. They know that if the United States remains the lonely figure at the top of the world pyramid with respect to full employment and wealth, sooner or later this will cause major difficulties for national security, economic growth, trade, and immigration policy (among other things).

Nevertheless, North America has made no notable progress in its relationship to Latin America. The promise to extend the North American Free Trade Agreement (NAFTA) to South American countries has so far remained empty. Trade barriers, moreover, remain at a quite high level, and U.S. foreign trade with Latin America is stagnating (Mexico is an exception). In the end, globalization is a process of opening to the outside world and not an institutional executive power. To help get this progressive process under way, the Americans, who call the shots, must first clean up their own front yard—that is, they must help South America to overcome centuries of backwardness. In order to rectify the harm done after the debacle of the WTO summit in November 1999, an active, purposeful U.S. policy to promote a socially harmonious globalization seems all the more urgent. The American protesters in Seattle stated explicitly that their goal was to protect the sovereignty of countries from the "dark forces of globalization" and anonymous international institutions. This thesis that globalization undermines the sovereignty of nation-states and causes harm to independent nations is voiced not only in America. One of the leading Social Democratic leaders in Europe, French prime minister Lionel Jospin, also spoke of the deluge of globalization at the November conference in Florence. The arguments of the opponents of globalization are identical: it is claimed that globalization and the WTO undermine democratic principles by regarding national laws as trade barriers that have a negative influence on international economic relations, environmental protection, and human rights. However, Jack L. Goldsmith and John C. Joo correctly state: "The progressive activists defend the sovereignty of America, not because they are concerned about indigenous democratic institutions, but because they are opposed to free trade and economic interdependence."[38] The WTO, moreover, is an institution that poses the least danger for national legal systems because no single country, whether that be the United States or Belgium, can block the jointly accepted regulations. The WTO agreements have no executive authority within a state, either in court proceedings or elsewhere. Thus the WTO, claim Goldsmith and Joo, is a model that is capable of coordinating international norms with national sovereignty.

Peter F. Drucker, one of the top experts on this problem, claims that while the withering away of the nation-state has been a topic of discussion for two hundred years, it is only in the last thirty-five years that it has been debated as a current problem of world policy. In 1795, Immanuel Kant wrote on this topic in his essay "On Eternal Peace," and Karl Marx dreamed of the "disappearance of the state" as the desired goal of the socialist movement. In many of his speeches in the 1950s and 1960s, Bertrand Russell also discussed this problem. Drucker comments that what Lord William Rees-Mogg has to say on this topic in his book, *The Sovereign Individual*, is fresh in our memories. "But," says Drucker, "the nation state has shown amazing resilience." Whereas Czechoslovakia and Yugoslavia have ceased to exist as multiethnic states as a consequence of the big turn, Turkey has developed a solid and cohesive state structure. Moreover, all the countries of the collapsed Euro-Asian empire, hammered together by the tsars and consolidated even more firmly by their Communist successors, have formed independent states.[39]

In all probability, says Drucker, the nation-states will outlive the globalization of the economy, as well as the information revolution accompanying it. What survives, however, will be a substantially altered nation-state with different powers in fiscal, currency, and foreign economic policy, as well as in such areas as the control of national enterprises. The sovereignty of the nation-state in modern history has never been unlimited, especially in reference to its fundamentals—namely, monetary, credit, and fiscal policy. According to Jean Bodin, a well-known French legal expert, these policies are responsible for determining the breadth of state sovereignty. Drucker refers to the limited executive powers of the nation-state in currency and credit policy in the nineteenth and twentieth centuries. By the end of the nineteenth century, coins or banknotes issued by the state had lost their hitherto dominant role in money circulation, giving way to the creation of money by private commercial banks. In order to exercise an effective control over these commercial banks, the state established central banks under its jurisdiction. The United States, for instance, established the Federal Reserve System in 1912. All other states have done the same. The fundamental principles of monetary policy in the nineteenth century, however, were determined not so much by national institutions as by the gold standard, an utterly international institution that could by no means be defined as an institution of the nation-state. This worldwide standard exercised a rigorous control over the monetary and fiscal policy of nation-states up until World War II. In 1944, the Bretton Woods Agreement replaced it with the gold exchange standard. Although the latter was much more flexible than the gold standard, it too did not give the member nations full sovereignty in determining their national monetary policy. It was not until 1973, when President Richard Nixon took the dollar off the gold standard and allowed it to float freely, that nations gained autonomy in setting their exchange rate. Nevertheless, full sovereignty—specifically, unlimited freedom in setting the exchange rate—proved to be more detrimental to inner stability in monetary and fiscal policy than the reserve and moderation (in regard to the interests of trading partners) that had been imposed by the gold and gold exchange standards. These worldwide control mechanisms were more favorable for international economic relations than full sovereignty.

When the Bretton Woods system was created, the disastrous consequences of the "beggar thy neighbor policy" of the period of the world economic crisis in the 1930s, in which countries radically devalued their currencies in order to gain advantages at the expense of their trading partners, was still fresh in people's memory. This devaluation policy had triggered a chain reaction that decimated foreign trade worldwide. Such a policy is unthinkable today. However, the temptation still exists to revert to deficit spending during times of recession or promote exports and restricting imports through economically justified devaluations in order to limit foreign trade deficits. For instance, the recent practices of Southeast Asian and South American countries, which found themselves in a financial crisis, are just two of many well-known examples.

The Economist points out that the postwar period has been oriented toward the dismantling of foreign trade barriers and the moderation of deficit spending. This has been abetted by the GATT, which, after coming into force in 1947, successively tore down the foreign trade barriers built up in the 1920s and 1930s and since the 1960s has been favorable to foreign investments by multinational concerns. Furthermore, deficit spending was not that high in the "golden years" of 1950 to 1973: in 1970 it was no more than 32.3 percent of the GNP of the twenty-two rich OECD countries (this is equal to the present spending level of the United States). In Germany, France, and Great Britain, it was 38–39 percent. Public spending reached a peak between 1970 and 1995 by expanding another 10 percent in the overall OECD domain. Since 1990, however, there has been a discernible tendency for state spending to diminish. At the world economic conference in Davos in January 2000, the prime minister of Saxony, Kurt Biedenkopf, said that in the EU 45–50 percent of the GNP would be distributed not through the markets but by governments and institutions. Globalization, he said, is and would remain a minority program.[40] Advancing globalization has given the term "economic sovereignty" a new meaning. It is more restricted than at any other time in international relations. Yet it would be wrong to assess this development as negative, since the dismantling of trade barriers; the opening of state borders to free commerce, goods, capital, and labor; and the moderation of customs tariffs are all within the common interests of the partner states and presume a certain reciprocity, a generally arrived-at consensus.

Susan Strange correctly points out that "globalization has fundamentally changed the nature of production and the source of finance, and has begun to change beliefs, perceptions, ideas and tastes. These forces and ideas, and the international institutions established to manage them, have eroded the traditional attributes of sovereignty and accountability, and have allowed the shift of power from states to firms."[41] George Soros writes: "We have a global economy, but the political agreements are still firmly grounded in the sovereignty of the state."[42] He asks: "How can the needs of a global society be reconciled with the sovereignty of the states?" Soros advocates an alliance of states that "would include the United States, the European Union, a critical mass of democratic countries from the periphery of the capitalist system." The most problematic member, according to Soros, "would be the United States, because at present it is unwilling to abide by the rules it seeks to impose on others."[43]

The global economy has forced governments to exercise stricter control over themselves than ever before and to display discipline and restraint in fiscal policy. Currency floating, an often misused policy that was introduced in 1973, has brought huge sums of money into circulation that have no lasting influence on economic activity, production, consumption, or investment. This "world money," which is created through and in currency trading, does not perform any of the traditional functions of money, such as being a form of value or an instrument of exchange. "It is totally anonymous. It is virtual rather than real money. But its power is real," writes Peter Drucker.[44] The volume of such money is gigantic. In a single day it is capable of reaching a turnover that would be enough to finance trade and investment for a whole year. However, this world money is extremely mobile and flees the capital market in panic at the slightest suspicion of devaluation. Recent events in South America have exposed this inglorious practice and its devastating consequences for the stability of the world economy. Although it exercises no traditional functions, the world money acts increasingly as a determining factor for the monetary policy of nation-states. Thus responsibility shifts more and more from nation-states to the world economy. There are winners and losers in the globalization of the world economy. As a rule, it is the strong economies that win at the expense of the weaker ones. But to argue, as the American protesters in Seattle argued, that the United States, the world's greatest economic power, is sacrificing its sovereignty and its economic interests to the benefit of its trading partners is, to put it mildly, illogical and seems to better correspond to the temptations of traditional American isolationism than to reality.

Economic power is not so heavily concentrated as one hundred years ago, however. In July 1945, forty-six nations signed the UN charter. Now the United Nations has 185 members. In 1946, the four superpowers accounted for three-fourths of world production. Fifty years later, the G-7 made up only 65 percent of total production. (The G-7 states are the United States, Germany, France, Great Britain, Italy, Japan, and Canada.) While in 1950 five great powers accounted for 82 percent of world spending for weapons, in 1993 seven countries account for only 70 percent of this outlay.[45] Yet Robert Pastor is obviously convinced that the influence of the great powers on economic events has, if anything, increased in these times of globalization. As evidence for this, he points to the swift increase in the capital transferred to the world money markets, an increase by a factor of eight since 1986, to $1 trillion daily. The principal recipients are the countries of the Third World and the reform countries of Central and Eastern Europe. Since national barriers have been dismantled, the influx of foreign capital has risen dynamically, says Pastor. He goes on to say that the United States, with its laissez-faire model, exerts the greatest influence on economic events. Japan, which is still trying to find a balance between the state and the market, and Germany, which despite all its cutbacks would still like to maintain a social market economy, also play weighty roles in the global economy. The United States influences international economic relations more than any other country. Thus Bill Clinton had to swallow much criticism at the world economic forum in Davos in January 2000. Among other things, in view of the existing worldwide constellation of power, the question was raised whether the world of the peace of Westphalia in 1648 had come to an end. The well-known French political scientist Dominique Moise admonished: "The United States must not become in politics what Microsoft is for the information sector."[46]

After the introduction of currency floating in 1973, which has brought a great deal of economically unjustified money into circulation, nation-states tried to take countermeasures by strengthening or establishing super-national regional communities. The community of the eleven EU states of Western Europe, which began to restructure its economic union into a currency union in early 1993, has gone the furthest in this direction. These nations have transferred their sovereignty in currency and fiscal policy wholly to the supernational European Central Bank. In January 1994, NAFTA entered into force with similar designs. As a result, foreign trade among Canada, America, and Mexico has doubled in five years. The Association of Southeast Asian Nations (ASEAN), founded in 1967, is still not a free trade zone, but it does contribute to the expansion of economic cooperation. The Asia Pacific Economic Cooperation (APEC), a group of twenty-one countries, agreed to establish a free trade zone on both shores of the Pacific by the year 2020. The United States joined a group of thirty-three Western nations in December 1994 with the intention of establishing a free trade zone by the year 2005. In South America, the trade bloc Mercosur, whose members consist of Brazil, Argentina, and Uruguay, with Chile and Bolivia as associated members, has initiated many jointly conceptualized projects. Thanks to Mercosur and the economic reforms introduced, Latin American foreign trade tripled in the 1990s. As noted above, the opponents of globalization who demonstrated in Seattle were described by Mexican president Ernesto Zedillo as a "curious alliance of forces of the extreme Left, environmentalists, and other self-appointed critics, who have joined together in the attempt to bar the peoples of the developing countries from participating in development."[47] In Davos 2000, it was not globalization and the related reduction of sovereignty that was criticized but the "protectionism of the rich." This criticism came especially from the Latin American countries. The Argentine president, Fernando de la Rua, and the president of Colombia, Andrés Pastrana, especially attacked the protectionism of the rich in agricultural production. Zedillo had similar things to say at the beginning of the deliberations. The fact that economic liberalism "now speaks Spanish" was pointed out by José Maria Aznar, the Spanish prime minister, who further emphasized that the Spanish-speaking world consisted of a population of about 600 million and that the United States would soon be the second largest Spanish-speaking country in the world, after Mexico. Aznar pleaded cogently for a greater opening of Europe to the other regions of the world and called for deep reforms of the European labor market and social system "in order to foster more motivation, creativity, and competitiveness."[48]

Nobel Laureate James Buchanan directed strong criticism against protectionist measures, especially those of his homeland, the United States, in a conversation with *Die Presse* in Vienna.[49] Buchanan said: "I consider the strengthening of protectionist forces that are against opening markets and free trade to be very dangerous. For example, we use our antidumping legislation to protect our own industries, such as the steel industry. At the same time, however, we chastise the Japanese, the Chinese, and others because we have a balance of trade deficit with them." In his opinion, the greatest increase in productivity in the past fifty years has been due to the revolution in telecommunications and computers. Buchanan is concerned with "what will happen when the bubble on the shares market bursts." In particular, Buchanan fears that U.S. central banks will panic and respond incorrectly by pumping too much liquidity too rapidly into the economy. A very serious inflation may be the consequence.

The WTO is gradually getting over the shock of Seattle. Mike Moore, the head of the WTO, would like to liberalize world trade through shuttle diplomacy. He has held talks with U.S. trade commissioner Charlene Barshevsky, traveled to India and Japan, and visited the EU trade commissioner, Pascal Lamy. The main topic was the proposal, which had already been discussed in Seattle, to eliminate all trade barriers for goods from the twenty-nine poorest countries. Nevertheless, Europe has some reservations with regard to certain agricultural products, and the United States is concerned about textiles. If nothing else can be achieved, as is mooted in WTO circles, Moore would at least like to put together an agreement for the poorest countries. That would be a good start for the liberalization of agricultural products and services, which account for 70 percent of the value of world trade. However, it is clear that a major breakthrough in this direction is not to be expected in the near future.

The Partners in Globalization, Big and Small

In the introduction to *The World in 2000*, a special edition of *The Economist*, its editor, Dudley Fishburn, presents a somewhat rosy picture of the world economy in the year 2000. The world will increase its wealth by 3.5 percent, but the huge U.S. economy will see its growth rate slowed. Europe, on the other hand, will experience an increase in its growth rate. The prosperity of one-third of the world population, living in China and India, will develop twice as rapidly as that of the "wealthy world." The Internet will "escalate to a world language," and, although there will be conflicts among states, there will be no war. Democracy will chalk up a number of triumphs: thirty parliamentary elections will take place, some in countries where twenty-five years ago dictators ruled. Russia will elect a president, but poverty will remain a problem. This is, Fishburn says, a sign that democracy is meaningless at the voting booth if there is no rule of law. The U.S. elections on November 7, 2000, will show that this "fortunate country" will put an educated person at the helm of the ship of state, for "America's system is easily mocked but it does not produce fools." Furthermore, after fifty years, Great Britain might surpass France's economic power. *The World in 2000* presents some important statistics on the principal actors in the global economy. Table 1.1 reproduces this information.

Of the thirty-three countries listed in the table, China and Italy may expect the highest growth rates. Japan's economy, on the other hand, will again fail to show growth in 2000. Of the major economic powers, Japan remains the problem child of the world economy. Japan's strong currency still functions as a break on economic development. The yen has increased in value vis-à-vis the dollar by 20 percent since January 2000. The Industry Bank of Japan (IBJ), which specializes in long-term credit, fears that a further rise in the exchange rate to 95 yen per dollar, as occurred once before in 1995, would mean a 1.7 percent loss in economic growth annually for the next two to three years. The government has opened all the floodgates to stimulate the economy with tax money and has allowed the state budget deficit to increase to 8 percent of the GNP. The debt rate is now 130 percent of the GNP. A debt of this magnitude harbors the danger of inflation and a rise in interest rates. Russia also remains a problem child for the world economy: its per capita GNP has declined to the level of Egypt's. Vladimir Putin, in the television program *Russia at the Turn of the Millennium*, said that his country must grow annually by a level of 8 percent over a period of fifteen years in order to reach the level of Portugal or Spain. Russia's GNP is at present one-tenth that of the United States and one-fifth that of China (which of course has a much greater population). The energy sector and the iron

Table 1.1

Statistics on the Global Economy, by Region and Country

Region and country	GNP (in billions of dollars)	GNP per capita (in dollars)	Population (in millions)	GNP growth prognosis for 2000 (in percent)	Inflation (in percent)
Western Europe					
Austria	217.9	26,740	8.1	2.4	1.0
Belgium	262.8	25,670	10.2	0.6	1.6
Denmark	173.8	32,576	5.3	1.8	2.4
Germany	2,260.4	27,337	82.7	2.3	1.4
Italy	1,236.9	21,393	57.8	2.1	2.0
Spain	576.8	14,623	39.4	2.9	2.3
Sweden	252.4	28,417	8.9	3.3	1.7
Great Britain	1,423.8	23,947	59.5	2.6	2.6
France	1,464.9	24,956	58.7	2.7	1.1
Central and Eastern Europe					
Czech Republic	57.1	5,580	10.2	1.5	4.6
Hungary	51.8	5,180	10.0	3.0	9.7
Poland	166.3	4,290	38.7	4.5	7.5
Romania	33.3	1,480	22.5	1.0	28.0
Russia	205.3	1,410	145.7	1.0	38.0
Ukraine	29.7	590	49.5	0.0	20.0
Asia					
China	1,001.0	790	1,266.5	7.0	2.5
India	539.7	540	1,002.4	6.1	8.0
Japan	3,913.3	30,720	127.4	0.0	0.1
Pakistan	65.0	430	149.7	3.5	8.5
Vietnam	29.7	367	80.9	5.7	12.0
Latin America					
Brazil	535.8	3,280	163.4	2.7	8.7
Mexico	496.5	5,040	98.4	3.9	12.9
Argentina	326.2	8,810	37.0	2.9	–1.5
North America					
Canada	692.0	22,394	30.9	2.8	1.6
United States	9,333.0	33,946	274.9	2.7	2.6
Africa					
Kenya	9.2	292	31.6	2.5	7.0
Nigeria	51.7	450	113.8	3.2	17.0
South Africa	138.2	3,150	43.8	3.2	5.0
Middle East					
Algeria	49.2	1,592	30.9	4.9	4.5
Egypt	98.6	1,499	65.7	5.6	4.3
Iran	68.1	1,050	64.8	2.1	25.0
Israel	100.7	16,100	6.3	3.6	5.8
Saudi Arabia	140.9	6,550	21.5	1.5	2.5

Source: Compiled from "The World in Figures: Countries," *The World in 2000* (London: *The Economist*, 2000), pp. 75–82.

and steel industries still account for 50 percent of Russia's total industrial production and 70 percent of Russia's exports. The proportion of high technology for civilian purposes accounts for only 1 percent of world trade, while this figure for the United States is 36 percent. Putin proposes to eliminate Russia's centuries of backwardness with the "Russian way." But his Communist predecessors wanted to do the same thing. The consequences are well known. In 1999, the Russian GNP increased by 3.2 percent, primarily due to an abrupt rise in oil prices. However, compared to 1997, the year before the crisis, the volume of investment decreased by 6 percent, retail trade by 11 percent, and foreign trade by as much as 30 percent. The unemployment rate rose to 17 percent.[51] The economy of Ukraine, the second largest Slavic successor state to the disintegrated Soviet Union, has declined even further. Its GNP per capita is $590—not much higher than that of India ($540). When radical change commenced, Ukraine generated a national product of $29.3 billion, which is half the level of 1991.

The forecasts in *The World in 2000* concerning individual economic branches are also of interest. The computer industry will bring smaller, quicker, and cheaper products to the world market. Between 1998 and 2003, the number of households with online PCs will grow by 13 percent in Italy, 17 percent in Spain, 34 percent in Great Britain, 42 percent in France, 45 percent in Sweden, and 81 percent in Greece. The auto industry can also expect dynamic growth: in 2005, General Motors will produce 5.1 million cars, Volkswagen 4.5 million, Ford/Mazda/Volvo 4.4 million, Toyota/Daihatsu 4.3 million, and Renault/Nissan 3.8 million. Europe, however, is already producing 20 percent more cars than can be sold. The prognosis for Peugeot and Fiat is gloomy. It is believed that if these two big European firms are incapable of increasing their production through acquisitions or alliances with other manufacturers, they will fall behind their competitors. In the meantime, Fiat has placed its stakes with a "big one" by allying with GM. Moreover, GM/Suzuki and Ford/Mazda will produce a small "strategic car" for Asia by the end of 2000, and Daimler/Chrysler is at present looking for new partners; Mitsubishi and Subaru are possible candidates.

Energy consumption will increase by 1.3 percent 2000 and by 2 percent 2001. At present, oil reserves on a scale of one billion barrels have been found, and an increase of 10 percent in investments is expected, mainly in the Caucasus region. The use of nuclear energy is declining, but a revival is not to be ruled out. Prices for raw materials also show a rising trend. The use of aluminum in car production will rise to 150,000 tons by 2005, whereas in 1998 it was only 22,000 tons. Copper mines in the United States will be abandoned, but production over the next two years will decline by only 2 percent. At 14.2 percent of the GNP, health expenditures for 2000 will be highest in the United States, followed by Germany at 10.5 percent, France at 10.2 percent, Japan at 7.5 percent, and Great Britain at 7 percent. The OECD also has a positive assessment of developments in the world economy for 2000. Its prognosis is based on the assumption of a "cautious decline" in the high growth rate of the United States. Perceptible rises in basic interest rates, estimated at 6.25 percent for 2000, will contribute to this decline. The developing countries, however, could suffer from the envisaged interest rate rises in the industrial countries. According to the OECD, growth of world trade in 2000 will be 7.1 percent, and in 2001 it will decline to 6.3 percent.[52] The former director of the IMF, Michel Camdessus, says that "uncertainties still plague the world economy, and it is necessary that, for the present, we avoid self-complacency." The international community will probably face "many difficult trials in the coming years." Camdessus warns that today's world faces the "specter of a new and complex sort of financial crisis."[53]

2

Transnational Corporations and Competition Among the Great Powers in the Global Economy

Today's transnational firms are truly world concerns. These global multis, which increasingly move whole production sectors abroad, where they use a local labor force and sell their products, are carrying out production less and less in their home countries. McDonalds, Boeing, ABB, and Nestlé produce more than half of their output outside of their domestic market. Ninety-eight percent of Swiss food manufacturer Nestlé's turnover is outside Switzerland, and 96 percent of its employees are also abroad. It is not competition among nation-states but among transnational concerns that is the determining factor for the international division of labor. Boeing, the biggest U.S. aircraft manufacturer, no longer views itself as an American firm but as a global concern that has created sixty thousand jobs in Europe alone. The megamultis divide the world markets among themselves. Like a global oligopoly, many multis dominate the most important economic sectors. Mergers and takeovers have reached such a scale that the sums exchanged are comparable to a major portion of the state budget of a European country. For example, German finance minister Klaus Grubelnik notes that the British mobile phone concern Vodafone made a takeover offer of $121 billion for its German competitor Mannesmann; this is several times larger than the sum the minister would have to raise to pay off the state deficit. The economic expert of the Viennese *Die Presse*, Josef Urschitz, justly poses the question: "Will we have in the foreseeable future a world economy in which Daimler/Chrysler builds cars, Time-Warner/AOL takes care of information and entertainment, Wal-Mart builds supermarkets, Exxon/Mobil supplies fuel, and Electricité de France supplies electricity?"[1]

There are two crucial forces driving globalization: technological innovation (especially information and communication technology) and the triumph of market ideology as a result of the fall of the Soviet empire, as well as the economic reforms in China and Vietnam. The hegemony of neoliberal ideology, as former Dutch prime minister Ruud Lubbers put it, is a catalyst that economizes our life habits and customs, enforces deregulation, and promotes mass consumption. The production strategy of large concerns has changed radically. As an example, Josef Urschitz points out the victorious "Welch doctrine." Fifteen years ago, Jack Welch, head of General Electric, called for the elimination of every product from the firm's range of goods that did not make the top three worldwide in its sector. The *New York Times* summed up the Welch doctrine with the phrase "dominate or perish." The globalized world economy is totally integrated through the telephone and the Internet. A pioneer of modern German entrepreneurship, Paul Neef, said in a talk with *Der Spiegel* that "there is practically no firm that has not recognized the role played by the Internet."[2] Whereas at first there were attempts to dismiss the Internet as a fad or "media hype" that had been cooked up by a few madmen in the United States, now it is taken seriously even by top management. According to the founder of the firm Pixelpark, which provides Internet business assistance to more than 150 customers, the question of a business strategy for the future is synonymous with the question of a strategy for the Internet, and anyone who does not have an answer to this question faces tremendous problems. U.S. President Bill Clinton has devised a $2 billion program for the next ten years to help U.S. citizens with low incomes meet their need for an Internet hookup. "Television, radio, telephones, and anything else that can be digitized will enter tomorrow's household" through a universal wall plug, says *Der Spiegel*; "cyberspace has become part of everyday life. Not even a carton of milk makes it to the shelf today without a computer optimizing the driving route of the delivery truck or a clever algorithm having calculated beforehand the needs of the consumer."[3] Connection to the Internet is as self-evident as having electricity. Although the Internet was regarded initially as a sales channel, Paul Neef insists that this view is too shortsighted. Moreover, it is much more important to adapt internal processes, to organize anew the recreation of value, thus reducing costs enormously. The loser will be traditional trade. In its place, new medium-sized firms will form that have nothing more to do with logistics but rather conduct "automated markets." Price competition will no longer take place among trade organizations but among the producers. Experts expect new impulses in the next century from small young enterprises in biotechnology, information technology, and E-business, where young researchers and "resourceful thinkers" will find work and dream of careers like that of Bill Gates, whose company, Microsoft, has made him the wealthiest man in the world. There is already a new archetype—namely, that of Jeff Bezos, who founded the Internet bookshop Amazon.com and now has the biggest virtual bookstore in the world. Since its posting on the stock market, the stock has risen by more than 3,800 percent. *Der Spiegel* mentions a similar discrepancy between economic strength and value on the stock exchange. For example, three German Internet firms that were founded a few years ago have a value on the stock exchange of about DM 30 billion, which is more than the total value of Volkswagen. However, while VW has an annual turnover of DM 147 billion, the three Internet firms do not even bring in half a billion. The experts ask, and with good reason, how far the stock exchange bubble can continue to inflate before it explodes with a big bang.

Globalization is driven not only by the global multis, but also by huge regional communities. The EU, for instance, plans to admit the reform countries of Central and Eastern Europe, as well as the Baltic countries, in the next few years. NAFTA, moreover, will further integrate the countries of North America. The region around the Pacific Rim has already decided to create a free-trade zone for its twenty-one members by the year 2020; together with the United States, Japan, and China, Pacific Rim trade accounts for more than half of world production. Finally, Rudi Dornbusch, the U.S. economist and MIT professor, prophesies that a tripolar economic world will form: North and South America on the one hand, Europe spreading to the Ural Mountains on the other, and a huge Asian bloc. This triad will be dominated by three currencies: the dollar, the Euro, and the Chinese yuan. China, according to Dornbusch, will overtake Japan as a world economic power. Furthermore, the technological level of developing countries will gradually reach the level of the industrial countries. Social backwardness, however, will remain an issue for some time. It will diminish, if at all, only at a very slow rate.

The total assets of the two hundred wealthiest persons exceed the total income of 41 percent of the total population. Three billion persons, half of the world population, must get along on less than $2 per day. The tremendous discrepancy between the research and high-tech levels aimed at by the developing countries and their overall efficiency is striking. For example, India has become the hottest spot for research and development, especially in information technology. Six of the twelve biggest data processing centers in the world are in India. Megamultis such as Daimler/Chrysler, the pharmaceutical concerns Eli Lilly and Astra, the aeronautics concern British Aerospace, the food giant Unilever, and the electronics concerns Texas Instruments and S.G.S. Thompson do research and develop models in New Delhi, Bombay, and Bangalore. A data processing specialist, together with a staff of 140 persons, processes about 4 million tickets per year on commission from the AUA Zentrale in Vienna and thus saves Austrian airlines $2.5 million per year. Although in such an undertaking a specialist from India earns only a fraction of the earnings of his European counterpart, in India he or she is considered a big earner.[4] Whereas the per capita GNP of India, which has outstanding research centers, is no more than $540 annually, in the United States it is $33,946, in Germany $27,337, and in Japan $30,720.[5]

If India and other relatively developed countries in the Third World are able to extend the perfection they have reached in the elite economic sectors to all branches of the economy, the depth of poverty and the still steadily widening gap between the rich and poor could diminish at least partially in the foreseeable future. Hans Peter Martin, Austria's member of the European Parliament and best-selling author, comments that globalization needs a political adjustment. The chairman of the Commission on Global Governance, India's Shridat Ramphal, puts it more clearly: "We must ensure that the first words of the United Nations charter, 'We the people's, do not mutate to We the peoples of the West.'"

The Globalized System Requires Adequate Coordination

Globalization, driven by the third of the industrial, computer, and telecommunications revolutions, is proceeding rapidly and can no longer be halted. It is changing the world and the lifestyles of people and nations, as well as traditional relations among nation-states. However, it has reached a level where supranational coordination is necessary in order to impede inevitable derailments and to pursue objectives that make human life on the planet more tolerable. Moreover, it is necessary to reduce the ever-growing gap between the rich North and the poor South, to establish a worldwide civil society, and, last but not least, to subjugate the megamultis, which elude control by the nation-state, and to control anonymous speculative capital, which is reaching an enormous scale. Anthony Appiah, the author of the introduction to Saskia Sassen's book, *Globalization and Its Discontent*, says correctly: "We must develop a transnational system of alliances if we are to deal with the political economy that, while it is organized in national regimes, increasingly escapes national regulation."[6] Just like the transition from an agricultural society to an industrial society or the three world-changing industrial revolutions, globalization is a free-running process that can no longer be arrested. Similarly, globalization is a natural progression of human civilization; it is an opening of nation-states to one another that accelerates the exchange of goods, services, ideas, and cultural values. The course of things so far, however, shows that a proper supranational coordination is indispensable. Indeed, the "creative destruction" globalization brings about accelerates an already massive accumulation, setting into motion a huge, anonymous, and uncontrollable capital, causing, according to William Greider, a "human exploitation that characterized industry 100 years ago."[7] Technology, ever improving, is forcing millions of people out of their jobs and driving the unemployment rate higher and higher, even in periods of economic boom. The environment is becoming increasingly polluted, the gap between rich and poor is growing deeper, and the number of discontented people is growing. The balance of control is visibly shifting away from the state to the market and away from the nation-state to the global world market. However, it would be a mistake to believe that this market could be a laissez-faire market steered in the right direction by the "invisible hand." This raises the question of how a worldwide supranational body could be established to integrate diversified national economies and what executive powers this body should possess.

The opinions on the relationship between the steering of the free market and the controlling functions of the state remain very controversial. Three are worth citing here. George Soros stated: "The market fundamentalism is today a greater threat to open society than any totalitarian ideology."[8] The thesis of Karl Polanyi is this: The origins of the cataclysms of his time can ultimately be traced back to the evils of laissez-faire. They lay, he writes, "in the utopian endeavor of economic liberalism to set up a self-regulating market system."[9] In contrast to these opinions, Brink Lindsey, director of the Cato Institute's Center for Trade Policy, supports the strengthening of the market mechanisms. He writes:

"I believe that the long term advantage lies with the liberal cause. Since the collectivist, top-down ideal is moribund, there is at present only one viable model of economic development—the liberal model of markets and competition."[10]

Brink Lindsey, as well as other contributors to *Global Fortune*, maintains "that the troubled nations have suffered not from unbridled capitalism, but from perverse forms of government intervention." It is indisputable that globalization is a free-running process driven by market forces; yet the assertion of these authors that a fundamental adherence by these countries to market principles will allow them to enjoy the full prosperity enjoyed by the United States overestimates the beneficent powers of these forces. The task of the greatest importance for the civilized world—that of diminishing the deep and rising discrepancy between the rich and the poor—can be and was initiated by the visible hand of the industrial countries. It has to be continued in cooperation with the most populous countries, such as China and India, as well as with the WTO, IMF, World Bank, and regional economic organizations. No utopian experiment, such as the "New Order" initiated by Willy Brandt is meant here, but rather coordinating endeavors to solve strategically important problems of common welfare that are needed to give the "invisible hand" of the market the right direction.

Francis Fukuyama attempts to make globalization and the WTO palatable to the Left. He is addressing, in particular, those who protested so loudly at the WTO's Seattle conference at the end of November 1999. Fukuyama, who became world famous with his thesis of the "End of History" after the fall of the Berlin Wall, writes: "By creating the WTO, global capitalism has solved the Left's collective-action problem. The WTO is the only international organization that stands any chance of evolving into an institution of global governance."[11] Nonetheless, there is no unified Left, in Europe or elsewhere. The question, however, is whether this brilliant sociologist has identified the proper group that should love globalization. To equate left-wing groups such as the PGA—which called for a "day of action" on November 30, 1999 (the opening day of the WTO conference) and called for resistance to the global capitalist system with slogans such as "The WTO kills people, kill the WTO"[12]—with thousands of other groups, such as trade unions, environmentalists, and defenders of consumer rights, is questionable. Innumerable groups came to Seattle to protest against the WTO as a symbol of every evil of capitalism. It is legitimate to ask Fukuyama precisely why the Left should love globalization since it represents the latest, highest stage of capitalism. The orthodox Left, which has not learned very much from the collapse of the Soviet Union, regards globalization as the realization of neither its collectivist nor international ideals, as Fukuyama claims. In fact, according to Marx's doctrine, those ideals are to be realized via the expropriation of the expropriators and according to the slogans "To each according to his needs, and from each according to his abilities," and "workers of the world, unite." It is of little concern to the Left that these objectives were realized by transferring responsibility for the means of production to the irresponsible state bureaucracy and through the conquest of Central and Eastern Europe by the Soviet Army after World War II, after which the Soviet system was imposed.

The United States is now and will continue to be in the future the economic front-runner. With a roughly sixfold rise in the U.S. living standard in the twentieth century, the improvement in the human condition for the country's citizens has been "more than for all people in all the previous centuries of human history combined."[13] With the experiences of unadulterated authentic capitalism, telecommunications, and the computer era, the United States has shown itself capable of triggering an economic boom that has lasted longer than any other in history. W. Bowman Cutter, Joan Spero, and Laura D'Andrea Tyson correctly state that "the United States enters the twentieth century as the greatest beneficiary of the global system it helped to create after World War II. As a power of unrivaled dominance, prosperity and security, it must now lead the peaceful evolution of the system through an era of significant changes."[14] Unlike other great powers, the United States was never an empire and has had better experience with liberal ideas than any other nation on this planet. It is more strongly committed to the laissez-faire idea than Europe. It has a liberal, extremely flexible labor market. "I believe," says the Nobel Prize laureate James Buchanan, "that the difference between prosperity in the United States and prosperity in Europe in the 1990s is attributed mainly to the fact that the European institutions, especially the labor markets, are by far not so flexible as ours." Furthermore, "In the United States we have a tradition of personal mobility that they do not have . . . in Europe."[15] Moreover, the United States has achieved a record growth in the creation of jobs: 54 million since 1970.[16] However, on the occasion of the conference of Social Democratic heads of government in Florence in November 1999,

Bill Clinton had to listen to the reproach of Romano Prodi, the president of the EU Commission, that the United States should give due consideration to the "success of the old continent in achieving a more just income distribution." This may be true, but Europe is no paradise of equality. It is, however, a long way from the scale of inequality that exists in the United States. Michael Milken, former investment banker and philanthropist, had an annual income of $550 million a few years ago. The CEOs of big concerns earned four hundred times more than their employees; in 1988, the difference was still only 4:1.

In the United States, it is not equality per se but equality of opportunity that is the desirable but hardly realizable objective. Nevertheless, thanks to the rapid development of the capital market, citizens are experiencing more and more opportunities to acquire property and wealth. For instance, about 50 percent of Americans are already stockholders. The difference between the economic achievements of U.S. firms and European firms lies above all in the fact that the Americans invest more than their colleagues from the old continent. Whereas in the last ten boom years Americans have invested twice as much as in the preceding decade, during the same period, Europeans have increased their investment by only 16 percent. The Americans have invested 8 percent of their GNP in the computer sector, the Europeans only 5 percent. But it would be inaccurate to say that the European multis had weakened competition with American firms. The year 2000 was for them a year of transatlantic mergers and acquisitions. According to Thomson Financial Securities Data, in 2000 the European multis purchased nearly eight hundred U.S. firms for a total price of $263.9 billion. This took place despite the heavy losses of Chrysler, merged in 1999 with the German Daimler. Deutsche Telecom purchased U.S. VoiceStream for $50 billion; the Spanish Internet company Terra Networks swallowed U.S. Lycos for $12.5 billion. The British–Dutch Unilever acquired U.S. Bestfoods Group for $20 billion; the Crédit Suisse took over the U.S. investment bank Donaldson Lufkin Jenrette for $13 billion. UBS of Switzerland acquired the U.S. investment bank Paine Webber for $12 billion. Thomson Financial makes it clear that takeover fever by the U.S. multis in the year 2000 was at a peak too. Chase Manhattan acquired the J.P. Morgan group for $32 billion; America Online purchased Time-Warner for $112 billion; General Electric took over Honeywell International for $45 billion; PepsiCo paid $13.5 billion for Quaker Oats; Texaco took over Chevron for $35 billion. The development in the United States of a stocks and bonds society, however, has had some dangerous results. For example, Americans are becoming increasingly indebted to buy stocks. In January 2000, stockholders owed $243.5 billion to brokers who are members of the New York Stock Exchange.

More than any other country on this planet, America has understood the significance of using globalization to open its economy to the outside world for an expanded exchange of goods, and services, and thus has liberalized foreign trade. In the last three years, considerable progress has been achieved through the Global Information Technology Agreement" and multilateral agreements on telecommunications and financial services, as well as in regard to the terms of China's entry into the WTO. On the other hand, the United States has had some bad experiences with sanctions against trade partners for every sort of transgression of the agreed conditions. Sanctions, which have caused export losses to the tune of $20 billion, as well as a loss of two hundred thousand jobs, were applied to twenty-six countries containing half of the world's population. Global developments, however, would have been much better served had these countries received economic help instead.

Globalization and liberalization have served America better than other countries and have helped it to become the greatest exporting country in the world. Alongside increasing productivity, U.S. exports have contributed most to the tremendous economic growth of the 1990s. One-third of economic growth is due to exports. The cost of this growth, however, has been the historically largest and steadily growing foreign trade deficit ($33.18 billion in October 2000, according to the Department of Commerce), especially with Japan and China; the deficit is covered principally with dollar deposits used by these countries as reserve currencies. The deficit in the trade with China in the first ten months of 2000 was $302.53 million. This deficit represented an increase of 41.6 percent in comparison with the same period 1999. Nevertheless, the share of U.S. dollars in the world's foreign exchange reserves was 60.3 percent, whereas it makes up only 17.7 percent in the national currencies that have now given way to the Euro.[17] Since the introduction of the Euro in early 1999, little has changed in its currency composition established in 1998. According to data provided by the governor of the Austrian National Bank, the share of the Euro in the world's currency reserves is now 13 percent.[18] Moreover, in regard to the progressive devaluation of the common EU currency, no essential change is to be expected in the near future.

The United States has made a considerable contribution to the globalization of the world economy since World War II—above all thanks to its crucial role in the creation of the Bretton Woods Agreement of 1944, which established the IMF and the World Bank. Furthermore, the it has guaranteed the stability of the exchange rate against its own gold reserves, an unchanged gold price of $35 an ounce. This system has substantially contributed to the stabilization of monetary and trade relations since World War II. Yet, because of the continuing dollar inflation and the drastic reduction of the gold reserves, this guarantee is no longer effective. In 1971, the dollar was devaluated. And in 1974, Richard Nixon entirely closed the "gold window" and rescinded all the commitments in the Bretton Woods Agreement. Money and capital relations would henceforth be subject to the rules of the free market game. The price of gold rose from $35 to $380 an ounce and later oscillated around $300.

A further step toward opening national markets to one another and the globalization of economic relations was the easing of controls over the transfer of capital outside the country. Germany abolished such controls in 1981, and Japan has done so gradually, although even today it is still preoccupied with this matter. The consequence of these reforms has been a swift rise in the trading stocks and bonds: from $30 billion daily in the 1980s to $500 billion daily in the first half of the 1990s.[19] Stock trading increased at the beginning of the 1990s at a rate of 17 percent, seven times stronger than the economic growth rate of the OECD countries. The liberation of capital transfers from state controls afforded the possibility of reaching the market where the greatest profits could be expected. The foreign exchange reserves of central banks are much too small to be able to withstand this superpowerful current. In 1992, whereas the most powerful central banks in the United States, Germany, Japan, Great Britain, and Switzerland had reserves of $278 billion, trading activities had already reached $623 billion daily.[20] When the United States decided to take the dollar off the gold standard and thus allow it to float freely, it was capitulating to the superior strength of the free market. The IMF has not been responsible for the stability of the exchange rate of its members since 1974. The IMF's functions, set in 1944, have been limited. It now primarily serves as the lender of last resort and as a bail-out financier for countries that have fallen into financial crises, like the recent crises in Southeast Asia, South America, and Russia. This function, however, has come under increasing criticism since it better serves the incautious lenders, by ensuring they get their invested money back, than the crisis-beset borrower. The call to reform the IMF in order to enable it to adapt to worldwide events is becoming ever louder. However, it is becoming increasingly more clear that the almost thirty years of floating, in which the IMF members have been able to change their exchange rate without any restrictions and have often misused this policy to stimulate exports and restrict imports through currency devaluations—a "beggar thy neighbor" practice used throughout the 1930s—has allowed mountains of money to accumulate that elude national or international control. This money is of little utility for production, and increasing prosperity drives stock prices, which are becoming sky high and ever more remote from real values, thus increasing the danger of a devastating collapse. Alan Greenspan's efforts to induce a soft landing have all been ineffective. Keynes's notion that government knowledge is to be valued more highly than market knowledge (which Robert Skidelsky, the biographer of Keynes, interpreted as "the state is wise and the market is stupid") has again fallen into disrepute. The free and ever freer market of the global economy, the megamultis, and the vast and steadily growing speculative capital, which eludes all control, dictate developments on the world market. National governments and young international institutions are unable to adjust for the inevitable derailments. Just as Keynes in his time overestimated the influence of governments on economic events, now Lori Wallach, the symbolic figure of the opponents to globalization worldwide and head of Global Trade Watch, seems to overestimate by far the influence of the young international institutions. She voices her opinion in the following "firm conviction": under the guise of globalization, "power is shifting increasingly from democratically elected governments to anonymous international institutions, which take into account primarily economic interests, and are making the self-determination of nations a hollow concept." In an interview with *Der Spiegel*, Lori Wallach claims that governments are "losing their authority."[21]

One can see from the above example of the IMF, however, that although this organization continues to lend money to prevent national or regional financial crises from spilling over onto the whole world, since 1974, it has in fact lost its powers to influence the exchange rate. The progressive globalization of the world economy can no longer be stopped. Nevertheless, inevitable derailments and counterproductive decisions must be stopped at any price. This task, however, is above all a task of international institutions created by sovereign nation-states, even when they restrict sovereignty in the interests of a community of nations. The task of the opposition is to prevent the derailments but not to prevent the positive developments of international economic relations. It is doubtful if the leader of Global Trade Watch did the world any real service by attempting to torpedo the WTO's conference in November 1999. After all, it was the WTO's goal to liberalize world trade and complete an international agreement for foreign investments, which had been worked on by twenty-nine countries over a three-year period, and to channel investment money into the newly emerging markets, stimulate the economy, and reduce poverty. Lori Wallach overestimates the power of her movement if she believes that her activities can hinder the advance of globalization.

A protest movement, however, can prove useful by making its objective the righting of the incorrect course of globalization. The 1944 Bretton Woods Agreement also created the World Bank, with the goal of facilitating credit for the modernization of infrastructure; the building of dams, streets, and power plants; and the reduction of poverty in developing countries. More than five decades have passed since then, but the gap between rich and poor has not diminished. "With the important exception of Asia and a few other scattered countries, the overall gap in incomes and wealth has grown much wider. Scores of nations around the world are now concretely in worse shape than they were twenty years ago," writes William Greider.[22] Greider goes on to state even more clearly that the IMF and the World Bank "serve as the paternalistic agents of global capital–enforcing debt collection; supervising the financial accounts of poor nations, promoting wage suppression and other policy nostrums . . . instructing and scolding aspirants on the principles of neoclassical economics."[23] Poverty continues to grow. In its "poverty statistics" published in Geneva, the United Nations Development Program (UNDP) points out that the fortunes of the three wealthiest individuals in the world are greater than the GNP of the forty-eight poorest countries, which contain a tenth of the world's population (600 million people). Their share in world trade is no more than 0.3 percent, half as much as twenty years ago. These "poverty statistics" indicate that 100 million of the 1.3 billion people who live in "absolute poverty" inhabit industrial countries.[24] The situation of Africa is in this regard the worst: 16 million people will starve if they receive no outside help, report the newspapers. This continent is most heavily hit by AIDS: as noted, 2 million people have already died of this disease, and several million more are infected with HIV. Therefore, the 250 organizations that have joined together under the umbrella organization Mobilization for Global Justice (on the incentive of a meeting of the IMF and the World Bank) to demand an easing of debt for the poor countries could be a useful proponent of this cause. There can be no doubt that the success of globalization must be measured in terms of the extent to which the ever-growing gap between the rich North and the poor South is reduced.

At a summit meeting of the Third World Group of Nations, which was founded in 1964 by 77 countries and has since increased to 133 countries, held at the same time as the April 2000 meeting of the Bretton Woods Institute, its chairman, Nigeria's president Olusegun Obasanjo, said, "From now on we will play our part in making this world into one that is just, fair and naturally beneficial to all sides." Jamaica's prime minister, P.J. Patterson, added, "We will not be mendicants content with the crumbs that fall from the table of the North." The presidents and vice presidents expressed their frustration that the technological revolution that has brought wealth to the rich has not improved the situation of billions of people in the South, most of whom live in poverty. Fidel Castro stated in especially aggressive tones: "I hold the firmest conviction that the economic order imposed by rich countries is not only cruel, unjust and inhuman . . . but is also carrier of a racist conception of the world which in its time inspired Nazism."[25] The summit adopted a resolution to "bring into being a new humane global order that will even out the growing disparities between rich and poor" and to give the South the right to participate on an equal basis in decisions that concern it. But there have been innumerable resolutions of important international and regional institutions that have been passed without being able to alter the situation. The protesters at the WTO's November 1999 meeting in Seattle and in April 2000 in Washington on the occasion of a meeting of the IMF and the World Bank, as well as during the WTO Prague meeting in September 2000, correctly attacked the inaction in regard to the question of Third World poverty. They targeted mainly the idea of globalization and the development policy of financial institutions, which, according to their slogans in Washington on April 15, "destroy the environment and do harm to the poor people of the Third World." The president of the World Bank, James D. Wolfensohn, replied: "There is no organization on this planet that helps the poor more than we," and further, "neither the World Bank nor the IMF are capable of abandoning globalization. However, what we can do is to help countries and people to adapt to the circumstances in order to reduce the gap." That is precisely the point. The gap is, however, becoming greater.

There can be no doubt that the Bretton Woods Agreement of 1944, as well as the international organizations created some years later, did contribute considerably to postwar reconstruction and to the later economic boom. After World War I and after the devastating world economic crisis of the 1930s—which lead to the rise of fascism in Italy and Germany, militarism in Japan, and finally World War II—the picture of the world changed fundamentally in the second half of the century. Germany, which Charles de Gaulle wanted to "break up into pieces" and Hans Morgenthau wanted to transform into pastureland in his 1944 plan, with Italy and Japan, was brought into the democratic camp thanks to a reasonably rational postwar solution. Colonial domination was brought to an end. The British Empire, with its 450 million inhabitants, broke apart. The jewel in Great Britain's crown, India, gained its independence in 1947, followed by Burma, Ceylon, and Palestine in 1948, and the other British colonies in the early 1960s. Thus Great Britain was able to avoid a devastating colonial war. France was less wise. To affirm its colonial rule, it waged and lost bloody wars against Indochina (1946–54) and Algeria (1954–62). Great Britain established a commonwealth on a volunteer basis, leaving it with the appearance of imperial greatness even as it ceased to exist as a great power.

After 1945, the United States moved into the first ranks. The most far-seeing postwar undertaking of historical significance was the Marshall Plan, which the United States established in 1947. By instigating this plan, the United States showed that it did not intend to operate as the only island of prosperity on earth. The Europe of both the losers and the winners lay in ashes. A great portion of the national economies was destroyed or incapable of functioning. But the Americans as well, whose economy had suffered little from the war, were unable to develop their production capacities because there were no solvent client countries. The purpose of the Marshall Plan was to promote the reconstruction of Europe and thus enable the United States to put to use its production capacities, which had expanded during the war. A certain far-sightedness was discernible in the decision to include the defeated Germany in this plan. This inclusion was a precondition for the economic miracle brought about under the governments of Konrad Adenauer and Ludwig Erhard, which turned Germany into the most powerful social market economy in Europe.

On the other hand, Stalin's decision to prevent the participation of Czechoslovakia and Poland in the Marshall Plan was fateful, although understandable from the standpoint of power politics. Their participation would obviously have been an attempt to remove these two countries from the Soviet Union's influence and claim to absolute power. However, the Soviet Union and its allies still had fifty long years to suffer under the "Iron Curtain" and the trials of the "Cold War." The Marshall Plan helped the economies of Western Europe, which had been devastated by the war, to flourish once again. This laid the foundations for a globalization of the world economy, which would eventually lead to the victory of the West, and the disintegration of the Soviet empire, which could no longer compete in the murderous and costly arms race that it itself had caused. There is no doubt that it was the Marshall Plan that began the process of Europe's transformation from a continent rife with belligerent conflicts to a European common home for the fifteen members of the European Union. No one single country would have been able to reconstruct its devastated economy without it. The preconditions for the evolution to democracy and a social market economy were established and gradually led to a universalization of Western moral values and the West's economic and political system, and, as a consequence of the technological revolution, to a globalization of the world economy. The war not only had destroyed the economy, but it had also devastated the economic and political system, and it was entirely unclear what form of social system would be put in its place.

The leader of Germany's Social Democrats, Kurt Schumacher, who languished for ten years in Nazi concentration camps, stated unequivocally that postwar Germany would replace capitalism with nationalization and central planning. In 1947, the Christian Democrats also promulgated a program that stated that the capitalist economic system had failed. They claimed that "the national and social interests of the German people made it necessary to establish both public ownership at the command heights of the economy," and relatively long-term central planning. Yet these considerations were dropped within a single year. A lot of state and not so much market was Jean Monnet's motto for France's reconstruction plan. Will Clayton, a U.S. undersecretary of state for economic affairs and one of the architects of the Marshall Plan, made it clear to French politicians that France's government had to come up with a precise program for achieving internationally responsible economic parameters as a precondition for U.S. economic aid. This was necessary, he stated, regardless of whether France became liberal or dirigiste, returned to capitalism, or steered toward socialism.[26] Jean Monnet, dubbed the father of Europe, prepared such a program. He redefined the investment goals and resources for the restoration of the most important branches of industry by nationalizing electricity, coal, and railroads and internationalizing steel, cement, and the agricultural branches. Monnet established the Commissariat Général du Plan under the ministry that was to coordinate the reconstruction and modernization of France's economy. His plan created the prerequisites for the French economic miracle of the 1950s that served as a model for the other states of Europe. He helped the economy find its place in international competition, which it had lost even prior to the war. In 1939, the average French industrial plant was four times as old as that in the United States, and three times as old as that in Great Britain.[27]

After the Labour Party under Clement Attlee unexpectedly won the election in 1945 against the undisputed war hero Winston Churchill, the state sector was to play a defining role in the reconstruction of Great Britain's war-wrecked economy. One of the most important decisions of the Labour government was the nationalization of the coal industry, which was later reversed by Margaret Thatcher. The nationalization of innumerable economic branches followed. Central planning played a major role in the coordination of reconstruction. A "mixed economy" was one of the most important components of Labour governments. The first years of the postwar period under the Atlee government were the most difficult in the country's history. In July 1946, bread rationing, which had been avoided throughout the war, was introduced, and it was not until July 1956 that state controls on meat and butter could be lifted. Currency convertibility, which was introduced in July 1947 under pressure from the United States, was abandoned after five weeks, and in September 1949 the exchange rate was reduced to $2.80 per pound sterling. Aid from the Marshall Plan helped Great Britain's economy to get on its feet again. The 1950s and 1960s have entered into the country's history as a golden age.

Because of the volatile political landscape, with its alternation of Labour and Tory governments, with their nationalization and denationalization respectively, Great Britain was unable to keep up with the dynamics of economic growth in Western Europe. In the 1960s, Great Britain's per capita GNP ($1,357) was higher than France's ($1,336) and Germany's ($1,300) and three times higher than Japan's ($463).

However, twenty years later, in 1980, while the per capita GNP of Great Britain was $9,080, Germany's was already $13,410, France's $12,300, and Japan's $9,400. Moreover, while Great Britain's economic growth increased by 1.4 percent annually between 1971 and 1981, this figure was 2.5 percent for Germany, 3.1 percent for France, and 4.8 percent for Japan.[28] The electoral victory of the Tories, led by Margaret Thatcher, in October 1979 marked a radical turn in Great Britain's economic policy. Thatcher broke with collectivist traditions, introduced a far-reaching denationalization, and drove back the often abused, inordinate power of the trade unions. The per capita GNP estimated by *The Economist* for the year 2000 was $23,947, not far from France's ($24,956) but lower than Germany's ($27,337) and much weaker than Japan's ($30,720).[29] Tony Blair followed Margaret Thatcher's economic policies and eliminated nationalization from the party program.

After its devastating defeat in Word War II, Germany developed steadily into Europe's leading economic power and finally achieved the reunification of its divided country. This result was thanks to the policies of the first postwar chancellor, Konrad Adenauer (1949–63), which Josef Joffe has described as a policy toward economic integration without the relinquishment of sovereignty that achieved a steadily increasing level of self-determination with every step.[30] Adenauer was the most zealous advocate of the Coal and Steel Community, the predecessor of the European Economic Community, which was founded in 1957 in Rome. In 1955, the occupation regime ended, and the Federal Republic of Germany joined NATO. Ludwig Erhard continued the policies of his predecessor under the motto "Prosperity for all," and by 1965, West Germany had reached its prewar level. The mixed economy that had been propagated in the first postwar years lost its attractiveness. The SPD's policy, "Market as far as possible, state as far as necessary," which was set down in the party program in Bad Godesberg in 1959, was exactly the policy pursued by the SPD governments of Helmut Schmidt and Willy Brandt. Gerhard Schröder has completely joined Tony Blair in his policy of enterprise and economic efficiency.

France also developed into a competitive partner in the globalization of the world economy, especially when the government abandoned the ambitious nationalization plans from 1945–46 and much later under François Mitterrand, who was elected in 1981 as president of the Fourth Republic. In the 1990s, privatization was again the order of the day, and the state retreated from direct control of the economy. It was de Gaulle's intention to divide the economy into three sectors: private, state-controlled, and nationalized. Nationalization was meant to promote investments, modernization, and technological progress and to adapt economic structures to the requirements of the world market. The government took over control of the banking system, the energy sector, gas, and coal, as well as firms such as Renault and others that had collaborated with the Vichy government. Ironically, the Communist minister of industry at the time proclaimed himself a zealous opponent of nationalization. He claimed that nationalization was an instrument of capitalism to protect the capitalist state against communism. In May 1947, the Communist Party withdrew from the coalition government. Although the mixed economy of the postwar years had played an important role in economic reconstruction, it became an obstacle to further development when France's industry reached the level of maturity at which independent enterprises become a precondition for competitiveness. Denationalization and liberalization created these preconditions. France rose to the fourth strongest economic power in the world, ahead of Great Britain.

The Marshall Plan provided the code for liberalization: reduce trade barriers among European countries in order to make use of U.S. aid more efficiently. The European Economic Community, established by Jean Monnet and France's foreign minister, Robert Schuman, has transformed the markets of the fifteen member countries to a common, internal market. Furthermore, the 1991 Maastricht Agreement laid the foundations for a currency union. Helmut Kohl gave up the all-powerful German mark as a sacrifice for gaining consent for Germany's reunification. Henceforth, the European Central Bank and the central issuing banks now determine the exchange rates of the national currencies; the "beggar thy neighbor" policy has thus come to an end. By early February 2000, in comparison to January 1999, the Euro had lost 18 percent of its value against the U.S. dollar, 15 percent against the British pound, and 21 percent against the Japanese yen. Nevertheless, price stability was guaranteed among the EU members. In fact, the devaluation had a positive effect on the competitiveness of domestic enterprises. The EU became the second most important partner in the global economy. Table 2.1 shows the EU's economic strength in an international comparison.

From Table 2.1 one observes that both the economic strength of the EU and its population are almost the same as that of North America. In the upcoming years the EU will expand to include some of the states of

Table 2.1

Economic Strength of the European Union in Comparison with Other Regions

Region	GNP (1996)	Population	Proportion of world trade
EU	$8.45 trillion (28.6% of world GNP)	373 million	$5.08 trillion (37.2%)
United States, Canada, and Mexico	$8.34 trillion (28.2% of world GNP)	388 million	$2.43 trillion (17.8%)
East Asia	$7.35 trillion (24.9% of world GNP)	1.72 billion	$2.83 trillion (20.8%)

Source: World Bank Indicators, 1998.

Note: East Asia includes Brunei, China, Hong Kong, Indonesia, Japan, Malaysia, the Philippines, Singapore, South Korea, Taiwan, and Thailand.

Table 2.2

Indicators for Four EU Candidates

Indicator	Poland	Czech Republic	Hungary	Slovenia
Area	312,685 km²	78,866 km²	93,035 km²	20,273 km²
Population	38.7 million	10.3 million	10.1 million	2 million
GNP as percentage of the EU's per capita average	39	60	49	68

Source: "Finanzplatz Zentraleuropa," *Die Presse*, March 3, 2000.

Central and Eastern Europe. The reform countries shown in Table 2.2 have the best chances of joining the EU.

An impressive economic area will grow from the EU and its enlargement to the east. A community of twenty-five nations will form from the fifteen EU states and the ten candidate countries of East and Central Europe, thus creating an economic and political zone of almost a half billion citizens in which one-fourth of all world trade will take place. Nonetheless, the distribution of prosperity within an EU of twenty-five will be more differentiated than it is in today's EU. With an average of only 8,400 Euros, the annual GNP per capita in the candidate countries was only 35 percent of the EU's 1998 level. The wage costs are spread over an extremely wide range. For example, in 1997, the labor costs per hour in the manufacturing industries were DM 1.42 in Bulgaria, DM 4.80 in the Czech Republic, DM 3.67 in Estonia, DM 4.81 in Hungary, DM 3.24 in Lithuania, DM 3.37 in Latvia, DM 5.48 in Poland, DM 1.81 in Romania, DM 4.85 in Slovakia, and DM 19.93 in Slovenia. In a currency union such discrepancies in prosperity harbor the danger of economic and social conflict. Whereas entry into the EU would be possible in 2003, according to the Deutsche Bank AG, entry into the currency union would not be possible until 2006. Banking experts warn that an overly early participation in the currency union could entail considerable risks for both the candidates and the EU itself.

Japan is the second largest industrial country in the world, with 70 percent of Asia's national product. However, the land of the rising sun finds itself at present in a phase of economic decay for which no adequate remedy has been found. Since 1992, ten stimulus programs in the amount of about 120 billion yen ($1.2 billion) have been applied, yet the "industrial colossus is still bobbing about in troubled waters."[31] Never in its recent history has Japan's government been so helpless as in the last decade of the second millennium. Since the Meiji renaissance (1868–1912), Japan has sought and found a place among the most developed nations of the world. Young, determined Samurai came to power, putting an end to Japanese feudalism (the longest lasting feudalism in world history) and set loose an industrial revolution with unprecedented dynamics. Better than any country in the world, a determined Japan made use of the best achievements of world technology to improve itself and enter into the world market. Nonetheless, the highly developed economy was not used to raise the living standard: 50 percent of the state budget was used for military ends and for arming and conquering other territories (at first independently and then in alliance with Hitler and Mussolini in World War II). On September 18, 1931, Japan started a war against Manchuria and in 1937 against China, in order to "establish a new order" in all of Asia. In 1942, Japan brought Hong Kong, Burma, the Philippines, French Indochina, and Thailand under its control, thus establishing Japanese hegemony over 350 million people. By the end of the 1930s, the United States had become Japan's main supplier of raw materials and fuels—80 percent of its energy needs, 70 percent of its crude, 93 percent of its copper, and 60 percent of its machinery components. But Japan's self-confident generals started a wholly unexpected war against the United States in 1941 and sank the American fleet stationed at Pearl Harbor. The end results are well known. The Potsdam

Conference in July 1945 decided to destroy the Japanese empire, punish its war criminals, and establish a democratic regime. Just before an end of the war, the Soviet Union joined in the fight against Japan.

On September 12, 1945, proud Japan signed an unconditional surrender on the battle ship *Missouri*. For the first time in Japanese history foreign troops occupied its territory. Three million people were lost in the war, and one-fourth of its industrial plant was destroyed. Japan, however, understood more than any other country on earth how to translate the lost war into a victorious peace. High tech has taken over the function of the military. No more than 1 percent of the GNP was to be used for military purposes. The United States covered the archipelago's defense costs, and a defeated Japan was able to start an unprecedented economic offensive. Imported raw materials were transformed into products of the highest quality and brought onto world markets, especially American markets. Japan's strategy had undergone a fundamental change: the army receded into the background, and the economy was to become Japan's best army. In the 1980s Japan overshadowed the Western world. Prestigious real estate in America was bought up. However, in the 1990s, a recession began, and this self-assured country has not yet surmounted it. Not only has the economy been affected, but so has the entire social system. The Liberal Democratic Party, which had been in government for almost forty years, no longer listens to the voice of the people. The "five wise men" determine the country's destiny. They are the kingmakers. They have chosen eight prime ministers in the last decade, including the enthusiastic rugby player and former minister of trade, Yoshiro Mori, who took power after Keizo Obuchi had a heart attack in early April 2000. The new prime minister is confronted with a mountain of difficult challenges. With an unemployment rate of 4.7 percent in 1999, lifetime jobs are a thing of the past. In 1998, the economy receded by 2.8 percent, but then recovered with a meager growth of 1.4 percent in 1999. Before his heart attack, ex-premier Obuchi claimed he was the most indebted king in the world. With a state debt of 645 billion yen, or 107.2 percent of the GNP, Japan has become one of the world's major debtors. Moreover, no other industrial country is aging as fast as Japan. Demographers have calculated that by the year 2002 more than every fourth Japanese person will be over the age of sixty-five. Furthermore, a wave of violence is troubling its citizens. The multiplying symptoms of crisis are giving a lift to the nationalists. The governor of Tokyo, Shintaro Ishihara, has become their idol. In a public opinion survey he was rated one of the most popular politicians in the country. Japan's bureaucratic system, he said in an interview with *Der Spiegel*,[32] is reaching its limits: "Politicians must finally lead the nation out of its paralysis with new ideas." Japan's foreign policy is not made in Tokyo, he confided to *Der Spiegel*, but in Washington or Beijing. Article 9 of the constitution, in which Japan renounced war "for eternity," must be rescinded, he said. China causes the nationalist politicians the greatest anxiety. "Therefore," according to the militant governor of the country's metropolis, "it would naturally be better if China's huge empire were broken up into several small states. . . . Japan should further this development as much as possible." Ishihara nurtures ambitious and by no means friendly undertakings against the Americans: "Over a third of the world's financial capital is Japanese money with which the Americans do what they want." Japan is America's greatest creditor. In order to become more independent of the United States, Japan "should get rid of some of [its] state loans" and build a "greater Asian yen sphere." This influential Japanese politician claims that a yen sphere could free Asia of the domination of the dollar.

One-fifth of the world population lives in China. Its per capita GNP is estimated at $790.[33] While China has nuclear weapons, Japan, with its outstanding technological potential, is capable of producing them. China has been through many civil wars but has rarely attacked a foreign country. Japan, on the other hand, has subjugated many of the countries of Asia, including large parts of China. And those defeated countries were not treated especially mildly under Japanese rule. Japan still denies the atrocious massacre of Nanking. Specialists estimate the number of victims at 260,000. Tokyo's mayor had something to say on this account: "If there was talk of a figure of 20,000 or 50,000 victims, I would not get so worked up. But our Asian neighbors harbor a deep distrust against Japan because it has not yet apologized for the wartime atrocities."[34]

The greatest danger for Asia is a revitalization of nationalism and militarism in Japan. This danger has become a tragic reality. China's industry is growing unabated with an above average growth rate—as high as 11.2 percent in the first half of 2000. Japan has not yet completely overcome its recession, but it remains a highly developed industrial country. China, conversely, is still a country of peasants with three-fourths of the population living in rural areas. The industrial revolution is still a long way from completion. Meanwhile, the presence of no fewer than 50 million unemployed, many as a result of mass emigration from the overcrowded countryside to the overcrowded cities, hangs over the economy. The conflict between state enterprises, which are losing money, and the booming private sector, as well as between the latter and the totalitarian regime, is wholly under way. Furthermore, China has opened its doors wide to foreign trade and investment. The industrial states are becoming increasingly convinced that China's integration is a better way to bring about the democratization of the country than its exclusion. The enormous market of 1.26 billion inhabitants cannot be neglected, of course. During the last months of his presidency, Bill Clinton paved the way for China to enter the WTO, in spite of human rights violations in the country. The damage to the environment is estimated by the World Bank at $60 billion annually. Acid rain alone causes damage of $13 billion; 1.6 million people die every year because of poisoned drinking water and polluted air, which are the fifth largest cause of the death in the country. Eight of the world's most polluted metropolises are in China. Beijing is one of the world's most unhealthy cities, according to World Bank expert Songsu Choi.[35] But expenditures for the protection of the environment are no more than 1 percent of the GDP (as compared to 1.8 percent in Germany, for example). China's role in the world economy can hardly be underestimated. Cooperation between China and Japan could bring economic stability and promote prosperity in all of Asia.

Vladimir Putin as Protagonist of a More-State-Less-Market Policy

Russia, the fifth largest country on earth in terms of population, is bound to be a principal player in globalization. Vladimir Putin, appointed prime minister in August 1999 and later acting president (at the end of 1999) by his predecessor, Boris Yeltsin, won the presidential election on March 26, 2000, with 52.7 percent of the votes. His prior experience was largely in the middle levels of the internal security apparatus of the Soviet Union and later Russia. Yeltsin, who did all this and resigned "voluntarily" in exchange for immunity, was acting on the command of the head of state security and the ruling oligarchy. Putin's only serious opponent, Communist leader Gennady Zyuganov, was able to gain no more than 30 percent of the votes. Two other popular candidates, ex-prime minister Yevgeny Primakov and Moscow's mayor Yuri Luzhkov, withdrew in a timely manner. The other twenty-one candidates had no chance. In the end, the state security man triumphed over his competitor from the Communist Party. It should be noted, however, that the propaganda apparatus was concentrated wholly on Putin, especially the television station of the oligarch Boris Berezovsky. Putin had promised in the election campaign to eliminate the oligarchs as a social class. Berezovsky does not take Putin's threat seriously. "That's only meant for the voters," he said, and moreover, "if Putin puts me behind bars tomorrow, he would get applause." Berezovsky is convinced that if a capitalism in which Putin's promise of legal security to foreign investors is to prevail, it can be achieved only by people of his potency. Finally, he says, the president is dependent on the forces that have put him into office—namely, the secret police, the generals, and the entrepreneurs. Berezovsky's presumption that the threat of liquidation of the oligarchs was solely propaganda for the voters was correct. In any case, he invited the newly elected president to a birthday celebration for his beautiful wife Yelena. Once again the entrepreneur was not wrong: Vladimir Putin showed up and celebrated with the other guests, powerful entrepreneurs, and the host himself. Was the election carried out properly? There are no clear indications of electoral fraud. *Der Spiegel* reported that "two hours before the close of Moscow's voting booths, participation throughout the country was noticeably below the requisite 50 percent. Shortly before the end of the election, another 20 percent of the ballots that were later counted found their way into the urns."[36] Nobel Prize laureate Aleksandr Solzhenitsyn, the conscience of the nation, expressed his unease in somewhat clearer terms: many Muscovites, according to him, voted on voting machines whose results are difficult to check. But no one will ever know exactly.

The constitution of 1993, devised by Boris Yeltsin to satisfy his own aspirations and confirmed by a referendum, affords the president enormous powers. Thomas F. Remington characterizes them as follows: "The effects of centuries of bureaucratic authoritarianism in Russia have made the presidency the heir to the position of Tsar and general secretary."[37] The Russian president can issue decrees with the force of law; he can nominate the prime minister and the government. The president's power is, however, not unlimited. The constitution states that the president's decrees may not contradict an existing law or a provision of the constitution; the parliament may refuse to confirm a nominated prime minister, and it did so in September 1998.

Putin has been able to avoid any serious conflict with the parliament until now. The only party that supports him, Yedinstvo (Unity), enjoys success due only to the financial and organizational support of the Kremlin. Without a majority in the Duma (the lower house of parliament), Putin can gain the support necessary to continue his policies only by skillfully plying divide-and-conquer tactics. A good example of this was provided by Putin's resuscitation of Stalin-era music for the Russian national anthem.

After the election, the newly elected president said to his voters that there would be no miracles, but rather a "difficult journey on a winding course." Putin promised much as acting president—for example, to raise pensions by 20 percent and curtail the omnipotence of the bureaucracy—and he even offered a beauty case to the 1,500 female soldiers on the Chechen front. Putin criticized NATO and participated in the burial of sixteen police officers and eighty-four parachuters killed in the war in Chechnya, all buried in the presence of the good patriarch Alexei II. However, Putin started a second atrocious war against the rebellious Chechens after the Russian Army's humiliating defeat in the first war and the compromise peace that was concluded. The patriots of the country have greeted the disgraced army's revenge with extraordinary satisfaction. Moreover, two months before the election, a document was drafted that disturbed NATO but pleased patriotically minded citizens. A new security concept was formed whose basic tenor was patriotic, with a clear tendency toward a policy of distancing from the West. It especially stresses Russia's external threats and points out the most important aspects of these threats—namely, the declining role of the United Nations and the advance of foreign outposts to the Russian borders in connection with NATO's enlargement to the east. The document demands that "danger should be recognized early, Russia's sovereignty and integrity should be guaranteed, the economy should be socially oriented, and dependence on foreign technology should be reduced." Furthermore, "Russia's military should be armed, and aggression shall be deterred." The next passage of the document, which is especially important and threatening to the West, radically alters Russia's traditional strategy: "Russia can use any means, including nuclear weapons, to strengthen its defense." Moreover, "in the face of armed aggression, if all other means to a resolution of conflict have been exhausted and are ineffective, the use of nuclear weapons could be necessary and justified."[38]

Western commentary on this security concept shows that Vladimir

Putin has lowered the threshold for the use of nuclear weapons and put special emphasis on Russia's status as a great power. But just after the election, Russia's president undertook precautions to underscore his peaceful intentions. On April 2, 2000, the Duma, with an overwhelming majority, ratified an agreement on the banning of nuclear tests. However, this agreement will come into force only when forty-four countries that have the potential needed to make such tests have approved it. So far, twenty-nine nations have ratified this agreement. The next and most important step followed two weeks later: the Duma ratified the Start II agreement with a yes:no ratio of 288:131. This agreement calls for the reduction of the nuclear arsenal of the United States and Russia to between 2,300 and 3,500 warheads by the end of 2007. Start III, which is now being discussed, provides for a further cutback of 1,500–2,500 warheads. For years the Duma refused to ratify Start II, but the American Senate had already ratified the agreement in 1996. At the same time, the Russian president issued a statement that Moscow would withdraw from the concluded agreements if the United States did not annul the antiballistic missile treaty from 1972. Putin stressed that not only would the Start II agreement be vacated, but so would all other hitherto concluded agreements on the limiting and control of strategic weapons.

It is no coincidence that the newly elected president turned his attention immediately to security problems. After all, Putin is a professional security service man who resided in Dresden during the Soviet period in order to spy on West Germany and other subjects. After 1991, he was head of Russia's security system, which was based on the old Soviet one. The fact that he does not know very much about economics is evident in his forecast that Russia's present per capita GDP of $3,170 would rise to the British level of $20,700 within fifteen years. His adviser, German Gref, is more modest: he would be happy if in ten years Russia's per capita GNP came as far as Brazil's today ($6,500). However, the new Kremlin boss is lucky. The swift rise in the price of crude oil and gas brought Russia $20 billion more in 1999 from exports than in the previous year. The economy finally began to grow again by 3.2 percent, industrial output grew by 8 percent, and tax revenues increased by 3 percent of the GNP. But per capita national income decreased in 1999 by 30 percent.[39] Furthermore, the $31.8 billion debt from the Soviet period was cut in half by Western banks, mainly at Germany's expense. But the situation can change. Oil and gas prices are again falling, and the Ministry of Finance calculated that expected revenues could decrease by $2 billion in 2000. The preconditions for truly stable economic growth are not yet in place. Whereas the perils are well known, the means to combat them remain unidentified. The above-mentioned national security concept named some of those perils: a shortage of innovations and investments and the fact that businessmen, who have no confidence in Russia's economy, prefer to deposit their export proceeds in Western banks. The new managers, most of them "red directors" from Soviet times, have little entrepreneurial initiative and even less creativity; the school of a planned economy was not suited for cultivating such qualities. Moreover, this security concept does not make coping with any of the other handicaps any easier. This applies, for example, to the stagnation in the agricultural sector, where collective work methods predominate and appropriate prerequisites for massive privatization are not in view. The imbalance between the export of raw materials and fuels and the import of finished products and the huge and steadily growing mountain of domestic and international debt are causes for concern.

The ecological situation is devastating. The internal political and social instability of the country is regarded as threatening. This is a result of (among other things) separatist tendencies, tensions between the federation and the provinces, political extremism, organized crime and corruption, the growing gap between the small stratum of new rich and the overwhelming majority of the poor, and alcohol and drug abuse. The government intends to strengthen the role of the state in order to stimulate investment and competition, to reinforce the struggle against organized crime and corruption, and to organize the decision-making process more effectively. It should be noted that the structural, social, economic, and political difficulties mentioned here have accompanied Russia throughout its history, under both the tsars and the Communist Party's general secretaries. A tour de force by Vladimir Putin will not be sufficient to eliminate them. However, Putin, as a former intelligence agent of both the disintegrated Soviet Union and the new regime on its way to democracy and a competitive market economy, is the right personality to provide more discipline, legal security, and equality before the law. All of these things are preconditions for evoking greater confidence from domestic and foreign investors in the country's economy. If he succeeds, Vladimir Putin will be able to say he has fulfilled his mission of integrating Russia into the Western world.

Vladimir Putin cuts an impressive figure with his single-mindness of purpose and energy. For months on end a think tank under the leadership of Putin's confidential adviser, the "German-Russian" German Gref worked on a model for the rehabilitation and development of the country's devastated economy. (The president flirted with Ludwig Erhard's reform project and liked to listen, as he said, to the advice of German experts.) On June 18, 2000, the time was right. Mikhail Kasyanov, who had recently come to power as the chief of government, presented the Duma with the reform concept for the next ten years. There was nothing surprising about its contents. The only surprising thing was how quickly and easily the Duma, which Putin had entirely subjected to his control, accepted the proposal. Growth was to expand at a 5 percent average per year, and in order to accelerate investment activities, taxes were to be lowered and private property guaranteed. Indeed, the East European Bank (London) expected an increase of 6.5 percent in Russian GNP in the year 2000.[40] Moreover, subventions for failing businesses were to be reduced, the delay of salary payments was to be put to an end, and free health care would be provided. Finally, the bank and energy systems would be entirely reformed in order to double the value of the ruble within just a few years.

The *New York Times* cites the opinion of Goldman Sachs expert Al Breach on this subject: "A strong, liberal reform project was presented." Although similar projects had been formed before by the IMF and the World Bank, "this time, it's the Russians themselves doing it."[41] The domestic and international public, however, is more concerned with the government's project of reorganizing the upper house. An entirely new house has been promised. In the place of the upper council, made up of eighty-nine governors and an equal number of their legislative representatives, a freely elected senate should be chosen. Boris Yeltsin, who suggested that the governors "take as much sovereignty for themselves as they could swallow," was in the process of handing the responsibility of power to the "subjects" of the federation, the regions, the member republics, and the districts. This had a terribly damaging effect on the entire federation. Putin, however, desires a return to unified federal power. This is partially due to the fact that the governors have increasingly taken on competencies that pose a danger for the upholding of the unified state.

At the end of May, at a conference of the Akademie für Internationale Politik of the Renner-Institut in Vienna, several examples of the abovementioned danger were cited. For instance, during the last decade nineteen of the twenty regional governments of the federation passed constitutional regulations that stood in crass contradiction to the federal constitution. Although according to the federal constitution defense and security policy falls under the jurisdiction of the federal power, the member republic Tuva, located in southern Siberia, even retained the right to make decisions on war and peace. Moreover, in contradiction to the law, the governor of the Far Eastern region of Primor′e demanded that the central government annul the border treaties agreed upon with China. In the member republic of Tatarstan, only a single article concerning citizenship, is in agreement with the federal constitution. Finally, only 10 percent of the eighty-nine federal subjects contribute more to the federal budget than they receive. The remaining 90 percent hide their revenues in order to feign a need for federal monetary aid.

A member of the Carnegie Center, Nikolai Petrov, who took part in the Renner conference, said that under the "pleasantly sounding name of Russian federalism a quasi-half-feudal regional princedom" had been created.[42] Vladimir Putin has already announced a new legal initiative to limit the power of the governors. An administrative reform was introduced that divided Russia into seven federal districts, each with its own authorized governor, to be named by the central power. These governors would control the enforcement of federal decisions and the translation of the president's body politic into action.

One is fully aware of the inherent difficulties of returning power from the member states to the central government. The head of the federal council, Yegor Stroyev, has already explained that the transformation of the federal council into a senate would require a change in the constitution. In order to achieve this, according to Stroyev, "a new constitution must be written."[43] Even if this present administrative reform succeeds, one is not sure if the new order of relations between the central government and the regions can guarantee the necessary results.

Low Efficiency of Western Financial Assistance

The increasing disproportion between the enormous financial help provided by the IMF, the World Bank, and private commercial banks and the low performance in the transition to a market economy and democracy raises a question regarding the rationality of the investment. Sergei Khrushchev, the son of the former leader and now senior research associate at Brown University, has stated that in the years of transformation the Soviet GNP has dropped by nearly 50 percent, investments have decreased by 80 percent, and living standards have fallen by 60 percent.[44] The weak and underdeveloped Russian market was hit by the financial crisis in Southeast Asia much harder than other countries. The inflation rate reached 86 percent in 1999, and the national debt has doubled owing to the lack of resources to service it. Mass privatization increased the share of the nongovernmental sector to 70 percent of the GNP, yet according to Putin's chief economic adviser, Andrei Illarionov, the privatized companies perform more poorly than the state firms. The Russian population has dropped in the nine years of transformation by 4 million.[45] The country's record in controlling the spread of AIDS is dismal: the number of infected persons rose from 23 in 1987 to 69,120 in November 2000. According to the chairman of the Duma, Nikolai Gerasimenko, the epidemic now endangers the security of the country. The increase rate is 1,000 per week, with the unofficial estimate tenfold higher.

The assistance of the West to Russia on the way to a market economy has been considerable. Western advisers, who recommended quick reforms and first of all swift privatization, also recommended the support of shock therapy. Former premier Yevgeny Primakov stated, "We obey your instructions." But Illarionov blames the executors, Yegor Gaidar and Anatoli Chubais, who he feels played the decisive role in the collapse of the Russian ruble in August 1999. Russia's debt in the post-Soviet era reached $150 billion; the loans of the IMF amounted to $27 billion.[46] "The Fund watched," writes Ariel Cohen, an expert on Western assistance to Russia, "as the Russian currency collapsed by 75 percent, while its banking system and securities collapsed, causing over $20 billion losses to Western investors."[47] The largest share of the money invested by Western financial institutions in Russia was not invested in the economy but funneled out, mixed with the revenues from oil exports and illegal weapons sales, to be deposited in Western banks. A massive capital flight, which began in the last years of the Soviet Union and continued with dramatic speed during the transformation period, amounted to some $120–200 billion in 1985–99. This sum is larger than the total of Western loans and investments. The enormous extent of money laundering included the Yeltsin family's involvement in the Mabatex firm's Kremlin renovation.

The question arises whether this lax credit policy with Russia will continue during the Bush administration. There are strong signals of change. "The watchword for this government will be pragmatism. . . . Gone will be the romanticism of the early Clinton years," according to

Thomas E. Graham, Jr.[48] The statements of the administration's architects of foreign policy, Colin Powell and Condoleezza Rice, confirm this. The latter believes that the Clinton administration spent too much time and money trying to transform Russia into a Western look-alike democracy and market economy. The Bush approach will be to focus much less on what the Russians are doing at home. The trebling of oil and gas prices, the main Russian export items, improved the economic situation there. After years of decline, the GNP rose by 3.2 percent in 1999 and by 6.7 percent in 2000; the rate of inflation dropped from 84.5 percent in 1998 to 16 percent in 2000.

Yet the discrepancy between Russia and the West is enormous. Professor Boris Mironov of the Russian Academy of Sciences offered a few figures during a lecture in Vienna in December 2000. The lag in the culture is 25–30 years, the lag in industry is no less than fifty years, and the lag in agriculture is even longer. Russia's credit rating occupies one of the last places in the listings, alongside Pakistan, Burma, and Zimbabwe. The lack of skilled managers demanded by the emerging new economy is in part a cause of reliance on the Soviet command-economy methods, accompanied by the newly surfaced criminal contract enforcement. Structural reforms needed to overcome the anarchy and mismanagement will take at least a generation—assuming that a coherent reform program can be worked out and pursued.

3

Demographic Explosion in a Differentiating Global Economy

Two centuries have gone by since the British economist Thomas Malthus formulated his thesis that the world population would increase more rapidly than its food supply. At that time, his conclusion was that nations were doomed to a miserable existence and starvation. Meanwhile, enough time has gone by to confront this thesis with the realities of the modern age. Malthus's assertion, *New York Times* economist Nicholas Wade writes, "is much more than plain wrong."[1] The figures given by Wade seem to bear out his opinion: in 1804, the world population reached its first billion, and it took no less than 123 years to reach the second billion. However, in order for the population to rise from 5 billion to 6 billion, it took no longer than twelve years. The long-term prognosis is somewhat more reassuring. Because of declining fertility and longer life expectancy, the world population in the year 2025 will be no greater than 10 billion. The population has not undergone a geometric progression as Malthus had predicted. Benjamin Franklin predicted a doubling of the U.S. population every twenty-five years. The reality, however, is a long way from that. Nicholas Wade writes that the United States "is almost static and suffers dreadfully from obesity, not from starvation."[2] But the vision of overpopulation still persists. In the early 1970s, the Club of Rome, in its study *Limits to Growth*, warned that the danger Malthus predicted between the population explosion and the capacity to feed it was just on the horizon. A forecast for 2020, published in November 1999 by the International Food Policy Research Institute in Washington, D.C., is not exactly optimistic: the world population will increase by 73 million people annually. To feed them farmers will have

Table 3.1

Comparison of Population and Income Figures for 1900 and 2000

	1900	2000
World population (in billions)	1.6	6.0
United States		
Population (in millions)	76.0	273.0
Life expectancy	47.0	77.0
Real GDP (in billion dollars)	336.6	8,100.0
White population (in percent)	88.0	82.3
Black population (in percent)	11.6	12.8
Other (in percent)	0.4	4.9
Average number of children per family	3.5	2.0
Income per capita (in dollars)	9,964.0	49,774.0

Source: Bureau of the Census, National Center for Health, cited in *Wall Street Journal*, September 16, 1999.

to increase their grain production by 40 percent, and the demand for meat in Third World countries will double between 1995 and 2020. Moreover, the demand for meat in the industrial countries will also increase, although somewhat less—by 25 percent, say analysts. Since the agrarian surface area is almost wholly in tillage, the only way to meet the demand for grain will be to increase productivity—not an easy task. Millions of people will live in misery, despite the fact that according to predictions national incomes in the Third World will increase by 4.32 percent annually, twice as fast as in developed and industrial countries. China alone will need one-fourth of the increased global demand for wheat and 41 percent of the same for meat. The main supplier will remain the United States, whose grain exports were expected to increase by 34 percent between 1995 and 2020. Although other exporters will emerge, analysts forecast that U.S. farmers will cover 60 percent of the rising needs of the developing countries in 2020. The United States will certainly not be affected by Malthus's predictions. The population will continue to rise, but the efficiency of the economy will increase at an even greater rate. Table 3.1 confirms this view.

One can see from Table 3.1 that demographic growth is matched by even greater economic growth and that the average number of children per family has declined from 3.5 to 2.04. Not only the United States, but all industrial countries, including the whole of North America, Europe, Japan, Australia, and New Zealand, have nothing to fear from Malthus's prediction. Most population growth will be in Third World countries in

Table 3.2

Demographic Growth and Child Mortality in Developed and Underdeveloped Continents

Continent	Life expectancy per woman	Fertility, children	Use of contraceptives (by percent of married women)
Africa	51	5.1	20
Asia	66	2.6	60
Europe	73	1.4	72
Latin America and Caribbean	69	2.7	66
North America	77	1.9	71

Child mortality (deaths per 1,000 births)

Highest mortality rates		Lowest mortality rates	
Sierra Leone	170	Japan	4
Afghanistan	151	Singapore	5
Malawi	138	Norway	5
East Timor	135	Germany	5

Source: UN Population Division; cited in *New York Times*, September 19, 1999.

Africa, Asia (with the exception of Japan), and Transcaucasia; the Central Asian republics of the former Soviet Union; all the countries of Latin America; and the Caribbean islands and Oceania (with the exception of Australia and New Zealand). The net population increase in the last fifty years has occurred mainly in the poorest countries of the Third World; ten countries account for 60 percent of this population growth. Between 1995 and 2000, India's population increased by 16.0 million annually, China's by 11.4 million, Pakistan's by 4.0 million, Indonesia's by 2.9 million, Nigeria's by 2.5 million, the United States' by 2.3 million, Brazil's by 2.2 million, Bangladesh's by 2.1 million, Mexico's by 1.5 million, and the Philippines' by 1.5 million.[3] The world's two most populous countries, China and India, contributed approximately 21 percent to demographic growth between 1995 and 2000, while the most populous industrial country—namely, the United States—increased only by 2.3 million people. A good portion of this increase, however, was due to immigration. Between 1970 and 1995 the United States received 16.7 million immigrants, many more than all the countries of the world put together. Table 3.2 shows the considerable differences in demographic growth between developed and underdeveloped continents.

In comparison with the other continents of the world, demographic developments in Africa are far behind: life expectancy is 51 years, there are 5.1 children per married woman, and 20 percent of married women use contraceptives. Asia's figures are much more hopeful: a 66–year life expectancy, 2.6 children per family, and 60 percent of women use contraceptives. The narrowing gap among Asia, Europe, and America in this regard is due above all to China's rigorous population policy of one child per family, which is also subject to strict family controls. In contrast, there is little if any population control in India, which according to predictions will probably exceed China's population in the next twenty years. According to estimates of the Population Division of the United Nations, 2050 Asia will account for 59 percent of the total world population, Africa will account for 20 percent, and Latin America for 9 percent. Moreover, life expectancy will continue to rise, having increased by twenty years since 1950 to sixty-five years today. The increasing migration is also noteworthy: in 1965, 75 million people were immigrants from different countries. Today that number is already 125 million. As noted above, between 1970 and 1995 the United States receives the majority of these immigrants, followed by Russia with 4.1 million (mainly ethnic Russian immigrants who had resided in the former Soviet republics and have returned to the Russian homeland), Saudi Arabia with 3.4 million, and India with 3.3 million. The immigrants came mainly from Mexico (6 million), Bangladesh (4.1 million), Afghanistan (4.1 million), and the Philippines (2.9 million). The UN Population Division breakdown into older and younger countries is interesting: the oldest are Italy and Japan, with an average age of 40.2 years, followed by Germany and Sweden with 39.1 years. The youngest countries are Uganda, Nigeria, Yemen, and the Republic of Congo with an average age of 15–15.9 years. A worrisome demographic development is at present taking place in Russia. Because of the falling standard of living and the uncertain future, during its period of transformation, Russia's population has decreased by about 4 million, from 152 to 148 million, and life expectancy for men has fallen to 58 years. This is much lower than in Asia (66 years) and Europe (73 years). Japan and Italy also exhibited a demographic decline, albeit for completely different reasons.

The combined population of the fifteen nations of the EU was larger in 1995 than that of the United States by 105 million; yet by 2050 it could be smaller by 18 million, according to some forecasts. Spain and Italy will see their populations shrink by more than a quarter during that period. The birthrates are declining and the population is aging. European policymakers are grappling with the problem of sustaining the pay-as-you-go social security system with an ever-smaller number of workers and an ever-growing number of retirees, who will outnumber the workers by 2050. Higher levels of legal immigration could ease labor shortages and increase the number of taxpayers, propping up pension funds. Over the next half century, the EU, according to some estimates, will need as many as 75 million immigrants.[4] The EU stresses the need for more proactive immigration to ensure the economic growth and viability of the social welfare systems. Yet the individual governments are under pressure from a number of politicians who are willing to capitalize on anti-immigrant sentiments.

The Population Is Growing More Rapidly in Democratic India; the Standard of Living Is Rising More Rapidly in Totalitarian China

China and India, which account for over 30 percent of the world's population, will undoubtedly have an important influence on demographic trends throughout the world. China has a rigorous, though gradually diminishing, birth control. India has very lax demographic control, if any at all. Whereas in China the economy is growing more rapidly than the population, in India the contrary is the case. The demographic trends of these two highly populous countries are of special interest. By drawing on international experts, the *New York Times* thoroughly analyzed the above problem.[5] Ashish Bose, a demographic researcher, is convinced that India's people will never accept obligatory family planning since if it is not linked in some way with other social and economic aspects of the country, it will not bring the desired results. Adrienne Germaine, president of the International Women's Health Organization, is also convinced that autocracy or the violation of human rights are not unconditionally necessary for the implementation of a successful demographic program. However, she adds that in order to make China's demographic policy understandable, China's autocratic government operates in an authoritarian manner by demanding that all children should attend school, and all people should have basic health care and . . . housing. India's Nobel Prize laureate Amartya Sen adds to this opinion that "China under the Great Leap Forward endured one of history's greatest famines, as did the Ukraine under Stalin and Cambodia under the Khmer Rouge."

However, in the last twenty years the situation has changed fundamentally. China is becoming more modern and more open to the outside world; even elections are become more democratic than had previously been the case. Poverty in the countryside is diminishing. Furthermore, in the course of just a single generation, economic reforms have given Chinese cities a more progressive complexion. Democracy alone, says Professor Sen, is not the most crucial factor for prosperity, "but that doesn't mean that democracy is not important." Moreover, Sen adds, "political democracy may be only one of a number of components; another is population control." India's most critical journalist, Tavleen Singh, has a similar train of thought. She asked the following question: "Would, for instance, our political parties like to explain to us why the image of the average Indian child, 50 years after Independence, is that of a scrawny, spindle-legged, barefoot creature who ekes out an existence by begging at traffic lights?"[6] She views the deficient population policy, as well as the continued existence of the caste system, as the main causes of India's decline to the social level of sub–Saharan Africa. Will the fact that every year India's population increases by 16 million finally make more effective population control the order of the day? Mark M. Brown, the administrator of the UNDP advises patience: "India is changing, if not as rapidly as we would like."

The question, though, is more one of dynamics than the end result. In this regard, China presents a better picture: 83 percent of Chinese know how to read and write. Only 53 percent of India's citizens, however, possess this art, and most of them are men. Whereas one-third of India's girls attend school, the figure in China is 99.9 percent. In China 16 percent of children under the age of five are undernourished, while in India the figure is 50 percent. Moreover, half of India's population must survive on a dollar a day. There are 56 telephones per 1,000 Chinese but only 19 per 1,000 Indians. Furthermore, while 6 of every 1,000 Chinese have a personal computer, in India it is only 2.1 per 1,000. China's exports are five times the exports of India. Professor Sen says that the Chinese are creating freedoms, but in another way than is normally the case, and further, China's critics often do not see that educational opportunities and universal health care allow people to live longer, more fulfilling lives. India, says Professor Sen, has the possibility of raising its performance to China's level. In order to raise the standard of living, China sacrificed one of the basic principles of its social order: planned economic control of industrial enterprises based on state property is no longer the dominant form of management in China. Private property is no longer seen as a necessary evil; rather, in March 1999, it was underscored in the appropriately amended state constitution as an important component of the "socialist market economy." In the amended constitution, a state based in law was also set down. Nevertheless, the practice of rigorous birth control will continue. During a research and lecture trip by this author in 1992, prominent Chinese politicians informed him that if this birth control policy were abandoned, the fruits of the vitally important reforms would be devoured by the additional population, and the ultimate end goal of prosperity would not be obtained.

India has both a pluralistic democracy and capitalism, but it is still one of the economically most backward countries in the world. One of the reasons for this is its explosive demographic development. India fundamentally dropped the elements of a planned economic policy from the country's economic management during the lifetime of Jawaharlal Nehru, the leader of liberated India. Birth control, however, is still in its beginnings. The population has increased almost threefold since India threw off the yoke of British colonialism in 1947. Draconian controls have been out of the question in democratic India since Indira Gandhi's fruitless initiatives in this direction. Nonetheless, birth control is no longer just the affair of totalitarian states. Indonesia and Bangladesh introduced control measures long ago. Indonesia's president Suharto, overthrown in 1998, built condom factories and encouraged the operation of "supermarket style" family planning centers.

The following prognosis is probable: the social systems in China and India will steadily converge on their way to overcoming their centuries of backwardness. India, which recognized long ago that the caste system has nothing in common with a democratic system—India's president is a member of the lowest caste in the country, the untouchables—will continue to dismantle this archaic, inhuman division of the nation and will introduce birth control, which had been previously prevented by the caste system. China, on the other hand, will shape its socialist market economy more efficiently through the allowance of more private property and more democracy. The result will be greater prosperity for the two most populous countries of the world, which will in turn have an important influence on the social constellation of both Asia and the entire world.

Let us return to Malthus's thesis of an expected discrepancy between dynamic population growth and a moderate, halting growth in goods. It is now two hundred years since Malthus presented his thesis to the public. The Industrial Revolution in Great Britain, at that time the most economically developed country in the world, was only in *statu nascendi.* No one could have foreseen that the incipient technological revolution would improve economic efficiency to such a degree that the scarcity of goods would no longer be an issue. Indeed, the problem has become overproduction, which has led to economic crises and unemployment every seven or eight years. In Malthus's time, 70–80 percent of the population lived in rural areas. Then it was very difficult to satisfy the rather moderate food needs of the ever-growing population. No one could have foreseen that a tiny percentage of the population working in the agricultural economy—namely, 3–6 percent—would be able to bring grain and meat production to such a level through the use of artificial fertilizers and farming machinery that the main fear would no longer be scarcity, but rather surplus, which caused prices to fall catastrophically.

However, surpluses and prosperity are relevant issues only in Europe and North America, which account for just one-fifth of the world population—that is, in those areas where the first and second industrial revolutions and the last one, the computer and telecommunications revolution, have been successfully completed. Because the production of goods is growing more rapidly than the population, there is no need to persuade the population to limit births. Whereas in Europe and North America there are 1.4 and 1.9 children per woman respectively, the situation in developing countries is much different. In Africa, for instance, there are 5.1 children per woman. The billion people living in prosperous countries are matched by the billion people living in developing countries. Without a social and technological revolution it will be impossible for the Third World to overcome its centuries of backwardness. Moreover, in order to alleviate the acute poverty of the rapidly growing population and reduce swiftly rising infant mortality rates, a combination of radical social measures seems indispensable in the upcoming years.

The aid programs introduced by the industrially developed countries and the international financial institutions in the form of credit, the transfer of technologies, and the training of qualified management where necessary must, however, also include birth control as the most urgent precondition for success, especially in Africa and India. Of course this must take place without violating the traditions of the peoples affected. According to a study done by the UNDP on the situation in Southeast Asia, Bangladesh, India, Nepal, Pakistan, and Sri Lanka are among the "worst governed countries on earth." Southeast Asia is the "most corrupt" region on earth it is asserted. The principal victims are the poor segments of the population. In Pakistan alone, 5 percent of the GDP disappears every year in bribes.[7] The bribery scandal of the oil giant Elf Aquitaine in early November 1999 shook public opinion. Apparently, African heads of state had profited regularly from the bribery system of the oil giant, called the "parallel bonus." One major recipient was apparently the president of Gabon, Omar Bongo. Corruption in Southeast Asia and Africa thrives in fertile ground. Poorly paid government officials who grant licenses for important services are especially susceptible to bribery, and the top levels of government receive their goodies as well. In these countries, it is the poor that pay the bill. Hope is placed in Western aid, which, however, can be effective only if it brings about self-help. One of the most important self-help measures could be an effective birth control policy, which would alleviate the most acute poverty. Such a policy seems to be one of the most important instruments in combating poverty. The initiation of birth control measures in the countries of Southeast Asia, especially India, which spends tens of billions of dollars for tapping atomic power, as well as in Africa, is becoming an international affair.

Universal Capitalism: Product and Driving Force of the Global Economy—with Many Faces

"At the threshold of the twentieth century, it looks as if it could be a century of humanity and brotherhood among all men," wrote the *Chicago Tribune* on January 1, 1901. Within but a few years the dream would turn to dust, and the *Tribune's* vision would turn into its opposite. Two world wars, with millions dead, and the world economic crisis of 1929–33, made the twentieth century, one of the bloodiest and most deadly of all times. Hitler "took the ground out from under mankind's basic confidence in civilization, which had sustained it up until the present," wrote *Der Spiegel.*[8] Nevertheless, mankind regained hope in the second half of the century. "The fin of this siècle has been an astonishingly positive period," writes Bill Emmot, the editor of the *The Economist.* It was much more positive than people in the 1980s and the pessimistic 1970s could have foreseen: "The threat of war casts its dark shadow over a smaller proportion of the world's population, and fewer people live in constant fear of arbitrary arrest, torture or worse."[9] The expansion of democracy is noteworthy: only 6 of the 43 countries of the world had a democratically elected parliament in 1900, but in 1980 it was 37 of 121 (35 percent of the world's population), and in 1998 it was 117 of 193 (53 percent of the world's population). Emmot warns, however, of a "paranoid optimism." The 1990s were not free from war: four wars raged in Yugoslavia, and hundreds of thousands of people were driven from their homes. Authentic genocide occurred in Rwanda, and India and Pakistan tested their nuclear weapons. Furthermore, drug abuse, and the crime it causes, spread. Mass misery continues to reign in the economies of Africa, India, and some Latin American countries. However, the 1990s did see the collapse of the Soviet empire and the flourishing of foreign trade. The countries of Western Europe entered an economic and currency union with the Euro as the common currency of eleven of the fifteen EU members. This marked an important step in the direction of the globalization of the world's economy and in the perfection of its steering mechanisms, even though an activation of worldwide competition, inter alia between the United States and Europe, was still expected. The prominent expert on globalization, William Greider, writes about the significance of this phenomenon: "The global economy is the leitmotif of the end of the twentieth century. Driven by the logic of modern capitalism, the global economy, a product of the Third Industrial Revolution, is a wondrous freerunning system that is reordering the world as it transforms the lives and economic prospects of workers, corporations and nations."[10]

The Soviet Union collapsed under the burden of its size and its monstrous military-industrial complex, which absorbed 70 percent of the national product and reduced the satisfaction of mass consumption to a remnant, thus making consumer goods scarcity a chronic property of the retail economy. This collapse paved the way for capitalism as the universal steering system of the global world economy. The Soviet Union imploded at precisely the moment when Mikhail Gorbachev had begun to reform it, once again confirming the famous thesis of Alexis de Tocqueville that things become dangerous for a regime precisely when the regime, after falling into difficulties, begins to carry out reforms. Under Boris Yeltsin, the move to a Western social system began. In contrast, in 1978 China, under Deng Xiaoping, opened the way to capitalism by introducing the socialist market economy, which allowed considerable space for privatization, especially in agriculture (80 percent of the population) without changing the totalitarian political structures of the country. Ten years later, Communist Vietnam followed China's example. After a long test of strength in a competitive struggle with the practice of planned economy, capitalism has finally established itself as the most efficient steering system on the planet. Capitalism brought an end to the collectivist social system of the inefficient planned economy, which could no longer afford to fight the costly Cold War.

This capitalism is, however, different from the capitalism that the October Revolution in 1917 overthrew. Moreover, it also differs fundamentally from the capitalism in today's developed and undeveloped industrial nations. In Russia, for instance, an oligarchy, a handful of powerful new rich, has accumulated fabulous assets in the billions of dollars. But this accumulation is hardly the result of the pioneering achievements of the entrepreneurial spirit, like in the days of the Rockefellers, Carnegies, Fords, or Krupps, who built the steel, oil, and auto industries in the wake of the first industrial revolution. Russia's new rich did not have to build factories or oil fields but received them ready-made and intact thanks to their relationships with the new political elite of the country. A unique form of capitalism was introduced in Russia, a capitalism in which there is no longer a written or unwritten moral business code, a capitalism in which the mafia controls almost half of the economic and banking system and invests its earnings not in the homeland but in secure foreign countries. In a situation such as this, a large segment of the economy disappears underground to evade taxes. In no other country in the world is the gap between a handful of new rich and the majority of the new poor as broad as in the former collectivist country of Russia. A country in which, as Winston Churchill once wrote, "misery is evenly distributed." Churchill's statement is of course somewhat oversimplified since the ruling Soviet elite were able to build an extremely privileged existence within real socialism, and foundry workers and miners, who enjoyed an above-average wage, formed a kind of labor elite. However, it is they who have had to endure months of waiting for their miserable wages during Russia's period of transformation. In the former collectivist society, some people were "more equal than others," as George Orwell put it so beautifully. The standard of living was lower, as was economic efficiency, than in the industrial countries of the West. There were, however, fewer hungry and homeless. Those who have reaped the benefits of the new social order are above all the Communist "red directors," who have become a capitalist elite by transforming the enterprises that they once administered in the service of the party and the government into their own property. There is no entrepreneurial middle class in Russia that could free the country from its misery and no civil society that could link up Europe's poorhouse with Western civilization in the near future. No civilized country in the world is being exploited by an economic oligarchy so mercilessly as Russia in this period of transformation. True, there are democratic institutions—a freely elected parliament, free media, etc.—but they have no roots among the people. The main concern of the populace is how it will be able to eke out a tolerable existence under these unfamiliar conditions. Surveys show that many long for the "good old times," in which big brother took care of his citizens from the cradle to the grave, even if he could not provide prosperity.

Poor Russia, which has become even poorer during this transitional period, still has superpower aspirations, though it lacks a functioning economic base. It will not find it easy to integrate into today's capitalism with its modern social structures, its up-to-date technology and information institutions, its computer and blue chip systems, and its astute marketing and advertising arts. The modern capitalism of the global economy is more sophisticated and competitive than it has ever been in its long history. As noted, the capital structure of capitalism today is different; speculative capital, which can move previously inconceivable quantities of money on the stock markets, has evolved alongside production capital. Heinz Kienzl, the vice president of the Austrian Society for European Policy (Gesellschaft für Europapolitik), wrote that globalization and information technology, which "make trade in stocks and bonds around the globe, and around the UN, possible, have made events on the stock market even more unpredictable, more volatile, and more irrational." He goes on to say, "A zero-sum game is being played on the stock market through skillful maneuvering, in which some win and some lose, but no benefits to general prosperity are visible."[11] These maneuvers, in which the volume of speculative money exceeds the volume engaged in industry, could, under the right conditions, shake the stability of nation-states, regions, and even the whole world. The super speculator George Soros, for instance, shook the powerful British pound and in the process earned a billion U.S. dollars. Furthermore, this speculative capital, which has no ties to an economy and can be sent at the press of a button around the globe at the speed of light, is not without blame for the crisis in East and Central Asia in 1997–98 that carried many countries down with it. First, billions of dollars were invested for the construction of prestige objects; then flight began when the suspicion arose that the currency would be devaluated. The IMF's bail-out policy, though it primarily helped big speculators get their money back, stopped this crisis from spreading and thus becoming a world crisis. But as Heinz Kienzl fears, "The funds of the Monetary Fund may also eventually run out, and then it will be a rapid downhill fall for the world economy."

Modern capitalism has become more complicated and more aggressively competitive. William Greider writes, "The global economy divides every society into new camps of conflicting economic interests. It undermines every nation's ability to maintain social cohesion."[12] International multinationals are increasingly determining the fates of the national economies. Their sales increased from $721 billion to $5.2 trillion between 1971 and 1991, and they control a steadily increasing share of foreign trade. They move one-third of exports in the manufacturing industry and four-fifths of the turnover from technology, management, and the service industry.[13] More than 40 percent of exports and about 50 percent of imports are accounted for by goods that no longer reach the consumer directly through the open market but rather via internal company channels. The multinational corporations are the "muscle and brains" of the new system, Paul Krugman says: the Robespierres of this revolution, are finance capital. Marxism is dead, he continues somewhat drearily, but "the gross conditions that inspired Karl Marx's critique of capitalism in the nineteenth century are present and flourishing again. The world has reached not only the end of ideology but also the beginning of the next great conflict over the nature of capitalism. The inequalities of wealth and power that Marx decried are marching wider almost everywhere in the world. Fifty-five million workplaces have been destroyed by technological progress." Professor Krugman is not alone in his opinion on the social conflicts arising in modern dynamic capitalism. William Greider has also had similar things to say. The global economy, he writes, is spreading Schumpeterian "creative destruction" everywhere. It makes an enormous accumulation of wealth possible and activates the same variety of exploitation that was commonplace in industry one hundred years ago.[14] When confronted with impersonal market forces, questions on the relevance of the nation-state are raised with undiminished force. The fundamentals of capitalism are the same everywhere; it is as an economic system based on private property and the maximization of profit. However, what is not the same is the relationship between the market and the state, the relationship between the range of maneuver of that the invisible hand of market movement and the limiting hand of the state controlling these movements.

The United States, Leader of the Global Economy

Up to now, three models with various nuances have developed: the market-oriented Anglo-Saxon model, the state-centered French model, and the Scandinavian model based on the welfare concept. No country, however, has either an unrestricted, all-powerful market or entirely unrestricted state controls. In Europe—and especially among the twelve countries governed by either socialists or Social Democrats—there is continued speculation about a "third way," but the U.S. model is clearly directed toward the expansion of the power of the market. The American economy today is the most successful on the planet, and its success has accompanied the United States throughout the 1990s. *Der Spiegel* criticizes the "U.S. economic and employment wonder that is based on an overheated credit market, though it creates thousands of so-called McJobs, which often merely guarantee a minimum existence wage." Moreover, *Der Spiegel* reminds us that "the tradition of the welfare state is hardly developed in the United States" and that it was only fairly late in its history that a social security system was introduced with the Social Security Act of 1935 under Franklin Roosevelt. The market, and not the state, is "society's decisive regulation mechanism."[15] Nonetheless, the U.S. economy is the leader in the global economy, and no other country can challenge this leading role. William Greider mentions certain limitations. He begins, "America's basic superlatives endure—[it is] the richest, largest, most powerful economy," and he ends with a biting critique: "the essence of what is forming now is an economic system of interdependence designed to ignore the prerogatives of nations, even of the most powerful ones."[16] The success of the U.S. economy is thanks to the policy of progressive deregulation. The state increasingly frees itself from the economic areas under its control in order to hand control over to market competition. In this system the social component gets the short end of the stick. The loudly proclaimed health care reform has not yet been realized, and there are no signs that it will be realized any time soon. According to the U.S. president, medicine is much more expensive in the United States, and the portion of the price that the citizen must pay is higher than elsewhere. This fuels the drastically widening discrepancy between rich and poor.

James M. Schlesinger writes that "the entrance of capitalism could be just beginning—or disappear in the next recession."[17] He stresses the highly calculated deregulation of the U.S. government, for instance, in public services like mail delivery or the telecommunications monopoly, which were released to free competition. In 1999, even uranium enrichment, which up until then was considered a top matter of national security, was handed over to the private sector. Investment in the stock market, once the private domain of brokers and their clientele, has become the hobby of the middle class. "Around the world," writes Schlesinger, "communist countries and right-wing dictatorships have dropped their clumsy attempts to control supply and demand." The 1980s and 1990s, the author continues, became the prelude for a new "era of an unprecedented turn to competition and prosperity." After the United States gave up public control of the telephone network and airlines, a new deregulation was initiated. Half of the states leave it up to the budget to decide which company will provide them with electricity. Moreover, deregulation now encompasses social policy: private companies have established elementary schools on a profit basis, and it is expected that in the coming decades this type of school will make up 10 percent of all schools. Social security is also gradually becoming a private affair. President Clinton declared his intention to invest the unallocated social funds in the money market; control is to be left up to the insured themselves. The free market is already talking about a cultural revolution as a result of the growing number of private households participating in the money market, at present around 40 percent of the total worth. This development, experts claim, destroys the foundation of the democratic left wing. The average American is becoming a mini-capitalist more and more willing to embrace uncertainty, flexibility, and negotiability in daily life, money will permeate everything we make and do. The more America resembles Silicon Valley, the more the rest of the world imitates America, Schlesinger writes, and he goes on to quote international investment adviser Richard Medley: if things continue to develop as they are now, in the next three to four years 80 percent of the poor segments of the U.S. population will be able to reach the level of "a lower-middle-class style existence." However, the free functioning market, Schlesinger claims, negatively affects the form of social relations. The gap between rich and poor, which primarily developed in the 1980s, grew larger in the 1990s. A group of liberal Boston lawyers published information showing that between 1990 and 1998 the salaries of the highest managers grew by 48 percent; workers' salaries, on the other hand, grew by a mere 28 percent. There is fear that dynamically developing technology will not promote competition but rather introduce a new era of monopolies and lead to the creation of more giant companies like Microsoft, which will be able to utilize the various forms of technology available. Though Clinton emphasizes that the times of "Big Government" are over, it is necessary to stress that the all-powerful invisible hand of the market requires certain state controls. In a wealthy country like the United States, these controls are necessary in order to enable a better formulation of social services, especially in the expensive yet ineffective health care system, and in order to reduce, at least where necessary, the deep gap that continues to grow between rich and poor. For the inarguably leading economic power of the world to be able to define itself as a social state, these are the preconditions that must be fulfilled.

The Thorny Path to the "Third Way"

The old slogan of the "third way" was revived by British prime minister Tony Blair and German chancellor Gerhard Schröder in their common declaration in June 1999 entitled "Europe: The Third Way—the New Center," shortly before the European parliamentary elections. Both heads of government proclaimed a "Third Way" (Blair) into a political and social "New Center" (Schröder). Carried to its logical conclusion, this means nothing less than a historical break from the labor movement. This declaration threw the parliamentary left into a profound crisis of purpose. The introductory propositions of the common declaration made the intentions of the Social Democratic heads of government clear. Word for word, quoted according to the English text, the statement claims that "social democracy has found new acceptance—but only because, while retaining its traditional values, it has begun in a credible way to renew its ideas and to modernize its programs. It has also found new acceptance because it stands not only for social justice, but also for economic dynamism and the unleashing of creativity and innovation." Lord Ralf Dahrendorf accepts neither the opinion expressed in the above statement that social democracy has expanded its influence nor the somewhat misleading statement that Social Democrats "support a market economy not a market society." For according to Dahrendorf, the influence of this party was twice as great for twenty years.

The Social Democrats, however, did not win the June 1999 elections to the European Parliament; they unambiguously lost. While in the preceding parliament they had a relative majority, in the newly elected parliament the conservatives have the majority. In only four EU countries were the Social Democratic parties able to retain a relative majority—Spain (35 percent), Portugal (43 percent), Austria, and Sweden. In Belgium, Denmark, Finland, Ireland, Italy, and Holland, they won only about 20 percent of the votes, and in Germany, Greece, Great Britain, they got 16–33 percent of the votes. Lionel Jospin's socialists chalked up the best result but still got a mere 22 percent of the votes. The election results prove that those who voted for the European Parliament were not especially impressed by the Blair–Schröder declaration, published a week prior to the elections. The statement's introduction, which underscored that the traditional values of social democracy were being retained, hardly sounded convincing. Blair eagerly emphasized the abandonment of the class struggle. "The class struggle is over," Blair said at the Labour Party congress in Bournemouth. This is in crass contradiction to the over one-hundred-year tradition of strikes, often initiated by socialists, for higher wages and the improvement of working conditions. This abandonment of class struggle fundamentally alters the ideological profile of social democracy, as did the SPD's 1969 Bad Godesberg program, and opens the door to a totally new phase in Europe's left-wing movement.

Ralf Dahrendorf's criticism of the Blair–Schröder declaration, which envisions support for a market economy but not a market society, is well founded. An alternative, writes Dahrendorf, could be a command economy or a development as in Singapore. This would, however, conflict with the principles of a free society proposed by the "Third Way program." Dahrendorf's ambivalent statement resembles, inter alia, Deng Xiaoping's program of a socialist market economy, which was not socialist in the classical sense of the term since the classical model after all requires nationalization of property, which the Chinese wanted to denationalize in order to increase economic efficiency. Moreover, it was hardly a strict market economy since key industries remained under the control of the state and the Communist Party. A "third way" that wants to salvage the best elements from contrasting programs in order to craft a synthesis makes little sense in written declarations and even less in practice. In every country where attempts have been made to embark on a "third way," as in India under Nehru, the result has been failure, and there have been no further attempts to implement such a plan. The invisible hand of the global world economy has swept away the monstrous planned economy of the Soviet empire. Furthermore, in the face of steadily growing competition, India's mixed economic model, with its growing share of planned and state economics, has also proven unable to meet the requirements of the global economy. China's mixed economy, on the other hand, has guaranteed steady and respectable economic growth and improved the standard of living. This has been possible only by increasing the proportion of market components in agriculture, and to a certain extent in industry, and through China's openness to the outside world, which has resulted in growing trade relations and foreign investments. All of this has been achieved, however, under conditions of a somewhat loosened, though still powerful, state intervention in economic affairs and a totalitarian political regime that is reluctant to abandon the omnipotence of the Communist Party. The future will show whether this symbiosis between the market, which must be free in order to be efficient, and a totalitarian regime will be possible.

The global economy is clearly moving toward a single capitalist economic system that resembles the U.S. economy and represses a mixed economy. Hence what should a "Third Way" mean in Europe, with its functioning national and common EU markets and its pluralistic democracy? Blair's closest adviser, Anthony Giddens, the director of the London School of Economics and author of "The Third Way," attempted to answer this question in a talk with *Der Spiegel.*[18] Professor Giddens said that the question being debated is how the important "basic values of solidarity, equality, security, or the role of an active state are to be understood" in a world of radical change. It is not the values that are new, Giddens claims, but the realization that the old recipes are no longer sufficient to implement them. Furthermore, Giddens says, "we should not understand the world as a gigantic marketplace and expect that the market will somehow do away with all the problems." And further, "of course we need an effective market to guarantee prosperity, but at the same time we also need a functioning civil society and an active state." Every country must cope with its own specific national problems; the differences lie in the choice of solutions. Although Lionel Jospin may have other means in mind than those of Blair or Schröder, all three recognize the need to privatize public institutions (in his two and a half years in office, Jospin has privatized more than all of his predecessors combined), to reform the social system, and to solve the pension problem. "In a time of globalization," says Giddens, "we can no longer see social policy as something separate from economic policy because the labor market is much more dynamic than it was earlier and everything is changing much more rapidly as a consequence of the Internet revolution. We must invest more in human skills, in education and in continued education. Only in this way can we ensure social justice." But the labor protagonist Giddens comprehends social justice in the same way as other groups in his country—namely, "equality of opportunity and social solidarity." Thus according to Giddens, the "Third Way" consists in giving greater consideration to "human capital" instead of a direct financial redistribution from the rich to the poor. He then addresses the issue of the role of the state, insisting that the Keynesian approach of deficit spending is outdated. "The state," Giddens states with conviction, "can not alone solve the problems of society. It must act more flexibly. . . . Bureaucratic authorities and nepotism must disappear, and then democracy will regain the people's trust." What is necessary, he claims, is "a new social contract, in which there are no rights without responsibilities." In Europe, Giddens emphasizes, it would be intolerable for a manager, as is the case in the United States, to earn a few hundred times as much as his employees. Giddens, however, excludes a straightforward redistribution policy. The ideological climate must change and moral pressure must be strengthened.

The many problems raised by Professor Giddens in his attempt to better define social democracy's "Third Way" seem to point to the fact that it is not an entirely new method for forging a fundamentally different social system. The basic values stressed by the main strategist of the "Third Way"—that is, solidarity, equality, and security—remain intact; it is the recipe for their realization that is to change. However, the German chancellor, when asked what the "Third Way" actually meant, answered that "he did not even know the first two." Giddens's arguments seem to confirm that his strategy is one of adaptation to the challenges of a globalizing world economy; as he says, "people do not want to be unprotected and abandoned to be devoured by the global markets."

Nevertheless, a structural change is obvious, especially in the Social Democrats' rejection of class struggle. Class struggle, however, has been somewhat deemphasized since the1950s. Today, the British Labour Party and the German SPD are less the advocates of the ordinary citizen than previously. In an attempt to increase their competitiveness in the global economy, they expressly represent the interests of the entire national economy. Great stock is placed in the creativity and efficiency of the existing—ergo capitalist—society. The objective is not to overthrow but rather to perfect the existing social order. The slogans of the Social Democratic renewal are now "flexible markets," "performance and success," and "the spirit of enterprise" (among others). This strategy speaks to the new, steadily growing middle status level (i.e., management), thereby acknowledging the changes in class structure consequent to the industrial technological revolution. Workers and peasants no longer form the majority of the nation, as they did one hundred years ago. Elections can no longer be won by attracting only this small, ever-diminishing segment of the population, though of course one does not want to lose it. "The class struggles is over," said Blair to the delegates of the 1999 party conference, "but the struggle for a genuine equality has just begun." This means, as Blair's "Third Way" strategist Anthony Giddens declared, "the guarantee of the equality of opportunity for all." Nonetheless, they both know quite well that in a class society there are those who are "more equal" than others (Orwell) and that there is no real equality of opportunity between members of the upper middle class and the poor layers of the population.

The left liberal Parisian newspaper *Le Monde diplomatique* rails against the Social Democratic reformers who have completely forgotten goals such as eliminating the poverty and misery of 18 million unemployed and 50 million poor in Europe. Gerhard Schröder soon found himself confronted with strong pressure from the left-wing factions of his party. The Federation of German Trade Unions (DGB) and the German civil service union called for mass protests. Ten thousand demonstrated against the government's cost-cutting program. Schröder's SPD, which lost the 1999 September and October elections in all of the federal states, was able to regain some impetus only as a result of the corruption crisis in the Christian Democratic Union (CDU). However, in the fall of 1999 there was still no talk of reducing social services (at least not yet). The demonstrations were organized against the red–green coalition's intention of adjusting the income of 2 million civil servants and 1.3 million pensioners merely to the inflation rate. The demonstrators admonished the government for "dismantling social services with an axe." The head of the German civil service union, Erhard Geyer, proclaimed that the civil service would no longer allow itself to be ravaged.

In comparison, Tony Blair is in a better situation. Margaret Thatcher already did the "dirty work" of implementing cost-cutting measures to reduce social services and to curb the omnipotence of the trade unions. Therefore, Blair can dedicate himself to other problems, such as dismantling the feudal vestiges of state hierarchy. In October 1999, he thoroughly reformed the upper house, thereby ringing in the end of an era that had lasted more than six hundred years. The hereditary nobility in the House of Lords, the "most exclusive club in the world," lost its political power. The head of government was unimpressed by the Lords' protest—the Count of Burford, for example, screamed, "Betrayal! We are becoming witnesses to the abolishment of Great Britain." Lord Strathclyde said, "The Prime Minister has taken a knife and inflicted a huge scar on the face of history." The upper house gave the parliamentary reform its blessing with a large majority. The House of Lords was made up of 1,213 members, which included, in addition to the 646 hereditary lords, 541 lifetime lords (who were proposed by the government and appointed by the queen) and an additional 26 clergymen. The government and the upper house agreed on a compromise: ninety-two peers would remain for the time being in the upper house of British Parliament as an interim solution. In any event, this put an end to the greatest anachronism of modern history.

The discussion initiated by New Labour and the SPD about the "Third Way," as well as the shift to the right of these two powerful governing parties, continues unabated. An article by Ralf Dahrendorf entitled "The Third Way and Liberty,"[19] which linked the most recent developments with the progressive globalization of the world economy, is interesting. Among other things, Dahrendorf wrote, "The key issue confronting all European countries today is how to create sustainable economic improvement in global markets without sacrificing the basic cohesion of their societies or the institutions that guarantee liberty." In response to Anthony Giddens's opinion on the "Third Way," Dahrendorf insisted that in an open society there are not only two or three ways but innumerable ways that could lead to prosperity through the maintenance of social cohesion. "There are many capitalisms, not just that of the Chicago School of economics; there are many democracies, not just that of Westminster," writes Lord Dahrendorf. The capitalism practiced in the United States is different from European capitalism, and Scandinavian capitalism is different from Great Britain's. A "Third Way" that is the same for all countries would be harmful for a globalized world economy.

In response to the initiative of Blair and Schröder, France's head of government, Lionel Jospin, a left-wing pragmatist, proclaimed that "We are different." However, when the tire manufacturer Michelin chalked up a record 17.3 percent increase in profits in September 1999 while at the same time announcing the mass dismissal of 7,500 workers, this advocate of government intervention in the injustices of the market responded, "The economy can no longer be controlled." His coalition partners in the left-wing government, the greens and communists, chided their head of government for his lack of resolution against the "global capitalism [of the] neoliberal deviants." Moreover, they mobilized nearly fifty thousand demonstrators to back up their demands for a more energetic policy against unemployment. Jospin plowed his own middle way between the demands of his coalition partners for more government control and the neoliberal concept of Blair and Schröder; his slogan was "A modern country, but a humane society." In a TV interview, halfway through his five years in office, Jospin declared his credo—namely, that the state should keep out of the economy in the future but at the same time ensure the continued existence of a "humane society." However, he unequivocally rejected an administered economy. "Everyone accepts the market," the prime minister said, but his objective was to make a humane society a reality by rejecting economic liberalism in its "extreme forms." This was to be accomplished via initiatives for environmental protection, safer food, and a balanced relationship between producers and commerce. On October 19, 1999, Jospin welcomed the passage of a disputed law by the National Assembly that introduced the thirty-five-hour week but found himself attacked simultaneously by both employers and employees. The head of the organization of industrialists, Ernst-Antoine Seillière, announced on the same day that if the money for social security, unemployment benefits, and pension funds are to be drawn on for financing the additional free time of workers, then the government will have to make do without us as its social partner. An even greater threat for Jospin's government is the equally negative attitude of the trade unions, which likewise wanted to torpedo the financing, since it was planned with funds from social security and unemployment benefits. Accompanied by growing protests and faced with the danger of the collapse of the coalition, for which there was no alternative, Jospin reconsidered his left-wing platform. In mid-October, he published a hard-hitting document that was meant as a response to the Blair–Schröder declaration. Under the title "The Path to a More Just Society," this document states, among other things, that "globalization does not make the state impotent. . . . A redistribution must not be ruled out . . . [and] the excesses of the market must be fought."

Jospin is trying to tackle a new political identity, starting with the question of France's own tradition. He is trying to give new answers to new questions and to redefine the Social Democratic position in view of changed relations. Jospin is searching for new forms of coping with the modern age. "We want a complete modernity," he declares, one that must not limit itself to purely economic factors but also possesses political, social, and cultural elements. "The realities of life," he expounds in this document, "cannot be reduced to the market." Thus the answer to modern capitalism is "anchored in the guarantee of a true citizenship [*citoyenneté*]" which can be applied at all levels of reality. Nonetheless—and this is perhaps what is new in Jospin's declaration—"social security, which is a focal point of the debate, is a right of the citizen and not just of the working class." For this reason, he stresses, modernity must also be complete. It must be a modernity that is focused not only on the middle class, but also on those excluded persons whom modernity itself has created. Moreover—and now Jospin begins to sound somewhat conciliatory—social democracy cannot be an isolated entity but rather a representative of the common interest, and in this sense it defines legacy and continues it. This sounds similar to the dictum of the socialist-pacifist Jean Jaurès, its political project as a "new alliance." Thus the contemplation of one's own tradition means accepting the thesis of Jean Jaurès, murdered in 1914, who said that to "be true to a tradition [is to be] true to the flame and not to the ashes."[20]

The French minister for Europe, Pierre Moscovici, attempted to clarify some of the problems mentioned in the above declaration in a talk with *Der Spiegel*.[21] He views this document as a contribution to the discussion by his party that is "not aimed at anyone." Nevertheless, the differences between Jospin's declaration and the Blair–Schröder paper are more than obvious. The emphasis in the French document is on new forms of regulation, on a national as well as international scale. France's socialists accept globalization, but they also want to organize it, commented Jospin's minister for Europe. In order to accomplish this, in his opinion, some redistribution and *dirigisme* are indispensable. Moscovici distanced himself unequivocally from the idea that the "Third Way" was a legitimate alternative between traditional social democracy and neoliberalism. In his opinion, since the fall of totalitarian communism there are two ways but no third way. Though France's Socialist Party stands in the middle of French society, "it has not become a centralist party." Whereas the government is not powerless in the face of globalization, he said, national regulations are not enough to "protect our society against the excesses of the global market." Europe, then, needs an "organized and regulated economic, monetary, and legal space that can, because of its size and weight, also be strong enough for global regulations." Moscovici underscores the value of German–French cooperation in aviation and astronautics, as reflected, for example, in the merger that created Aerospatiale Matra Dasa. He goes on to say, "The French and the Germans are the heart of Europe." With this allusion to the absence of Great Britain in the currency union, he is calling attention to the fact that the British are not fully integrated into Europe.

Nonetheless, France's socialists are in a different situation from Great Britain's or Germany's. Their past is different; the French left-wing movement has deeper roots than anywhere else. Moreover, even a coalition with Communists is not something new in France. In 1936, the socialist leader, Léon Blum, governed a united front with the Communists and did so in the first years following World War II as well. But there are also traditional differences. For instance, before and after the war the Communist coalition partners pushed for more nationalization of private property than the socialists. As noted, in his two and a half years in office, Jospin has denationalized more than all of his conservative predecessors put together. What is new is the prime minister's retreat from the inherited left-wing tradition whereby he shifts the burden of the country's social security to the citizens. As is the case with New Labour and the SPD, Jospin focuses less on the workforce. Because of the steadily shrinking number of factory workers—now no more than 20 percent of the total number of employed—the workers no longer guarantee election victories. Instead the focus group is the middle class. The party, however, does reflect on its past, especially in its stress on state control. It still emphasizes the need for income redistribution and some *dirigisme* in national and international matters in order to create a more just and more humane society. In this sense, it has rejected the "Third Way." France's socialists accept globalization, but they would like to organize it. The realization of such an undertaking, however, will not be easy. The multinationals, which are in the process of bringing the most important domains of the world economy under their control through various transnational fusions and cooperative agreements, are no longer to be stopped in their marathon-like race. The assertion that "globalization does not make the state impotent" seems to grossly overestimate the powers of the nation-state, as well as the institutions of international finance and control. Indeed, so far it has not been possible, despite much effort, to initiate effective control mechanisms. The most recent example is the failed Seattle conference of the WTO. The 135 member nations left the deliberations without signing a communiqué. Nonetheless, the U.S. president was confident and expressed his conviction that the existing differences would diminish in the next few months and that a new basis for a successful round of talks would be created. He also said, "I am determined to move forward on the path of free trade and economic growth while ensuring a human face is put on the global economy."[22] The course of the Seattle conference, however, provides no evidence for such optimistic statements.

The representatives of India, Brazil, Egypt, and many other developing countries showed their manifest dissatisfaction with the U.S. position. The conflict between the United States and other countries exporting farm products, such as Canada, Argentina, and Australia, over the "elimination" of export subsidies that are disadvantageous to U.S. farmer was especially bitter. The EU was only willing to speak of "some reductions." The demonstrators, who marched in droves in Seattle with slogans such as "Stop the WTO," were also unsatisfied, yet they were unable to put forth a unified position. Whereas some of them demanded the dissolution of the WTO, the environmentalists and labor representatives demanded the establishment of a stronger international trade organization that would be able to enforce laws that represented workers' interests and protected the disappearing forests. The main victims of the demonstration, however, as a result of innumerable broken windows, were Seattle's citizens. The unsuccessful Seattle conference made clear just how powerless the most powerful nations of the world are when they attempt to create common solutions that primarily take the interests of the economically and politically stronger powers into account. Common solutions between the 80 percent economically underdeveloped and the 20 percent developed countries are out of the question. However, progress is possible if the poor countries recognize a process within the inevitability of globalization that could decrease their backwardness.

Jospin's socialists are not alone in their rejection of the New Labour and SPD shift to the right. Even the rather moderate Swedish socialists do not disguise their displeasure. The "Third Way" drives the new middle "radically to the right," they proclaim. The Scandinavian countries want to keep the welfare state, a model that promotes economic growth through rigid labor market programs and guarantees a high standard of living for the population through massive taxes on labor, assets, and environmental misuse. It was Sweden's head of government, Olaf Palme, murdered in 1986, who used his own version of the slogan "*Tredje vägen*," or the "Third Way," though at that time it still represented a path somewhere between capitalism and Soviet communism. However, Sweden's Social Democrats did not shy from rigid cost-cutting measures, and by 1994, after the end of a brief period in which the conservatives were in power, the budget deficit had increased to over 12 percent of the GNP. There was a real danger that currency stability would collapse. Unemployment and health benefits were reduced, a self-participation quota was added to the retirement system, and public employers had to eliminate one hundred thousand jobs. Nevertheless, Sweden's Social Democrats are determined to stick to one principle—namely, the welfare state.

Since then the situation has improved markedly. The unemployment rate has fallen by half, there is a budget surplus, and growth rates have reached top levels. Hence the government is prepared to compensate its citizens for the sacrifices they had to make during the period of cost-cutting measures. Denmark has also been profiting from its employment policy reform, which was systematically implemented in 1993 after years of deficit spending. In order to return to the state welfare system, social services were cut back, the pension system was made more austere, and generous early retirement regulations were cut back. Nyrup Rasmussen, Denmark's Social Democratic prime minister, recently declared that his country had shown that there was no contradiction between social security and a strong economy.

Denmark, with a population of 5.3 million, has achieved an employment miracle. Between 1993 and 1998, two hundred thousand new jobs were created, and the share of social services in the GNP (32.7 percent) is considerably higher than in Germany (29.4 percent), where Gerhard Schröder contemplated drastic cutbacks. A tax comparison, released by the Federation of Taxpayers in Europe on November 10, 1999, showed that Scandinavians had the highest tax burden. Sweden heads the list with 53 percent of the GNP, followed by Denmark with 49 percent, and Finland with 47 percent. Germany, which takes fourteenth place in these statistics comprising twenty-nine countries, has a tax burden of 37.1 percent and hence is below the EU average of 41 percent. Mexico is at the bottom with 15.5 percent, followed by 21 percent in Korea, 28.8 percent in Japan, and 29.7 percent in the United States. Nevertheless, with an average per capita income greater than $21,000 per year, the Swiss, Japanese, and Koreans have the highest incomes after taxes. Germany lies in the middle with an average of just $17,000 per year.[23] It should be noted that Germany's marginal taxation rates are ranked third after Denmark and Belgium, thanks to the high tax subsidies, deductions, and other tax advantages. The Scandinavian countries accept a high tax burden because this above average intensive policy of redistribution guarantees the maintenance of the welfare state, of which the Scandinavians are especially proud. Germany's government coalition, under better economic conditions, prefers to surmount its present budget difficulties by dismantling some of the benefits of the welfare state that had been granted in the past.

Differentiation of Social Services: The Consequence of Different Steering Models

Table 3.3 shows, through an examination of the most important indicators, the superior position of Denmark's welfare state in comparison with a selection of its EU partners. In Denmark, with a population of 5.3 million, a private household earns a much higher income than in France and nearly the same income as a private household in Germany, which has a population of 82 million and is the most technologically developed country in Europe. And all this has been accomplished with relatively higher social services and an unemployment rate lower than anywhere else. Denmark and its welfare model persevere, and the Danes are more likely to try to improve it than dismantle it.

In contrast, Germany's red–green coalition insists on its cutback package, which most likely has the dismantling of the welfare state in mind. Because of transatlantic mergers, Germany's big companies, such as Mercedes-Benz and Volkswagen, and the biggest banking institution in the world, Deutsche Bank AG, are finding themselves in the midst of increasingly bitter worldwide competition. At the expense of broad layers of the population, Gerhard Schröder is attempting to help the big

Table 3.3

Economic Indicators for Selected EU Countries

	Denmark	Germany	Britain	France	Portugal
Population (in millions)	5.3	82.0	58.8	58.4	9.8
Net monthly income of household with two children,1995 (in DM)	3,708.0	3,860.0	3,359.0	2,779.0	1,100.0
Inflation percent (as of July 1999)	2.4[a]	0.7	1.4	0.4	2.1
Unemployment rate (as of July 1999) (in percent)	4.4	9.1	6.1	11.0	4.8
Unemployed under twenty-five years of age (in percent)	6.4	9.0	12.9	25.2	9.8
Economic growth in 1999 compared with the previous year (in percent)	2.4	2.8	2.1	3.2	4.0
Social services in 1999 as percentage of GNP	32.7	29.4	26.7	29.2	19.3

Source: Der Spiegel 44 (1999).

[a]As of June 1999.

concerns in their competitive struggle and to accelerate economic growth by cutting back on state social services. In doing this, Schröder hopes to reduce the above average unemployment rate through forced growth. So far this tactic has been unsuccessful.

The Creation of the Currency Union Does Not Mitigate Tensions

The hope that the establishment of the currency union would eliminate tensions in Europe also remains unrealized. In a talk with *Der Spiegel*, Oxford professor Timothy Garton Ash offered his opinion on this: "It is to be expected that Europe will be exposed, not to a less, but rather to more tensions between leading states." The currency union was an eminent political decision; it was the price Germany "paid for France's consent to German reunification." In Garton Ash's opinion, the currency union was premature since "up till now a functioning currency union has always been preceded by a political union, be it in the USA, or Germany after unification in 1871." The claim that it was François Mitterrand who demanded that Germany's chancellor Helmut Kohl pay this price (i.e., abandon the national currency, the German mark, which, by the way, is the strongest currency in Europe), is also confirmed by the French mass media. The abandonment of one's currency sovereignty is a high price, especially if one takes into account that since January 1999 members of the currency union are no longer allowed to resort to traditional instruments of regulation, such as the use of currency devaluation to battle business ups and downs or the adaptation of interest rates to the needs of the national market. The nostalgia for a strong mark in contrast to the weak Euro fed the protests of managers and intellectuals against the European currency. Many of these were directed at the Constitutional Supreme Court in Karlsruhe. The protest movement has intensified with the approaching introduction of the Euro in the function of cash currency on January 1, 2002, and the ultimate liquidation of the mark.

Nonetheless, all of the EU members have not joined the currency union. Greece, for instance, was unable to meet the Maastricht criteria (this country was to become a member of the currency union in early 2001); Sweden stayed out for technical reasons and Denmark because of a referendum that rejected the Maastricht criteria. As in other strategic decisions concerning integration, Great Britain would like to wait and make its decision depending on the Euro's success. In the meantime, however, Britain is experiencing the development of a broad-based anti-Euro resentment within the country. Ash argues that this sentiment has arisen "because we have a different history, and in addition a press which, orchestrated by an Australian and Canadian tycoon, has been putting out an unbelievable anti-Europe propaganda for more than 10 years." Ash feels that the Euro debate will determine British policy over the next three to four years. Blair would first like to win the next elections; then he will take up the issue of the Euro. Helmut Kohl's prognosis that the city of London would see to it that England joins the currency union is, according to Ash, not so certain, for the city is not as powerful as one thinks. It is conceivable that Blair will call for a referendum on the Euro and lose. "In any case," Ash declares, "we British cannot continue to do things as we have for 40 years: always wait and see if everything is going well with Europe, and then, perhaps, be the last to join."[25]

The architect of the currency union was France's president François Mitterrand. He induced Helmut Kohl to go along with the plan as a price for the reunification of Germany. Italy and most of the small EU members were willing to join because of their dependence on the most powerful states of Europe, with their trade and political networks. "By swapping the D-mark for the Euro," *The Economist* wrote, "Germany is proving to nervous neighbors its continuing commitment to European integration. France and Germany still see a united Europe—whatever that means—as the best vehicle for advancing their interests in the world at large."[26] Because of their role as founders of the European Economic Community (EEC), the Benelux countries, which are more dependent on EU trade than other members and have fewer illusions regarding the importance of national borders, found it easier to agree to the Euro. The Netherlands had no other choice: since 1979 the gulden has been linked to the mark, and Germany accounts for one-fourth of Holland's foreign trade. Because of its early assent, the Netherlands was also rewarded more generously than the other EU countries; Dutchman Wim Duisenberg was appointed as the first president of the European Central Bank. This occurred, however, against the will of France, which wanted to install its own candidate. In view of declining national identity since the 1980s, *The Economist* claims that Belgium was interested in strengthening its "Euro identity." Hence for the Belgians, the Euro was a useful instrument of discipline from outside that could be used to carry out unpopular financial measures. Italy, on the other hand, because of its precarious fiscal and monetary discipline, was considered a candidate for later entry. The Italians, however, feared that any delay in casting their lot with France and Germany's program for Europe would degrade their country to the status of a minor state in the EU. Moreover, many Italians saw the acceptance of the Euro as an external means to strengthen their unstable economy and stabilize prices. The underdeveloped economies of Spain, Portugal, and Ireland also benefited substantially from membership in the EEC. Agricultural subsidies made up 4–5 percent of their GNP. Hence they viewed membership in the currency union as a means to gain more advantages and thus gave their consent to the establishment of the Euro without delay. Countries like Austria and Finland, which joined the EU only in 1995, accepted joining the currency union as part of the bargain. Austria agreed, among other reasons, because Germany is its principal trading partner and the schilling is linked to the German mark. Finland, on the other hand, saw this as a way of showing its commitment to Europe, though it did so with a heavy heart since its most important trading partners, Sweden and Great Britain, have elected to remain outside the currency union (at least for the time being). Europe's politicians had political objectives in mind when they established the currency union—namely, to bind Europeans more closely together by establishing supernational bodies. But nothing indicates that this will enable Western Europe to step onto the world market in the form of a single state, like the United States, for instance, in the foreseeable future. The Euro's first year (1999) was not a particularly auspicious one. Since the beginning of 1999, the Euro has lost 25 percent of its value. The value lost in the first half of the year could not be made up by the second half.

The response of Britain's EU commissioner, Chris Patten, to the question "Does whether or not war could return to Europe depend on the existence of the EU?" does not sound encouraging. The commissioner answered: "I believe that the Europe of the next century will probably more resemble the Europe of the Middle Ages."[27] As he himself said, the commissioner cannot dismiss the similarity between the situation at the end of the Middle Ages and the situation at the end of the twentieth century. He continued: "It was generally the view at the end of the nineteenth century that peace was secure in Europe. After the fall of the Berlin Wall I have the feeling that the ideological argument has now ended, and they are once again saying the same thing as in those days." Patten ended his comment with the warning: "We must not be complacent." One can certainly say that the EU neither wants to nor can eliminate rivalry in Europe. The EU will not enter the world global economy as a unified integrated business partner. But at least for the foreseeable future, customs duties, now abolished, will not be used as an instrument in the battle, and even if national rivalry does not disappear, the free transfer of goods and capital will not be restricted. Through mergers and all sorts of cooperative agreements the national economies of Europe will continue to grow together, centripetal tendencies will become stronger, and the near future will be marked by EU enlargement and an intensification of EU activities.

The Disintegration of the Soviet Empire Has Not Freed the World of the Risk of Major Wars

During a two-day official visit to Beijing in December 10, 1999, Boris Yeltsin fulminated in an ominous sounding manner: Russia has a tremendous nuclear potential capable of mobilization. The threat, which was doubtless aimed at the United States, was understood as such in Beijing as well. The hapless reformer reduced Russia's economic output by almost one-half with his ill-conceived transformations. He promoted unparalleled corruption, the use of Mafia methods, and a greedy oligarchy with the power to determine the course of the decimated economy. His saber rattling was obviously intended to keep the world out of Russia's dirty war in Chechnya. Unfortunately China's rulers, who after all have a potentially similar problem with Tibet and also regularly and overtly threaten Taiwan with force, stated that this war, unprecedented in its use of force, was Russia's internal affair. This new friendship among formerly irreconcilable enemies, which until recently were constantly bickering with each other over border disputes, lacks any constructive substance whatsoever; it is rather a concentrated joint policy of aversion to the United States, though they have much to thank the United States, especially for their latest technology.

Timothy Garton Ash rightly claims, "The great challenge of the next decade will not be in central Europe, nor in South Eastern Europe, but in the former Soviet Union."[28] Garton Ash evaluates the coming developments in Russia with extreme pessimism. "The worst for Russia," he says, "would not be a communist–nationalist seizure of power, but a total disintegration of state and society—and that has already begun. The provincial governors and men of big business are the new feudal lords in a new governmental system, a kleptocracy." In Chechnya, a country that is somewhat bigger than Germany but with only 22 million inhabitants, an outright war is being waged over Russia's role as a great power. Remarkably, the second Chechen war (the first ended in 1996 with Russia's defeat) is extremely popular among the country's population, at least in its early phase, and superpower pride is experiencing a renaissance. The popularity of the commander-in-chief, Vladimir Putin, increased to 45 percent of the surveyed voters just after the beginning of the offensive. Even Mikhail Gorbachev approved of the second campaign. Aleksandr Solzhenitsyn suggested that the rebel republic should be separated by "a kind of Berlin Wall." One of the main issues arising here is a confrontation with Islam. The local conflicts began immediately after liberation from the Soviet yoke. In 1992, a battle broke out over the right to live in Vladikavkaz, formerly a joint capital between the Muslim Ingush and the Christian Ossetians. A military operation followed: 12,000 Russian soldiers marched in, joined the side of the Christian Ossetians, and expelled 70,000 Ingush over the border to the east. To this day both peoples remain in a state of war. Twenty-two thousand policemen and 15,000 Russian troops are taking part in a long-lasting military operation. Unrest rules in the neighboring Muslim republic of Dagestan, in which over two dozen nationalities live. Since the collapse of the Soviet empire, 5,000 mosques have been built in Dagestan, with 3,500 religious teachers teaching the Koran. In August 1999, Russian troops bombed several villages. Furthermore, the three south-Caucasian countries of Georgia, Armenia, and Azerbaijan, which made their leap into independence after the collapse of the Soviet empire, have also failed to come to rest. Their wrecked economies are stuck in a crisis of transformation. In October 1995, kidnappers took seven leading politicians of Armenia hostage and executed the head of government and the chairman of parliament in front of running television cameras. The conflict between Armenia and Azerbaijan over the enclave of Nagorno-Karabakh has abated, but it has not been eliminated.

The Armenian and Azerbaijani foreign ministers met on December 1, 2000, in Vienna to seek support from the Austrian government for their respective positions in the Nagorno-Karabakh conflict. The Armenian minister demanded that Azerbaijan distance itself from "the Soviet inheritance." His counterpart demanded in his turn that Armenia release "occupied" territories, claiming that Armenia occupies 20 percent of Azerbaijan's territory. The conflict made refugees out of 1 million Azeris. The hope that the Commonwealth of Independent States (CIS) (the commonwealth of twelve former Soviet republics), whose chiefs gathered in Minsk (Belarus) in December 2000, would mediate the conflict has not been fulfilled. The conflict represents danger for the entire Caucasus region. The Georgian prime minister even alleged that Russia has a hand in the border conflicts of his country. The brutal war in Chechnya has made the centrifugal forces among the former Soviet republics stronger than the centripetal ones. In order to put pressure on Georgia and Azerbaijan, Russia supports their opponents, like Christian Armenia (with its 3.7 million inhabitants), Moscow's last ally in the Caucasus, where Russia has built up a military presence with new MIG fighter planes and defensive missiles.

The main issue in the Caucasus is oil and the oil pipeline that is to be built to pump the black gold from the sea. The Americans had already declared the Caucasus as a zone of their "national interest" years ago. Geydar Aliyev, the president of Azerbaijan and former member of the Politburo of the Soviet CP, has already offered NATO an air base. The consequences were not long in coming; new pipelines were conceived so that in the future they will avoid Russian territory. At the end of November 1999, a treaty was signed in Istanbul by Turkey, Georgia, and Azerbaijan that provided for the construction of an oil pipeline from Baku via Tiflis into the Turkish Mediterranean harbor of Ceyhan. Although the transportation of Caspian oil via Iran or the use of the extant northern route through Russia would be much cheaper, the United States wants to curb Moscow's influence in the Caucasus. Moscow is seeking allies and has found them in the former friends of the collapsed Soviet Union. As a response to the above-mentioned treaty, Russia's foreign minister, Igor Ivanov, traveled to Teheran and agreed on a "close partnership for the twenty-first century." Iran agreed that it would regard the war in Chechnya as an internal Russian affair, and Ivanov announced, despite American threats of sanctions, that Russia would continue the disputed construction of a reactor in the Iranian nuclear power station at Bushehr—a project valued at $2 billion. Russia and Iran, it was announced, would defend their common interests in the Caspian Sea and would not be driven from the Caucasus region. Georgia's president, Eduard Shevardnadze, correctly understood the announcement of the Russian–Iranian declaration of friendship and proclaimed that if "certain Russian circles" were to attempt to gain control over Azerbaijani oil, he would consider it an act of aggression.

Russia's flirtation with superpower status, however, stands in crass contradiction to its wrecked economy. A report published by *The Econo-*

mist Intelligence Unit (EIU) in November 1999 used seventy-seven different indicators, such as political stability, quality of government, monetary and fiscal policy, economic output, and liquidity, to evaluate the risk ratings for twenty-three countries. The report put Russia, with its score of seventy-seven out of one hundred possible risk points, in first place, followed by Indonesia, Pakistan, and Romania. According to the EIU, Singapore and Taiwan, with only sixteen and twenty-four risk points respectively, are among the most secure countries. Despite the crisis of 1997–98, Asia had forty-eight risk points, the Middle East fifty-three, Latin America fifty-four, and Eastern Europe fifty-eight.[29]

Recently, two profound analyses of Russia were published that shed more light on the tragic course of events in that country. The former adviser to the Russian government, Harvard professor Jeffrey D. Sachs, who correlates the persistent economic crisis with the devastating consequences of voucher privatization, writes: "The result all too often was corrupt asset grabs, managerial plunder of enterprises and paralysis of firms."[30] However, the consequences seem graver. Russia's immoral method of denationalization helped a small oligarchy to grab billions of dollars in assets almost effortlessly without the spirit of enterprise and is the cause of the immoral management. Moreover, cheating the state, tax evasion, and the illegal deposit in foreign banks of huge sums that should have been used for domestic investments are chronic problems. Had these sums been used for domestic investments, it would have been possible to trigger economic growth that would have reduced the incredibly huge gap between the rich and the poor. Russia would not need to go begging everywhere if these sums were brought back into the country. The use of shock therapy—a possibility for a country such as Poland, which was able to start its transformation into a market economy of the Western type with an already growing, blooming middle class and developed private economic activity—caused economic and social decline in Russia. The former prime minister Yevgeny Primakov, seeking Western aid, seemed remote from reality when he claimed in our transformation we did what we were advised to do. Primakov, a member of the Academy of Sciences, must have known that a historical turn from one economic and political system to an extremely different one could not be carried out on the basis of advice from foreign experts. Those experts may have been brilliant in aiding the struggle against recession and inflation, but they would not succeed in Russian conditions. For instance, Russia's collectivist tradition (not only in Soviet times) and the tendency to develop an inflated, greedy, and corrupt bureaucracy are unique. In order to have a swift transition to a private economy, one would be better off consolidating these properties, which is how things proceeded. Professor Sachs's hope that the Russian people would be smart enough to elect a real reformer as president in June 2000, and that the West would be wise enough to seize the inestimable chance to create a peaceful world this time seems somewhat unrealistic. The president's margin of maneuver and the influence of the West are not large enough to make it possible for them to start again—that is, to introduce a new reform for the failed transformation. The 1996 election of the president, who was financed by big capital but was billed as a big reformer and as the "lesser evil," escalated to the greatest evil in the last four years. The presidential candidates for the year 2000 are all well known, and all of them present themselves as reformers. However, whether any of them know and whether elected president Putin knows what reforms are necessary to bring the country out of its present chaos are not so certain. The most important reforms would be to ensure the continued cohesion of the Russian federation, which is currently threatened with collapse, and the development of a policy by the West and Russia that would lead to disarmament and the elimination of the world's nuclear arsenals.

A study of Russia published by the McKinsey Global Institute in November 1999 does not view the situation as especially tragic. Only 25 percent of Russia's industrial capacity, writes the director of the institute, William W. Lewis, is technologically so obsolete that the factories have to be closed.[31] On the other hand, if properly managed and equipped with modern technology, 75 percent of Russia's factories could reach a level amounting to 60–70 percent of U.S. efficiency (efficiency is now 20 percent). After all, Lewis writes, Russia does have a qualified, cheap labor force, as well as oil and gas resources that are greater than anywhere else in the world. An important precondition would be an economic policy that departed from the previous practice, in which, according to Lewis, "the most productive companies not only cannot make a buck, but are being driven out of business by government-subsidized laggards." Lewis closes his article with a call not to invest any Western money in Russia as long as government intervention in the economy undermines the stability that is supposed to further the credit that is granted. Here is a quite inspiring idea that could fundamentally alter credit policy in regard to Russia: instead of granting sector-earmarked credit that disappears into dark channels, one should grant purpose-earmarked loans for promising, expandable, export-oriented economic areas that can be effectively controlled.

Crisis-Ridden Ukraine

Ukraine, the second largest Slavic nation with 52 million inhabitants, is in an even more precarious situation than Russia. During its period of transformation, more than half of its economic output was lost, and its debt to Russia for oil and gas supplies, as well as its debt to the West, has increased considerably. The annual GDP, calculated at $650 per capita, was only 37 percent of the 1989 level.[32] Ukraine already has its presidential election behind it. On November 14, 1999, Leonid Kuchma, the incumbent president, won the second round of elections with 56 percent of the votes. His Communist challenger, Petro Simonenko, received 38 percent (in the first round, the left groups gained 45 percent of the votes). *The Economist* asked: "How to greet the re-election of the dreary leader who has presided over unremitting economic decline and political deadlock, who is surrounded by dubious cronies and who has fought a ruthless and unscrupulous campaign to stay in power?" To answer this question in the words of a leading reformer, the Ukrainians had to choose between a death sentence and a very severe illness. The election of Petro Simonenko, who, obsessed with Russia's superpower vision, proposed rejoining crisis-ridden Russia during the election campaign, would have been a death sentence, at least for Ukrainian independence. The serious illness was the consequence of the reelection of Leonid Kuchma. In the election campaign, Kuchma described himself as a leader in the struggle for independence, reform, and democracy, but in his previous term of office he was unable to create the preconditions for overcoming the country's economic and social misery. Just as in the 1996 elections in Russia, the Ukrainians chose the lesser evil, though this lesser evil, as was the case in Russia, could easily become a much greater evil. For Kuchma, reform means the ability to plunder the state's assets. The president, who endeavored to maintain a foreign policy balance in relations with East and West, downgraded his country's membership in the CIS and expanded links with Azerbaijan, Georgia, and Uzbekistan, whose purpose it was to shore up their independence from Russia. But Ukraine is very dependent on Russia's oil and gas supplies, and it cannot always pay its bills. Because NATO is aware that a weak and poor Ukraine could easily fall under Russia's influence, friendly relations with NATO are being cultivated. The Ukraine's attempts at closer ties with the EU, however, encounter no reciprocation. The Ukraine's economy will need many years to recover before it can strive to become a member of the EU. However, the West's ability to provide further aid has reached the limits of tolerability.

Both Russia and Ukraine have a highly skilled labor force and a tremendous wealth of raw materials and energy resources. But they lack the management and skilled class that is necessary for a modern market economy that would be able to secure their society's due place in today's global economy. Though there is much talk about reforms, only a few know what kinds of reforms are necessary to overcome the growing economic and social crisis. In order to protect the country from imminent collapse, what Ukraine needs now is not increased privatization, but a consolidation of the existing private economy. Furthermore, it especially needs to strengthen the state and expand civil society. The economic and political Mafia and widespread corruption must be stopped. "Organized crime," journalist and Mafia expert Jürgen Rath writes, "creeps into society from the state, through the police and into the media."[33] Therefore its structures become a part of the society. Sixty-eight percent of all Russian oil firms are in the hands of criminal organizations, and they have also successfully infiltrated Western companies. Russia and Ukraine have many of the preconditions that could bring the present transformation to a positive conclusion, but outside advice is of limited use. Unfortunately, Kuchma has not shown himself to be a democrat. He remains under suspicion of having inspired the kidnapping of a journalist who criticized him sharply. The most important thing is not merely the construction of an appropriate plan for reconstruction and development that conforms to existing conditions, but above all the creation of social forces that welcome and bring life into such a plan and are capable of assuming the burden of reconstruction. The issue is not to introduce a new version of capitalism but to find the right way that would lead onto the present worldwide global market.

At the CIS summit of December 1, 2000, Vladimir Putin showed how much he appreciates his cooperation with his Slavic neighbor. He not only postponed for ten years the Ukrainian debt for gas deliveries, estimated at $2–3 billion, but also promised to deliver every year 78 billion cubic meters of gas. The rest of Ukrainian gas consumption has to be covered with Ukraine's own production (918 billion cubic meters) and with deliveries from Turkmenistan (30 billion cubic meters). The price for Russian deliveries would be lower by $20 per 1,000 cubic meters than the world price. The agreement was concluded because in May 2000 Ukraine renounced its use of the Russian pipeline to cover its needs illegally. The agreement shows the importance of bilateralism for both countries now that the CIS has shown itself ineffective. Dependent on foreign assistance, Russia has lost its international standing as a superpower, and beyond that, it has little to offer other CIS members. Nevertheless, a necessary precondition is that Russia realize that there is no place in the twenty-first century for colonial domination and that only peaceful, friendly cooperation with former Soviet republics, not a divide-and-rule policy, will ensure the region's due place in the global economy. Furthermore, in order to avoid a devastating war, it would be even more important and constructive to develop a close cooperative relationship with the United States and other nuclear powers in order to bring about total disarmament (i.e., the liberation of the world from the present nuclear arsenals).

Central Europe on Its Way to the European Union

Unlike former Soviet republics, the historical transformation of "real socialism" into capitalism in Central Europe will go down in European history as a success story. Despite the intolerable pressure of the occupying power, these countries have shown that they not only remained faithful to European traditions of religion and culture, but also in some areas were even able to enrich them. They have returned to where they belonged. Moreover, a rather large middle class, especially in Poland and Hungary, has maintained its entrepreneurial spirit and, when the right conditions were again in place, moved into action. The market economy is functioning with all its advantages and disadvantages. There is no scarcity of goods, but because wages are much lower than in neighboring Western countries (20 percent of the EU level), there is an acute lack of effective buying power (disposable income per capita decreased by 30 percent in 1999). Pluralist democracy is also functioning. In Poland and Hungary, for example, the people first elected a conservative government, then an ex-Communist government, and in the last elections they put a Christian Democratic government in office again. In the Czech Republic there was first a conservative government under Václav

Klaus, an advocate of laissez-faire capitalism, and a social democratic minority government was elected under Milos Zeman. The ex-Communists in Poland and Hungary have for the most part renounced their Communist beliefs, and during their time in office they prevented the denationalized assets from passing into the hands of the former "red directors," thus protecting their countries from certain plundering. In Poland, a prosperous cohabitation between the Christian Democrats under Jerzy Buzek and the ex-Communist president Aleksander Kwasniewski has developed. And in both Poland and Hungary, the economy is growing at an above average rate; in fact, Poland's GDP is already 20 percent higher than it was in 1989. The Czech Republic is also beginning to show economic growth after a three-year recession. The foreign trade of these countries was quickly adapted to move to partners in the West, already two-thirds of their foreign trade goes to EU countries. The productivity balance deficit, however, remains at an unusually high level. Nevertheless, these progressive reform countries are obviously ready for Europe.

On October 13, 1999, the EU Commission decided to expand its membership talks, which began in 1997 with Poland, Hungary, the Czech Republic, Estonia, and Slovenia, to include Lithuania, Romania, Bulgaria, and Slovakia. Although the last five countries mentioned have not been able to fulfill EU economic criteria, the president of the commission, Romano Prodi, said it was enough that these countries were respecting the political criteria in areas of democracy and the protection of human rights. However, Prodi qualified, the talks with Bulgaria will be postponed until that Balkan country's planned reforms have been carried out and its promise to close several nuclear reactors has been fulfilled. Moreover, until Romania can stabilize its worrisome macroeconomic situation and end the violation of human rights in state-run children's homes, there will continue to be delays in talks with it. Romania's workers seem unsatisfied with the government's current reforms. The four largest unions organized mass demonstrations and strikes on November 25, 1999, and threatened to continue their protest until December 22, the ten-year anniversary of the fall of Nicolae Ceausescu, if their demands were not met. Many workers were primarily protesting against the progressing privatization. Nonetheless, the demonstrations were also aimed at raising low wages and pensions. A pensioner in Romania does not receive more than $10 per month. In response to the extremely tense social situation ex-president and head of the post-Communist party (now Social Democrats) Ion Iliescu won back the presidency in December 2000. The IMF relaxed its relationship with Romania and approved a credit package amounting to $574 million. Between August and November, 7.3 million people received payments from this sum. In return, Romania must reduce its state budget deficit and reform its banking system. Moreover, Romania, plagued by crisis, with 43 percent of the population living below the subsistence level, has also taken out a $64 million one-year credit package from twelve Western banks, thereby fulfilling some of the IMF's requirements that made it possible to activate the postponed payment of the second installment of standby credit.[34]

Of all the reform countries with EU membership negotiations, Romania will have the hardest time concluding them in a timely manner. In contrast, Romano Prodi praised Hungary and Estonia, which in his opinion, have made quick progress in regard to membership conditions, and he suggested that the EU think about setting a concrete date for membership. Prodi views January 1, 2003, as the earliest possible date for EU membership. In the first half of 2000, EU negotiations tackled the most difficult area for Central and Eastern Europe—that is, agriculture. With the membership of these countries, the EU's agricultural area will almost double, and the number of workers in this sector will more than double, from 7.5 million to 17.8 million. The enormous proportion of agricultural workers is a central problem for negotiations with these Central and East European countries. On average, the proportion of agricultural workers is four times as great as in the present EU states.[35] Experts say that to effect a structural change, jobs predominantly outside of agriculture must be created. However, there are major deficiencies in the production of agricultural goods, as well as in manufacturing and marketing. Because of the tremendous difference in wages and salaries, among the EU countries and those of East-Central Europe, which amounts to four-fifths of the EU average, EU countries, especially neighboring states like Austria and Germany, fear that there may be a mass immigration of the labor force. The Austrian Trade Union Federation demanded that Central and East European candidates for membership reach a wage level of 80 percent of the EU average. This is of course an absurd demand, says Austria's Organization of Industrialists. In order to satisfy this demand, wages in the candidate countries would have to increase by 17 percent annually, and the EU's enlargement to the east would take seventy-two years. Portugal and Greece had a wage level of 50 percent of the EU average when they entered the EU.

The idea that expansion to the east is an unavoidable economic and political question is gaining more and more support among EU officials, though not all candidates for membership will be able to meet the required conditions in the next few years. Commissioner Chris Patten says, "Enlargement is not just an economic and strategic question, but a moral one as well. The EU opened itself very quickly to Spain, Portugal, and Greece after the disappearance of their fascist governments. We should also show the same generosity and the same sense of urgency to the countries of Central and Eastern Europe." But the commissioner stipulates: "We must distinguish between the desire to become a member of the EU, and the desire to be seen as part of the European family." Patten said he attempted to make this clear to the ministers of the Ukraine. The considerable differences between the economic level of the EU and that of the candidate countries must be taken into account in making decisions on membership. However, these differences must not hinder or postpone membership *ad calendas graecas.* There are many conceivable options to help bridge the gaps—for example, by differentiating adaptation options and schedules for each of the candidates in accordance with their own special conditions. The prospective reform of the subsidy program, especially in agriculture, must be accelerated, though it must take the specific circumstances of Central and Eastern Europe into account. Perhaps one could consider the proposal made in the present study—namely, that the World Bank and the IMF be induced to grant long-term credit to finance the necessary restructuring in some of the reform countries, thereby accelerating the time it takes for them to adapt. Although the economic adaptations of the candidates for membership are the most important conditions, they are by far not the only ones. Chris Patten was correct when he stated that the acceptance of Central and East European countries into the EU was a moral question. Poland, for example, will have an especially difficult time meeting the Maastricht criteria because of the backwardness of its agriculture, which employs more than one-fourth of the able-bodied population. Moreover, if the borders were opened, the enormous differences in wages could encourage migration of the labor force into the prosperous neighboring countries. If one considers the moral component, however, one must also remember that Poland was the country that contributed the most to the fall of the Soviet empire, and during the occupation, Poland mounted the strongest resistance to sovietization. Finally, Poland has been a model for the successful transformation to a market economy and democracy;

the country has also led in economic growth despite a slight decline in the pace of growth in the past two years. The increase in the GNP was still 4.8 percent in 1998 and 4 percent in 1999. This was the result of a robust increase in internal demand: consumer credit had increased by 40.6 percent by the end of October 1999. The central bank was therefore forced to raise interest rates from 2.5 to 3.5 percent.[36]

The criteria for EU membership will worsen somewhat for Poland. Whereas its budget deficit exceeded 3 percent in 1999 and the balance of trade deficit reached a record high of 7.5 percent of the GNP, inflation decreased from 11.8 percent (1998) to 7.2 percent (1999). The unemployment rate rose from 10.4 percent to 12.5 percent, somewhat more than in 1998. All in all, despite a few weak points, this is a quite positive picture of a country moving toward economic growth, an improvement in the social structure, and a betterment of the social situation. However, Günter Verheugen, the EU commissioner for enlargement, considers Poland's chances for rapid EU entry questionable. At a meeting of Polish and European parliamentarians, Verheugen expressed his doubt that the Polish parliament would be able to complete preparations for EU entry by the year 2003. At present, says the Commissioner, "the country has a long way to go to fulfill EU laws." It is uncertain, he goes on, whether the Poles can appreciate the administrative effort and costs entailed in meeting EU criteria.[37] The results of a survey published in mid-November 1999 by the Warsaw Institute for Public Affairs show that Poland assesses the upcoming difficulties more dramatically than the EU commissioner. For the first time since the beginning of negotiations, fewer than 50 percent of Polish respondents supported EU membership. Every third respondent feared Poland's integration into the EU. Two years earlier, the number of Poland's EU supporters was 80 percent. The former head of government, and present chairman of the pertinent committee in the Polish parliament, Tadeusz Mazowiecki, attributes this precipitous decline to the government's inadequate information policy.

The EU skeptics' counterpropaganda has been much more effective. The politicians associated with the infamous ultranationalist radio station "Maria," with its 5 million sympathizers, proclaim, for example, that Poland's entry in the EU will destroy the nation-state and lead to a loss of sovereignty. The Catholic radio station, under the instigation of the fanatical priest Tadeusz Rydzyk, ignores the positive attitude of the Polish bishops toward EU membership, which they have been urging should happen as swiftly as possible. Nonetheless, the problems concerning membership criteria raised during negotiations have a negative influence on the growing skepticism of the population. Whereas in 1998 negotiations concerned relatively unproblematic questions, negotiations in 1999 dealt with contentious problems such as subsidizing agriculture and the sale of real estate to foreigners. Poland's minister of agriculture demanded them as a precondition for EU membership. Franz Fischler, the agricultural commissioner responsible for such issues, repudiated this demand and claimed it was simply economically unfeasible. Furthermore, the Poles fear that the free buying and selling of land and other real estate, which would be made possible by EU membership, could lead to a mass purchase of property by Germans who were expelled after World War II. Because of this fear, pressure from Poland's EU critics has led to the proposal of an eighteen-year transition period for the general sale of real estate to foreigners. This is a proposal that EU authorities are not prepared to accept.

Other EU membership candidates have similar, if not more difficult, problems. The latest progress report from Brussels shows that the Czech Republic is running up against even tougher criticism from EU authorities. The EU mainly criticizes the Czechs' slow tempo in adapting their legal system and expresses doubt in Czech ability to keep up with the competitive pressure of the market economy. Among other things, the adherence to the so-called Benes Decree, which was passed after World War II and led to the expropriation and exile of 3 million Sudeten Germans, could prove to be a stumbling block. Václav Havel, the current president of the Czech Republic, commented on his position as follows: "With certain 'subjects' we are doing better than with others."[38] "Unfortunately," Havel admits, "an apathetic mode of behavior has prospered among our political elite via the slogan 'We all want in the EU, and someday we will succeed.'" In regard to the subject of European integration, Havel says, "I believe that today's Europe has predetermined the present form of world civilization; it is responsible for all of its wonders as well as its contradictions. It is now up to Europe to pose the question of the general problems of civilization in such a manner that it may serve others as an example." In regard to the countries of Central and Eastern Europe Havel says, "I believe it makes sense to have concrete dates in sight. This motivates the membership candidates and hinders procrastination over uncomfortable decisions."

Romano Prodi set January 1, 2003, as a concrete date for the first membership candidates. Germany's chancellor Schröder insisted that the EU must be ready to take in members in 2003. Schröder primarily meant that in order for the EU to be ready to take on new members, it first needs to have the already proposed reforms behind it. These reforms include (among other things) the changes in agricultural subvention practices that are extremely important for membership candidates. The economic climate in Central and Eastern Europe, as well as in the Baltic states, has improved considerably. After a year of decline, growth rates in 2000 will once again increase, reaching more than 3 percent, and this in comparison with the highly prized 1.6 percent growth in 1999. This prognosis stems from the "Transition Report 1999" of the European Bank for Reconstruction and Development (EBRD). According to the EBRD, things will also improve in the CIS. After a decline of 3.5 percent in 1998, the GDP in 1999 rose by 2.5 percent and began to grow again at a rate of 4.8 percent in 2000. Vladimir Putin bragged that Russia's economy was growing by 7.5 percent over a part of the year 2000." The quick rise in oil prices, which according to Putin has brought in an additional $20 billion, has made a considerable contribution to this growth. The EBRD estimates that foreign investment in Central and East European regions will also increase by more than 5 percent, amounting in 2000 to a total of around $27 billion. Poland, Hungary, and the Czech Republic are currently the largest recipients. In 1999, the flow of capital to Russia also increased to around $3.5 billion, almost three times as much as in 1998. However, according to the EBRD, the greatest challenge for this region will be to motivate enterprise and improve public services.[39] The international multis' growing confidence in the solvency of the reform countries should be a substantial argument for their acceptance in the EU. There are no opponents to EU enlargement; the only questions regard the dates and mechanisms of adaptation most consistent with Europe's best interests.

The main obstacle to the entry of the reform countries into the EU is their economic retardation. The per capita GNP of the strongest of them—namely, Slovenia—is, according to the IMF, $10,981; in second place is the Czech Republic with $5,170; in third place is Hungary with $4,895; in fourth place is Poland with $3,984; the last places are occupied by Bulgaria with $1,540 and Romania with $1,523.[40] Slovenia, Poland, and Slovakia are the only reform countries to have achieved 1990 levels of employment in 1998. In worse shape are the former Soviet republics: Ukraine, Georgia, and Moldova achieved only one-third of the level before the transformation. The lowest is Tajikistan, with a per capita GNP of $1,045.[41] As noted, very low wages in the reform countries create the fear of mass migration. The level of wages of industrial workers in Hungary, the Czech Republic, and Slovakia is 13–14 percent of the level in Austria; in Bulgaria, Russia, and Romania, it is only 3–5 percent. The Austrian level could be achieved in ten years on the condition that the wages in Hungary, the Czech Republic, and Slovakia rose by 25 percent yearly and in Austria by 2 percent (now they rise by 4.2 percent)—and this is impossible. In Portugal, which was in the same position as the reform countries, wages over the last ten years rose by 6.1 percent annually and achieved only 25 percent of the Austrian level today.[42] The migration danger is real. According to the polls, 22 percent of the population in the Czech Republic and Hungary and 29 percent in Poland intend to emigrate to an EU country.

Not only do the candidates for entry have to become economically and socially ready to enter, but the EU also has to prepare its organizational structure and financial possibilities to incorporate very different members without damage to its goals. This problem was taken up at the EU summit in Nice in December 2000. After extensive discussions, the principal result was an allotment to each of the countries in the future Council of Ministers and European parliament. The future induction of populous new members will cause a very significant reallocation of power within the EU.

Principal deficiencies in the economic and currency policies of the EU remain unresolved after Nice. Beyond that, not all members are in agreement with the allotment of votes. Germany has 24 million inhabitants more than France, yet both countries are expected to have an equal number of votes, and French president Jacques Chirac did not agree to the German proposal to increase Germany's share by two votes. The fiercest battle was waged by the smaller countries to prevent their political clout from diminishing. Belgian prime minister Guy Verhofstadt expressed his dissatisfaction with these words: "There were some people around the table—but not many—who were working for the common good of Europe." The agreement fell short of the sweeping decision-making reforms proposed by France and some other countries to prevent the deadlock as the EU grows over the next decade. Another round of reforms is planned for 2004. The Nice summit assured the candidate countries that the door to membership will be open in 2004. The specifics will depend on the fulfillment of the Maastricht criteria.

4

The Prospects of Developing Countries in the Global Economy

Southeast Asia in Crisis

Bill Clinton assessed the economic crisis in Southeast Asia as the worst in the last fifty years. Although there have been may recessions in innumerable countries since the end of World War II, they have never caused such massive damage or had such a strong effect on other countries and continents as the 1997–98 crisis in Southeast Asia. As this crisis appeared to already have passed, the World Bank predicted that the growth rate in developing countries would not reach more than 1.5 percent in 1999, the lowest rate in seventeen years. Thus in Indonesia, for example, three-fourths of the 203 million inhabitants—around 150 million people—are still forced to get by on just one dollar per day. Pervaiz Musharraf, the general who overthrew the government of Pakistan in 1999 and seized absolute power for himself, commented: "Fifty-two years ago, we started with a beacon of hope, and today that beacon is no more. We stand in darkness. Our economy has crumbled, our credibility is lost, state institutions lie demolished."[1]

The economic situation in India is not much better. Since Pakistan split off from India following India's liberation from Britain's colonial rule in 1947, peace has never really prevailed on the subcontinent. The constant, often violent conflicts have depleted the bulk of the country's already meager resources. In 1999, these poorest of poor countries, India and Pakistan, tested nuclear weapons, costly and dangerous arms that they could use against one another. The National Defence Council Foundation declared in December 1999 that conflicts in developing countries, mired in constant violent disputes, were escalating. Nor did the IMF's prognosis for Latin America sound exactly optimistic. According to the IMF, even with a strong recovery in the next two years, Latin America's per capita income in 2000 would be lower than in 1997. The Reagan government's top adviser for developing countries, David Malpass, correctly maintains that the development of the Third World remains an important issue for the United States. He writes, "As the U.S. becomes more isolated in its full employment and wealth, economic conditions abroad raise major issues for its national security, immigration policy and future growth, not to mention morality."[2]

The true causes and effects of the economic crisis in the "tiger countries"—which had experienced decades of unprecedented boom and from being underdeveloped colonies had risen to join the ranks of the developed industrial states of the world—remain unclear. The editor of the *Asian Wall Street Journal* in Hong Kong, Peter Stein, points out that the causes of the crisis lie in a flawed allocation of credit, inefficient investment, and a weak crisis-management policy. Another factor was the mighty and steadily growing influx of foreign capital that was later withdrawn by foreign investors in panic, thereby throwing the capital and money markets into chaos.[3] One should remember that in 1996, just one year before Southeast Asia was rocked by its most serious crisis, five countries (South Korea, the Philippines, Indonesia, Malaysia, and Thailand) had succeeded in acquiring $102.3 billion in investments from the $327.7 billion that had streamed into the emerging markets worldwide that year.

The worst "crisis in the last fifty years" came only one year after the World Bank had called Malaysia, the healthiest growing country in Southeast Asia, an "economic miracle." But the economies of the region's other countries have also grown explosively. Thus the World Bank had seemingly sound reasons for its euphoric evaluation. But there is something wrong with a social system if it is able suddenly and destructively to transform an impressive, dynamic, and long-lasting period of boom into terrible recession. Moreover, international control mechanisms are malfunctioning if they first encourage an influx of money into a region, only later, as a result of vicious rumors of imminent insolvency, to allow that money to flee in panic and all but wreck a prospering economy. But powerful positive impulses will continue to exist in a country like Malaysia, where the yearly growth rate stood at an average of 7.8 percent in the 1970s and even higher from the mid-1980s. The growth rates of the other tiger economies of Southeast Asia were similarly high. The persistent opinion that the crisis in Southeast Asia was simply a "bubble" that popped under the pressure of the influx and outflow of casino capital is hardly tenable in light of the facts. Of course, the dramatic flight of foreign capital, as well as several incorrect investment decisions, and the construction of costly prestige projects helped to trigger the financial crisis. However, the view that thirty years of dynamic economic growth produced no more than a "bubble" is wrong. Growth in Southeast Asian countries has indeed been built upon a firm foundation.

The head of Malaysia's government, Mahathir Mohamad, has no patience with the claims that his country is an economic miracle. It is no miracle that his country, one of the world's biggest producers of semiconductors, has developed from a "rubber colony" to a country able to contend with the most powerful industrial nations of the world. Mohamad protests that what took place in Asia was no "miracle" but rather the realization of an idea. It is perhaps no accident that this dictum recalls a similar one uttered by Charles de Gaulle, who said, "France is an idea." Mahathir Mohamad continues this train of thought with pride: a new Asia is emerging that no longer looks to the West but to the East. Mahathir's spokesman adds that his country's success comes from the unprecedented opportunities for the creation of income and wealth that today's world has witnessed. Effective coordination of government decisions with the rules of the market has evolved into the concept of "state incorporation"—that is, the state as an umbrella firm. But by end of the 1990s it had become clear that this concept was no longer compatible with the challenges of the global economy. At the current stage of development, a watchdog and interventionist state was simply in contradiction with a modern market that is integrated into the global economy. Sights were set on a transition to a functioning free market economy.

The Asian crisis aside, impulses for dynamic financial growth are also clearly present in South Korea. After its division in 1945, the southern part of the country lost two-thirds of its industrial capacity in its war against North Korea. The actual founder of Korea Inc., Park Chung Hee, who took power in a military coup and ruled in an authoritarian regime from 1962 to 1979, introduced a management model based on Japan's. In line with Japan's *zaibatsu* model, which concentrates economic power in major concerns, President Park established the *chaebol* holding companies, which brought entire economic branches under their control. These large firms, buttressed by tax advantages, low-interest credit, and the like, developed into strong, influential, and diversified industrial entities. Several of them—for instance, Daewoo, Hyundai, Samsung, and Lucky Goldstar—have gained a worldwide reputation. Five strategically important economic branches—steel, petrochemicals, nonferrous metals, electronics, and mechanical engineering—have also enjoyed special support from the state. These economic branches, however, were subjected to iron discipline and a sixty-hour work week. Although the managers of these concerns earned a great deal, economic power remained in President Park's hands. Opposition to Park's authoritarian rule began to grow significantly, and in October 1979 the head of the secret police murdered Park. His successor, General Chun Doo Hwan, used all of his power to reduce the powerful influence of the *chaebols.* Chun's assistant, Kim Jae-Il, a Stanford University graduate, introduced a policy of stabilization and liberalization, reduced government control, and established the conditions requisite for the development of smaller and middle-sized enterprises. Kim also privatized state concerns, lowered the substantial import barriers, and exposed the inefficient branches of industry to healthy, external competition. Kim had no equals in his recognition that the growing complexity of the economy had made it impossible for the government to control it. However, he was killed in an airplane crash in October of 1983. Although the reforms he had introduced did continue, the powerful bureaucracy resisted them. From this point on, the *chaebols* began to invest outside of South Korea in an attempt to increase their competitiveness. But despite all of its attempts to stimulate growth, South Korea has not escaped the negative effects of massive state intervention, especially spreading corruption. For instance, the leaders of eight *chaebols* were sentenced to prison for bribing former president Roh; the sums in question were by no means small, amounting to $650 million. In August 1996, President Chun was sentenced to death, and President Roh Tae-Woo received a twenty-two-year prison term.

South Korea's economic growth was an uninterrupted success story for many years. Asia expert Ezra Vogel writes, "South Korea was unrivaled, even by Japan, in the speed with which it went from having almost no industrial technology to taking its place among the industrialized nations."[4] Hardly anyone would dispute the thesis that South Korea is comparable with West Germany and North Korea with East Germany prior to the reunification. Furthermore, there is great hope that a friendly reunification can be achieved on the basis of the stronger economic partner. However, in order to realize this goal and meet the challenge of the

Table 4.1

Comparison of North and South Korea

Indicator	North Korea	South Korea
Population (in millions)	21.4	46.9
GNP (in billions of dollars)	17.3	409.5
Soldiers (in millions)	1.082	0.672
Tanks	3,500.0	2,130.0
Ground-to-ground missiles	54.0	12.0
Submarines	26.0	19.0

Source: Der Spiegel 24 (2000), p. 192.

global economy, the country must first of all free its economy from the choking grip of the powerful, authoritarian state. Perhaps the Asian crisis has contributed to this. South Korea enters the twenty-first century as a developed industrial nation. Nevertheless, in order to be able to participate in the constantly intensifying worldwide competition, the country's modern market economy must function at full capacity.

A comparison of the most important indicators in Table 4.1 bears out the above thesis that developments in South and North Korea resemble the developments in West and East Germany. It is impossible to overlook the large discrepancy between the military and economic potential of both countries. Although the desire within the two Koreas to reunite has always remained, as was the case during the division of Germany, it is now actually possible to discuss real chances for the realization of reunification. For the first time since the Korean War (1950–53), the leaders of North and South Korea, Kim Jong Il and Kim Dae Jung respectively, came together in Pyongyang in the middle of June 2000 in order to discuss reconciliation between the two countries. It bears mentioning in this context that North Korea's president has his deceased father, Kim Sung Il, to thank for his power and that South Korea's president spent sixteen years in prison and was even sentenced to death for an attempted coup. It is still difficult to tell what the results of this meeting will be, although considerable progress has at least been made in reuniting separated family members.

In contrast, Taiwan's dynamic economic growth is perhaps built on a firmer foundation. After 1895, the island became a Japanese colony, and following World War II, although for just a few years, it became a part of the Chinese mainland. However, in 1949, after the Kuomintang leader Chiang Kai-shek, who was besieged by Mao's Communists, fled with

2 million civilians and soldiers to the island, Taiwan established itself as a separate, independent state. The viewpoint that Taiwan was a part of the Chinese state was shared by both the Communists and the Kuomintang leaders with one important difference: whereas Chiang wanted to unite continental China, with its over one billion inhabitants, with the island nation of less than ten million people, Mao aimed at exactly the opposite. Thus the fact that the Taiwanese government now questions the notion that the island belongs to the Chinese mainland is a revision of the original conception of the state. In its fifty years as an independent state, Taiwan has refuted the opinion of numerous experts that the Chinese are incapable of building a capitalistic social system. Of those experts, none other than the German sociologist Max Weber had claimed that Confucianism (Taiwan's present official state ideology) was incompatible with capitalism. In the course of its fifty year existence, however, Taiwan has proved that it is capable of not only building a prosperous state, thanks to its capitalistic social system, but also securing itself a top place in the ranks of the global world economy.

The mainland has also shown reverence for the effectiveness of the capitalist social system. As noted, save the economy from imminent collapse, in 1978 China began laying the groundwork for a socialist market economy. The result of this economy, which is still dominated by the role of state-owned concerns, cannot be compared to those of the capitalist island nation. The tiny island state has risen to the rank of an economic superpower. In contrast, despite continental China's above average growth rate and population of 1.2 billion, it still remains a developing country. Taiwan's success is the consequence of its substantial accomplishment in building a suitable regulatory model and its ability to continually adapt to changing internal and external conditions. Shortly after becoming independent, Taiwan carried out an agrarian reform that effectively raised the output of the island's farmers. Moreover, a determined anti-corruption policy strengthened the moral fiber of the young political elite. The government's deciding role in the formation of economic policy, predominant in the first phase of development, was successively dismantled in later stages. Once the preconditions for a flourishing entrepreneurial economy were created, Taiwan progressively turned away from an industrial strategy based on import substitution, and as industry diversified and product quality improved, it has become an important exporter of manufactured industrial goods on the international market. The figures for the founding phase of Taiwan's economy, between 1963 and 1972, when exports rose from $123 million to $3 billion, show just how lucrative this economic strategy was. The government placed great stock in the creation of a competent national economic and political elite, within which a smaller group of "supertechnocrats" would play a decisive role. Between 1963 and the end of the 1980s, K.T. Li, a Cambridge graduate, was considered the father of the Taiwanese economic miracle. He increased Taiwan's foreign trade many times over by utilizing Japan's concept of "competing outwardly and protecting inwardly." Protectionist precautions were successively dismantled, and large firms had to face international competition. In contrast to South Korea, the main architects of Taiwan's economic success valued the small and middle-sized businesses, thereby creating the preconditions for stable economic development. Although Taiwan and continental China function as two independent, politically separate states, economically they are slowly but surely growing together. In the 1990s, for instance, Taiwan invested tens of millions of dollars in the mainland and has become the most important foreign investor in China. It is entirely probable that the reduction in income differences, the success of the Hong Kong model of "one state, two social systems," the expansion of free market relations, and the relaxing of totalitarian rule in greater China will eventually produce a blueprint for reunification that would satisfy both states. Taiwan's recently elected president followed the example of the two Koreas by inviting the leader of mainland China to Taiwan on January 15, 2000, to discuss possibilities for reconciliation. However, mainland China will have a long way to go to catch up. For instance, Taiwan's per capita income has risen between 1949 and 1999 from $100 to $14,000 (China's per capita output is no more than a third of Taiwan's). Moreover, the island state is one of the most important computer producers in the world.

Southeast Asia is slowly overcoming its worst crisis in the postwar period. The economic situation in all of Asia has improved considerably. According to the most recent analysis of the Asian Development Bank (ADB) in Manila, the national economies of Asia will grow at 5.7 percent in both 1999 and 2000. (In 1997 and 1998 Asia saw the GNP decrease by 2.3 percent and 6.1 percent respectively.) ADB experts view 1999 as the beginning of a cyclical upswing in the region. Nevertheless, they have taken pains to be moderate in their positive remarks since, they say, this upswing is contingent on conditions outside the region, such as a "soft landing" for the U.S. economy, a stronger upswing in

Europe, and a relatively stable rate of exchange.[5] Foreign investors are also regaining confidence in the region. In 1999, $39.3 billion in private investment money streamed into Asia (in 1998 it was only $8.6 billion) and the ADB estimates an additional $27 billion for the year 2000. South Korea regained its precrisis growth level and in 1999 had a growth rate of 8 percent, strongest in the region. Taiwan, China, Singapore, Thailand, the Philippines, and Malaysia follow with growth rates between 3 and 5 percent. The original prognosis that India's growth rate would reach 7 percent for 1999 was corrected downward to 6 percent for both 1999 and 2000.

Signs of stronger economic cooperation are apparent: the members of the Association of Southeast Asian Nations (ASEAN)—Burma, Brunei, Malaysia, Cambodia, Indonesia, Laos, the Philippines, Singapore, Vietnam, and Thailand—intend, together with Japan, China, and South Korea, to expand the region into a common market. At the summit in Manila in late November 1999, the ASEAN states agreed to strengthen not only economic cooperation, but also cooperation in political and social matters. The establishment of a common currency was also suggested. In the closing statement, ASEAN acknowledged the possibility of establishing a customs union, a common market, and a unified currency. The countries of the region, as well as China, Japan, and South Korea, all declared their willingness to cooperate more closely in both financial and currency matters and to undertake common efforts for peace, stability, and prosperity. Agreements in political matters are of particular importance. Inter alia, a rule of conduct for the resolution of territorial disagreements was recommended to resolve the dispute over the Spratley Islands in the South China Sea, and Indonesia's territorial integrity was expressly reaffirmed.

It is no coincidence that China's architect of reform, Deng Xiaoping, began his reforms in the agricultural sector. Deng proceeded exactly as the economist Dwight Perkins suggested—that is, in a sector where success was certain. This was after a disaster in Anhui Province, where a drought in 1978 caused the starvation of hundreds of thousands. The police were called in to stop the starving people from streaming into the city of Shanghai. Members of the Politburo cried as they watched a film of the human tragedy. Afterward, they approved Deng's suggestion to let the farmers take over the communes, which the state had so inefficiently administered. The success of these agricultural reforms, which freed not only the farmers but the entire country as well from hunger and poverty, convinced the party and the people that Deng's reform strategy was legitimate.

The reform of industry was somewhat more difficult. For far too long, China had been used to setting low prices for agricultural products; this was supposed to serve the financing of industrialization. At the time of its introduction, this was the only development model in the enormous Communist empire. The party was frightened at the prospect that industry, which until 1978 had been entirely controlled by the party and the government, would be handed over to the "invisible, blind hand" of the market. Even Deng, who had been active in the Communist movement throughout its long struggle for power, had participated in building the state, and later became the top figure in Communist practice (sometimes in opposition to Mao), had no experience with how one could integrate a market economy into a state-dominated collective social system. While studying in France, Deng had become familiar with French capitalism through experience in several businesses, where he worked to earn the money needed to pay for his studies. He also had the opportunity to observe Communist practice in the Soviet Union, where he studied the Soviet version of Marxist theory at the Sun Yat-sen University for Workers of the East. At the end of the 1920s, Deng returned to China as a convinced Communist, and at twenty-three he was already the general secretary of the Communist Party. Deng took part in the Red Army's "Long March," as ninety thousand men fled the Kuomintang nationalists; only five thousand survived. Later, he defeated five hundred thousand troops of the Kuomintang army at Huan-Hai. Thus by 1949, he was already one of the most influential personalities besides Mao, the party prophet who pursued a utopian vision and established a tyrannical rule. But in contrast to Mao, whose rule was based on the maxims in his "Little Red Book" and not on the welfare of the people, Deng was a leader who thought in pragmatic terms. For Deng, communism was a means to an end, and this end was the overcoming of China's secular backwardness. As a provincial administrator, he steered the economy by promoting incentives and not through party directives, Deng was able to transform his thought into action. Already in those days, for him capitalism was not an enemy but rather a method of control and modernization that socialism could utilize for its own purposes. Mao appreciated his experienced comrade-in-arms, and in 1957, during Khrushchev's visit to China, he introduced Deng to the then Soviet leader as a man with a great future ahead of him.

However, the skies began to darken for the intelligent leader. Though his star shone brightly, it was quickly extinguished. Deng was made number four in the party hierarchy, but his rise lasted only for a short while. Although Deng was a willing participant in the "Great Leap Forward," Mao's plan to industrialize the backward country, he wanted to utilize modern technology, not primitive village blast furnaces. Furthermore, he did not want to promote progress through party orders and Communist propaganda, but rather via the experience of the modern, efficient, free market. Deng wanted to achieve the "great leap" to integrate the nation into the modern civilized world through the most modern technology—which China would first import but at a later stage would produce itself. Deng, however, wanted nothing to do with Mao's "Cultural Revolution," whose prototype was the Soviet purges of the 1930s, which took the lives of the most active and integral party leaders. General Secretary Deng Xiaoping was also on the list of those soon to be purged. When he was handed Mao's "Little Red Book," he refused it and returned it. Such a refusal to accept Mao's basic theses could not go unpunished. As the harbinger of capitalism, Deng spent two years in strict isolation and was then forced, with his wife, to repair tractors. Torture left his son a cripple. After Mao's death in 1976, Deng was freed and once again moved into the country's most intimate leadership circles. But he had first to fight a hard battle against Hua Guafeng, a stubborn party bureaucrat who had been appointed by Mao. It was only in 1978 that Deng finally managed to get rid of Mao's hapless successor and set forth on the path of reform. The historic plenary session of the Communist Party in December 1978 is a key date in China's modern history, alongside the republican revolution of Sun Yat-sen in 1911 and the Communist seizure of power in 1949. It marked an end to Mao's tyrannical, utopian methods for developing the country that had cost innumerable lives but had brought not prosperity, as was promised, but misery.

India: A Parliamentary Democracy with Antiquated Social and Economic Structures

The demographic explosion in India, the world's second most populous country, has greatly outstripped its economic growth. In 1947, the year of India's independence from Britain, it had 350 million inhabitants. In 1997, after fifty years of independence, the population had reached 917 million. Economic growth, however, lagged considerably behind. After freeing itself from the shackles of foreign domination, India proceeded to establish an inefficient economic system. The leader of the independence movement, Jawaharlal Nehru, was convinced that the Communists and socialists had confidently set out on their path because they "believed that science and logic were on their side."[6] Nehru thus attempted to impose the Soviet model on India, whose social system was entirely different. The architects of India's economic model were convinced that central planning, total state control, and state-set prices were better instruments for managing the allocation of resources and production than a million atomized producers and a competitive market. The state sector's share of the GNP rose from 8 percent in 1960 to 26 percent in 1991. At the end of the 1980s, 70 percent of the employed population worked in state-run industrial and service sectors. The consequences of this model were as disastrous as in the Soviet Union, which had fallen apart as a result of its economic problems. India's system of economic control, which consisted of state licensing in all areas of the economy, foreign trade, and investment activities, stifled any initiative on the part of participants in the economy. Every innovation in production, product range, and sales had to be approved by the state bureaucracy. This system, which was supposed to protect producers from internal and external competition, had a devastating effect on productivity and the quality of goods; along with the corruption it encouraged, it demoralized India's young market. State discipline could not supplant the natural discipline of competition. Moreover, the policy of economic self-sufficiency proved catastrophic since it cut India off from other countries.

The price for neglecting foreign trade relations and resisting foreign investment was technological stagnation at the level of the 1960s. It was not until the early 1990s that India opened up to the rest of the world—much later than the opening of China under Deng Xiaoping. But in contrast to China, India adopted the West's basic democratic principles after independence, and it has remained true to them to this day. India's first prime minister, Nehru, who governed the country for sixteen years after independence, had a deciding influence on India's politics and economy. Indira Gandhi, Nehru's daughter, took power upon his death. As Nehru's successor, however, she repeatedly neglected India's basic democratic principles and increased the federal government's authority at the expense of the states. After being accused of abnormalities in her electoral district in 1975, Indira Gandhi declared a state of emergency, introduced censorship, and limited civil rights. Only after mass protests did she concede and order new elections, in which she lost to a coalition of opposition parties. But this coalition was unable to revive the stagnating economy; foreign investors, fearing nationalization, left the country in droves. Indira returned to power in 1980 and renewed her authoritarian rule. This caused increased tensions in the states, especially among the Sikh communities. The head of state saw no other option than to storm the Golden Temple, the holy Sikh shrine, in which rebellious Sikhs had sought refuge. While walking in the garden of the government complex in October 1984, Indira Gandhi was murdered by Sikh members of her personal bodyguard. Her son and successor, Rajiv Gandhi, did not change many of the country's policies. The budget deficit, caused by the financial losses of state-owned concerns, was financed through domestic and foreign loans. But the initiation of reforms in state policy was not enough to substantially improve the economy. Although new loans were raised to cover due and overdue debts, a lack of money forced the cancellation of projects already under way, and production was cut back.

Rajiv Gandhi lost the 1989 elections. Once again, however, the opposition parties were unable to stop the economy's slide into a devastating crisis. Rajiv Gandhi started a new election campaign that might have seen his comeback had he not been killed in May 1993 by a Tamil suicide bomber. On June 21, 1991, seventy-year-old Narasimha Rao became president of the Congress Party and was sworn in as head of the government. Rao inherited a daunting economic legacy. The state domestic debt had ballooned to a shocking 55 percent of the GNP; interest payments for foreign debt were 23 and the internal debt 4 percent; the budget deficit had reached 8 percent of the GNP. Moreover, there was enough money in the country's currency reserves for only about two weeks of imports. The nature of India's stagnant economy becomes clear in a comparison with South Korea: whereas up until 1960 South Korea matched India's per capita output, by 1987 South Korea's per capita income was ten times greater than India's. A comparison between the two countries' export levels is even more telling: in 1990, OECD countries imported $9 billion of goods produced in India, but they purchased $41 billion worth of goods from South Korea, a country with a population twenty times smaller. Rao, India's finance and trade minister before becoming head of state, realized that his country's economy could be saved only through the introduction of comprehensive reforms. Within a few weeks, trade barriers were brought down, tariffs were reduced, the licensing process was revoked for 80 percent of the industrial branches, and the practice of requiring state approval for large firms to expand or diversify production was halted. Moreover, India opened to foreign investment and began liquidating the government's share in large concerns; state control of the economy was reduced, and the powers of the states and firms were extended.

Five years later, in 1996, the Congress Party lost its parliamentary majority. A coalition government was formed under Prime Minister H.D. Deve Gowda, who had initially enjoyed the support of the Congress Party. However, after a "no confidence" vote a year later, a new government, headed by diplomat Kumar Gujral, was established. The march of reform could no longer be halted. For instance, a nuclear power station valued at over $2 billion was built by an international consortium led by the U.S. firm Enron; other foreign investors followed. Yet the amount of foreign investment—$5.6 billion in 1996—was quite small given the country's size. The goal was to achieve progress through the privatization of nationalized industrial concerns, thus enabling a powerful private sector to slowly develop. Tatas and Birlas, two large Indian companies, were able to expand their operations in iron and steel, heavy machinery, tea growing, and publishing. A middle class of 300 million people emerged and increasingly began to influence the fate of India's civil society. Moreover, the influence of state officials on economic events diminished; their role was limited to education, social work, and health and to devising economic incentives in areas where they were urgently needed to attack poverty or alleviate unemployment. The positive results of this policy were visible after just a few years. Economic growth, which had stood at the "Hindu rate" of 3–4 percent for decades (and in times of stagnation was even below that level) has risen to over 6 percent. There is even hope that by the year 2020 the country will become the world's fourth largest economic power, after the United States, China, and Japan.

On the occasion of the fifty-year celebration of India's independence from British colonial rule, President Kocheril Raman Narayanan asked: Will there be economic growth with social justice? Mahatma Gandhi's grandson recommended that instead of building monuments to his grandfather, India should remember his legacy and put an end to the blatant injustice within the country. Today, India ranks as one of the world's leading software producers and has had a space exploration program for quite some time. Moreover, in 1974 India ran its first nuclear test, followed by five more in May 1977. Many Indians feel, however, that instead of constantly increasing military spending, it would be better if the country first concentrated on establishing mandatory school attendance and a functioning social security system. India's population grows by 16 million each year, and it will become increasingly difficult to keep the promise of food, clothing, and a roof overhead for every citizen. In fact, 400 million people today live below the poverty line in conditions of destitution. By 1990, India wanted to achieve its goal of providing every child with an education until age fourteen; with more than one-half of the population (i.e., 500 million people) unable to read or write, it will be difficult to fulfill this goal. Though poverty and illiteracy are considered the country's greatest shame, there are no signs that India will be able to overcome these conditions in the near future.

Although India is a functioning parliamentary democracy, its social structures are antiquated. The population is divided into four main castes and thousands of subcastes. Among these castes are 150 million people belonging to the most underprivileged layer of the population, the "untouchables," or Dalit. But much has changed within the caste system since India's independence. A few weeks prior to the fifty-year anniversary of India's independence, a member of the untouchable caste, K.R. Narayanan, was elected president for the first time in the country's history. And B.R. Ambedkar, the "great untouchable," was India's first minister of justice and the architect of the country's first constitution, which abolished the untouchable status—legally, at least. But the caste hierarchy continues to exist in everyday life, and the Brahmans remain the leading caste in the country, though their influence has diminished. Half of the representatives in the first parliament were Brahmans; today they make up less than one-third. Nevertheless, the 150 million Dalit are still considered "unclean," deprived of rights, despised, and often victimized by terrible violence. But because the Dalit have become one of the strongest political forces in the country, they can no longer be ignored. At election time, they are on an equal footing with other sections of the population. For the second time, a Dalit was recently elected prime minister in the northern state of Uttar Pradesh: forty-two-year-old Mayawati. However, Mayawati governs in a coalition with the Bharatiya Janata Party (BJP), a Hindu faction that hardly counts itself among the friends of the underprivileged Dalit. Along with seventeen other parties, the BJP is a coalition partner in the federal government and belongs to the "Buy Indian" lobby.

Even in the age of globalization, divisions in India continue to exist among the growing superwealthy industrial class of the Tatas and Bajaj; the 300 million members of the middle class; and India's other poor and suffering classes. Nevertheless, the Indian subcontinent's progress in terms of civilization is unstoppable. China and India, which together account for 40 percent of the world's population, will play an ever-increasing role in the globalized world economy. The deepening integration of these two countries with the West brings hope of disarmament efforts that would help decrease absurd levels of military spending, thus allowing China and India to raise their citizens' standard of living.

The Difference Between Global Capitalism in South America and North America

Jonathan Friedland, editor in chief of the Mexico City bureau of the *Wall Street Journal* and a Latin America expert, wrote an interesting piece about recent developments in South America: "The free market revolution promised so much. To many in Latin America, it has delivered so little."[7] Whereas the United States can thank the explosion of the free market for its lightning quick rise in the 1990s, South Americans are generally dissatisfied with the free market revolution, which has failed to fulfill expectations of higher income, a better living standard, and a secure future. The South American manifestation of capitalism remains a social order that brings little advantage to the majority of the population.

In order to understand the latest developments in South America, a brief look back is necessary. For a long time, the region's official theory of economic control, "*independencia*," enshrined the state's dominant role in the economy as national law via high import barriers, autocratic rule, and a debasement of market rules. This system, which prevailed until the 1980s, enabled the state to subjugate the most strategically important branches of the economy. According to a prominent Argentine economist, Raúl Prebish, who coined the principle of *dependencia*, the economy is divided into an industrial center (United States and Western Europe) and a goods-producing periphery. The terms of trade in this division have always worked to the advantage of the center and to the disadvantage of the periphery, to which the countries of Latin America belong. Thus world trade is not an effective method for raising the living standard of Latin America's population. The periphery must instead go its own way: import-substitution industrialization (ISI), with high customs tariffs and other protectionist measures. Moreover, in order to acquire the necessary imports of equipment for industrialization as cheaply as possible, currencies would be overvalued; other imports would be rationed and transacted through licenses. The prices of internal trade were subject to state control, many industrial concerns were nationalized, and the market was deprived of many of its traditional functions. The system of "*independencia*," which lasted until the end of the 1970s, created the necessary preconditions for a twofold increase in per capita national income between 1950 and 1970. The conviction that the economy, which was led by the state and not the market, would more likely approach the Soviet model than the competitive market of the West, found its explanation in the economic practices of the time.

It bears mentioning that the growing component of planning and administration was used not only used in Latin America, but also in India under Jawaharlal Nehru and in Tanzania and Ghana under Julius Nyerere and Kwame Nkrumah respectively, the fathers of African socialism. The situation in Latin America, however, developed differently: the economy, mainly controlled by the state, had already lost its vigor by the 1970s. These countries could keep their economies going only with credits from the World Bank and the IMF. Whereas in 1947 debt in developing countries amounted to $135 billion, by 1981 this total had reached $751 billion. Ten years later, at the beginning of 1991, it was almost three times as much: $1,945 billion. In 1993, the total debt of developing countries amounted to 40 percent of their GNP.[8] The Latin American countries accounted for a large proportion of this debt. Between 1975 and 1982 long-term debt rose from $45.2 to $176.4 billion; if one takes short-term loans and IMF credit into account, the total was $333 billion.[9] No one, Daniel Yergin and Joseph Stanislaw claim, paid attention to the rapidly growing debt in the Third World; good money was simply thrown at poorly managed countries to prevent a string of insolvency cases. It was only after Mexico declared its insolvency in August 1982 that the alarm began to sound. The result was both financial and intellectual bankruptcy. The belief that "*independencia*" could function as a reasonable control mechanism for Latin America had broken down.

Latin America's era of economic transformation has gone down in history as the "lost years." In 1990, per capita income was lower than at the beginning of the previous decade. The autocratic tendencies of "*independencia*" had protected the national economies from worldwide competition and the advancing technological revolution and thereby condemned them to inefficiency, while galloping inflation decimated people's savings. The only solution was to abolish total state control. In order to create an efficient, competitive economy, Latin America needed to bring down trade barriers and eliminate protectionist practices. To overcome the recession, half-hearted measures clearly would not suffice; an urgent shift from the state to the market was needed. The IMF made this transformation easier by postponing collection of due credit payments. Moreover, the collapse of the Soviet Union decisively undermined any remaining belief in the soundness of a planned economy. Latin America's leading economists began to change their ideas. These "technopols," often with PhDs from Harvard, MIT, or Yale, have not only enriched the field by founding research institutions, but have also substantially altered the economic policy of their countries.

The main tenets of "*independencia*" had been more or less the same throughout Latin America: reduced reliance on market mechanisms; a dominant, controlling state role in the economy; protection of the domestic economy against international competition; and an abnormally high inflation rate. However, new and radical reforms began to be introduced in Latin America. Although designed to reduce state intervention and strengthen market mechanisms throughout the region, the specific form these reforms took was contingent upon various factors.

South American Roots of Economic Shock Therapy

Gonzalo Sanchez de Lozada (nicknamed "Goni"), Bolivia's president from 1993 to 1997, was the father of shock therapy as a means of rehabilitating an economy rocked by crisis. Jeffrey Sachs, the Harvard professor behind Leszek Balcerowicz, the successful architect of Poland's transformation from a planned economy to a market economy, also supported Gonzales Sanchez. However, Sachs also advised Yegor Gaidar, Russia's hapless reformer. Ten years after the beginning of Gaidar's transition program, the Russian economy lay in ruins. Even today, the Russian people suffer from the terrible shock caused by these reforms. GNP decreased by almost one-half during Russia's transition period; at least one-third of the population now struggles below the poverty line. Although under certain circumstances shock therapy can be an appropriate method for the rehabilitation of a crisis-ridden economy, architects of economic transformation both great and small have not yet realized that shock therapy is not an effective means for converting a collective planned economy into a competitive free market economy. This is especially true in Russia's case since that country has such deep-rooted collective traditions and lacks a middle class that could steer the private economy. The power-hungry, seldom sober ex-president of Russia, Boris Yeltsin, had promised that his voucher privatization would bring about a just division of state property. But the gap between a handful of rich, powerful, and influential oligarchs and the impoverished majority is greater in Russia than anywhere else on earth, even South America.

Back to Bolivia: in 1985, when Gonzalo Sanchez became minister of planning, the country's economy was mired in crisis. The government had lost control over the country. Because the state could no longer effectively levy taxes, tax income made up a meager 3 percent of the state budget. State spending was financed through the printing of money, which resulted in a hyperinflation rate of 24,000 percent by the middle of the 1980s.[10] Goni came to the conclusion that Bolivia's regulatory system, in which the private sector was paid for at the expense of the state sector and vice versa, was condemned to bankruptcy and thus no longer viable. Two possible solutions to the crisis made a strong impression on him. One, which had been put into effect in New Zealand, used a labor team to quickly end the administrative economy and bring about the requisite conditions for successful economic growth. The second solution, which had especially impressed the Bolivian president, was Deng's policy of erecting a private sector within Communist China. Goni did not hesitate to take dramatic action in order to boost Bolivia's ailing economy. His historic decree of August 1985 removed price controls, made drastic budget cuts, reduced the customs tariff for imports, restructured the public sector, and slashed state subsidies. It bears mentioning that when these far-sighted, radical reforms were carried out, the treasury was empty; the resources of the state bank amounted to no more than $1.5 million. Hence the Sachs-inspired reforms proved valuable. The goal was to end galloping inflation, and this was achieved by reforming the tax system. Prior to this, taxes were difficult to collect in Bolivia; in fact, an enormous variety of tax types (450) existed. As a result of the tax reform, taxes were reduced to three clear and easy-to-collect types. Moreover, a corresponding state control apparatus was established, and the activity of the central bank was brought in line with Western practices. Between 1985 and 1987, the economy stabilized and the inflation rate dropped from 24,000 percent to 7 percent. "A market economy was established overnight," said Bolivia's main economic architect. In Bolivia's case, the shock treatment versus gradualism dilemma had been resolved; there was simply no time left for a policy of gradualism.

Bolivia's example became the accepted model for all of South America. The dominance of the state in regulating the economy had ended, and the preconditions for a free market economy were in place. Entire branches of production were privatized and freed from state control, trade barriers dismantled, and the way for democracy was cleared. Although Bolivia remains a developing country, it is expanding its economy and raising its population's standard of living.

Chile's Economic System: A Prime Example for South America

During the 1990s, Chile's economic growth accelerated and the country fought inflation. These developments were due to Chile's policy of distancing itself from the theoretically totally free market economy, which had been maintained under the rule of General Augusto Pinochet. Instead, the country applied several of the regulatory controls used by Asian countries to direct their economies—for example, forced savings and the control of capital. Chile's government tells foreign investors where they are allowed to invest their money and close certain financial sectors to foreign investment. In the middle of December 1999, the Social Democratic candidate for president, Ricardo Lagos, appeared to want to continue this policy by promising that the state would intervene only when it was necessary to correct the market in order to secure the state's employment contributions. The new president explicitly distanced himself from his socialist predecessor, Salvador Allende, who initiated a massive nationalization and expropriation policy after his election in 1970, which resulted in economic chaos. Allende perished during a putsch led by Pinochet, who then ruled the country for seventeen years, oppressing labor unions, journalists, and students; thousands of Chile's citizens were murdered. Although the general knew very little about economics, he took the El Ladrillo reform project, which had been prepared for the presidential candidate by the Catholic University, as his government program.

According to Yergin and Stanislaw, under Pinochet "the Chicago Boys" (conservative economists connected with the University of Chicago) then turned their Chilean project into practice.[11] A free market economy was established to replace the troublesome, predominantly state-controlled mixed economy that had been set up by Allende. With the help of the Chicago Boys, the system was fundamentally reformed, price policy was liberalized, foreign trade was freed from stifling barriers, and a large proportion of state concerns was privatized. Between 1973 and 1980, the number of state-owned concerns was reduced from five hundred to twenty-five; the military dictatorship had reduced state intervention in the economy to a minimum. Experts on South American relations called it an unprecedented and paradoxical event: although reforms brought a few positive results, they lasted for only a short period. In 1982 symptoms of an imminent and severe crisis emerged: serious mistakes and scandals discredited the entire financial system, the country was hit hard by debt, the economy stagnated, and the banking system collapsed. A second wave of reforms was initiated in 1985, but this time the Harvard experts played a larger role and had more success than the previous attempt; growth rates increased considerably, inflation decreased, and exports, especially of wine, rose. But at the end of the 1980s, the military junta was brought down thanks to a people's referendum. Alejandro Foxley, economics minister in the new government, continued the reform program with undiminished momentum. The new government focused on attacking poverty and social problems that had been neglected under Pinochet and expanding the rules of the market. It proclaimed that a competent state should establish a progressive social policy along with a conservative fiscal policy. Eduardo Frei's government also continued this course of reform. Frei insisted that the market should produce wealth, and he vowed to protect its powers. President Lagos, who was elected in January 2000, seems to adhere to this economic strategy as well.

Mexico: Between NAFTA and the Rest of America

In contrast to most countries in South America, Mexico has never been ruled by a military dictator. The revolution of 1910 brought political power into the hands of the Partido Revolucionario Institucional (PRI), which guaranteed order and stability within the country for seventy years. Although there have been opposition parties and groups, the PRI's clever power consolidation policy has enabled it to maintain unbroken domination over the country. A single labor confederation mediates between employees and employers, thus securing, without serious conflict, social peace within the country. Mexican presidents have enjoyed considerable authority and have been able to control events in the country, as well as to avoid dissent within the governing party. Their term of office, as set in the constitution, may not exceed six years, and no candidate who has held a government position in the prior six months is allowed to run in elections. Nevertheless, an unwritten yet unshakable practice called "*dedazo*" prescribes that the president may "point to" and thereby designate a suggested successor at the end of his term of office; this designate has always been elected head of state, without exception. The most popular president of the republic, Lázaro Cárdenas, created an immortal reputation for himself by nationalizing the oil industry and oil reserves in 1938. In contrast to other South American states, Mexico was able to guarantee stability, a relatively democratic government, and social services after World War II, thus avoiding inflationary developments.

All of this changed in the beginning of the 1980s. During the postwar period, Mexico made ISI one of the main principles of its economic strategy. The results are well known: the country closed itself off from worldwide competition, became heavily indebted, and piled up a state budget deficit as a result of deficit spending and subsidies for ailing state concerns. Moreover, former president José López Portillo squandered state funds. Yet the debt crisis of 1982 did not affect Mexico more than any other South American country. Miguel de la Madrid, elected president in December 1982, distanced himself from the policy of his predecessor by initiating austerity measures and cutting subsidies for state concerns. At the end of 1982, there were 1,100 national concerns; besides strategically important ones such as the electric company and railways, there were also hotels and restaurants (among others). The reformers drastically reduced deficit spending within two years and transformed the state deficit (7.3 percent of the GNP) into a budget surplus of 4.2 percent. Nonetheless, the dramatic drop in oil prices in the mid-1980s, as well as a terrible earthquake in 1985 that caused enormous damage amounting to 2 percent of the country's GNP, substantially hurt the Mexican economy. While the inflation rate reached almost 100 percent at the end of the decade, average income sank dramatically. Only Carlos Salinas, elected president in 1988, succeeded in gaining control of the economy, which was falling into an acute recession. Public finances were rehabilitated, and the foreign trade strategy was at least partially freed from the damaging practice of import substitution. NAFTA, which was approved by Salinas and the United States in 1993, opened the Mexican economy and intensified foreign trade. But two years later, Mexico's economy was in ruins. The banking system went bust, damaging the entire financial system and many industrial firms. More than 1 million jobs were eliminated, the real value of salaries dropped by one-third, and productivity shrank by 7 percent. Corruption grew, even in the most intimate circles of government. President Salinas fled abroad, and his brother was arrested on charges of stealing millions in state funds and on suspicion of being an accessory to murder. Indians in the province of Chiapas declared open war on the state, and the number of disturbances in other regions multiplied.

The economic boom in the early 1990s, which was restricted to the financial sector and supported by borrowed money, did not really benefit the economy. An investor could lend money on the inexpensive New York capital market at a low interest rate of 5–6 percent, and make a profit at 12–14 percent in Mexico.[12] Within three years, prices on the Mexican capital market quadrupled. But the bubble burst in December 1994. Panicking foreign investors withdrew about $25 million from the Mexican market and transferred it abroad. The result hurt not only Mexico, but also other emerging South American markets. Two months later, the market price in Latin America decreased by about 38 percent. In order to calm Mexico's market and halt the devaluation of its currency, a bailout of $50 million was needed. It seemed that NAFTA had not significantly improved Mexico's economic situation. Emigration of the poor sections of the population to the rich north grew; Mexico still ranks first among countries with the United States as the primary emigration goal—and by a wide margin. The infamous one-hundred-year-old motto of President Porfirio Díaz still rings true: "Poor Mexico, so remote from God and so near to the United States."

The situation in Brazil seems much rosier. After twenty-one years of military dictatorship, Brazil, the most populous country in South America, welcomed a democratic regime in 1985. But the new government had to tackle a sobering economic legacy: Brazil was $87 billion in debt, making it the greatest debtor in the world, and the country's inflation rate had reached 1,500 percent by the end of the 1980s. Moreover, corruption flourished: the first freely elected president of the country resigned in 1992 in order to escape impeachment for suspected corruption. Yet Brazil placed more confidence than any other South American country in the introduction of a free market economy. The architect of economic reform, President Fernando Henrique Cardoso, decreased state subsidies, coupled Brazil's currency to the dollar, and reduced the inflation

Table 4.2

Wealth Distribution in Latin America as Compared to Other Continents
(in percent)

Proportion of total income in:	Latin America	Africa	Southeast Asia	Industrial states
30% of poor inhabitants	7	10	12	12
5% of rich inhabitants	25	24	16	13

Source: Wall Street Journal, September 27, 1999.

rate from 7,000 percent to 10 percent. Cardoso also introduced a process of privatization that brought the state around $29 billion in earnings by the end of 1997. He believed that neither less state intervention nor an all-powerful private sector would be able to rid the country of misery and poverty. Nonetheless, even Cardoso's reforms could not protect Brazil from the recession of 1998, in which the country's and region's economy was terribly shaken.

The worst affliction in Latin America is the enormous gap between a small layer of superrich and the impoverished majority of the population. Table 4.2 compares Latin America's distribution of wealth with that of other continents. It was only in the beginning of the 1990s that Russia's failed transformation created an even larger gap between rich and poor than in South America. In a conversation with *Der Spiegel*, Mikhail Gorbachev condemned Russia's disastrous transition course, which has "forced 80 percent of Russians into poverty and misery" and made a tiny band of "robber barons" into multibillionaires.[13]

Jonathan Friedland points out that among Latin American countries, only Costa Rica and Uruguay have relative social harmony. In countries like Argentina, Brazil, and Mexico, a handful of businessmen with close relationships to the dominant political elite have made themselves rich. The middle class, the main pillar of sustained economic development, has not prospered. South America is still severely indebted and remains caught between short-term economic booms and repeated recessions. The blossoming North will need to help its neighbors to the South achieve long-term economic and political stability. But ironically, the United States was at its stingiest during its "generous" South American bailout, which primarily helped U.S. investors who had gotten themselves into financial trouble. South America remains a developing region. Although there are plenty of ostensible efforts to help, there is a real need for farsighted aid strategies that could create crucial structural change. The world reacted with astonishment when Bill Clinton declared at the September 1999 meeting of the IMF and World Bank that the United States was prepared to write off the debt "not just partially, but rather entirely" of thirty developing countries. The U.S. president knew, however, that the resulting costs would not be more than $90 million. If North America really wants to speed up the globalization of the world economy, which, of course, is led by the United States, it should provide better bailouts for crisis periods instead of constantly transporting production sectors into the cheap wage regions of the South. The United States needs to help reduce the enormous economic and technological discrepancy between North and South by contributing its vast economic resources and powerful experience.

The Players and Forces in Globalization

Globalization is an unmistakable feature of today's world economy. The interconnection of national economies through foreign trade, foreign investment, and transfers of mountains of money is growing at an unstoppable rate. Since 1950, world trade has increased faster (+6.5 percent yearly) than production (+4 percent). Between 1985 and 1997, the foreign investments of OECD countries rose sevenfold, from $47 billion to almost $360 billion. Today, $1.2 billion in assorted currencies is zigzagging around the globe.[14] The leaders of globalization are the megamultis; their branches, production centers, and sales activities extend throughout the world. Two hundred and fifty thousand branches of 40,000 transnational concerns have settled worldwide: 45,000 are active in China, 11,000 in Singapore, and 55,000 in Central and Eastern Europe. The one hundred largest multinationals account for more than 30 percent of all world trade. The ten megamultis in Table 4.3 play a growing role in production and sales, as well as in the worldwide labor market.

Every country integrated into the world economy is affected by global forces. These include, above all, modern technology and in particular telecommunications. But a demographic development different from that in First World Countries, a backward societal and technical infrastructure, and horrendous corruption reduce the potential positive outcomes of the computer revolution for the Third World. When the population count of the rich countries plunges, it rises explosively in the Third World. Most African countries face a demographic explosion that erases economic gains. The per capita GNP of Niger, Sierra Leone, and

Table 4.3

Top Ten Multinational Firms

Rank[a]	Multinational	Turnover (in billions of U.S. dollars)	Number of employees
1	General Electric	90.8	276,000
2	Ford Motor Company	153.6	363,000
3	Royal Dutch/Shell Group	128.0	105,000
4	General Motors	178.2	608,000
5	Exxon	120.3	80,000
6	Toyota	88.5	159,035
7	IBM	78.5	269,465
8	Volkswagen	65.0	279,892
9	Nestlé SA	48.3	225,808
10	Daimler/Benz AG	69.0	300,068

Source: Klaus Grubelnik, "Vors uns das goldene Zeitalter," *Format* (Vienna) no. 119 (November 29, 1999), p. 91.

[a]By volume of foreign trade in 1998.

Chad is less than $500. In the context of this study it is important to observe that the countries of the Third World that have been able to adapt their social, political, and economic mechanisms to the mechanisms of the modern industrial countries and have above all brought their demographic evolution under control have become developed industrial countries. The Newly Industrial Economies (NIES) of East Asia—Singapore, South Korea, and Taiwan—now produce a higher per capita GNP than Eastern Europe or Portugal. South Korea's per capita GNP in the 1960s equaled that of Ghana ($230), yet today it is twelve times higher.[15] South Korea, like other NIES, adapted the steering mechanisms and the structure of its economy to the demands of globalization and decreased its population growth. Table 4.4 illustrates the difference in the living standards between the reformed and the underdeveloped countries, as well as between them and some of the developed countries of the First World.

The ratios of these indicators did not change very much in the 1980s and 1990s. Niger and Togo remain underdeveloped in every area decisive for the living standard. India has not achieved much with its democratic, pluralistic system. It is on its way to getting ahead of China in the population count. Totalitarian China owes the significant growth in its per capita GNP to its birth-control policies. Singapore and South Korea are now nearer Spain and more distant from the developing countries of Asia and Africa.

Table 4.4

Comparison of Living Standards in Selected Developed and Underdeveloped Countries

Country	Life expectancy, 1987 (years)	Adult literacy rate, 1985 (in percent)	GNP per capita, 1988 (in U.S. dollars)
Niger	45	14	300
Togo	54	41	310
India	59	43	340
Singapore	73	86	9,070
South Korea	70	95	5,000
Spain	77	95	7,740
New Zealand	75	99	10,000

Source: Paul Kennedy, "Preparing for the Twenty-First Century," in *Globalization* (Bloomington: Indiana University Press, 2000), p. 33.

Due to the dynamic GNP growth in China, Taiwan, South Korea, India, and other countries of the region, the growth of Southeast Asian economies is higher than in Latin America and much higher than in Africa. Further differentiation of the economies of the Third World is unavoidable. It will depend on the systemic evolution of the big players in the regions and, above all, on the cohabitation of the private and state sectors, as in China. The success of globalization will depend no less on the demographic evolution in India and on overcoming the remnants of the caste system there. The progress of globalization in South America will depend on the possibility of enlarging NAFTA to include other countries and on overcoming the recessionary symptoms evident in the biggest players in the region, such as Mexico, Brazil, and Argentina. The situation in Africa leaves little room for optimism.

The December 2000 report of the World Bank, entitled "Economic Prospects and Developing Countries," is generally optimistic: "Many developing countries prepared reform programs, with the purpose of fighting against inflation, intensifying the integration into the world economy, and improving health care and education of the people," said the vice president of the World Bank Nicolas Stern.[16]

Many things overshadow this optimistic picture. Finance markets are volatile; prices are unstable—those of crude oil above all; not much is done to reform management. The architect of the above report, Bill Shaw, stresses that the developing countries have to intensify their endeavors to adapt modern technology to the needs of their backward economies.

Table 4.5

Growth Indicators for World Trade and GNP, 1998–2002

	Estimates of growth rates (percent)				
	1998	1999	2000	2001	2002
World trade	3.5	5.8	12.5	8.0	6.8
GNP	1.9	2.8	4.1	3.4	3.2

Source: World Bank, cited in *Frankfurter Allegemeine Zeitung*, December 5, 2000.

Table 4.6

Third World Exports to the United States (in billion dollars)

Country	Worldwide exports	Exports to the United States	Exports to the United States as percentage of total
Mexico	68.89	58.05	84.3
China	144.63	41.20	28.5
South Korea	75.52	16.68	22.1
Brazil	26.31	5.59	21.2
Thailand	33.29	6.80	20.6
Hong Kong	80.87	14.91	18.4
Chile	9.14	1.57	17.2

Source: New York Times, January 7, 2001.

The countries of the Third World have not been able to follow the rapid growth rates of the world economy. Table 4.5 shows the growth indicators of world trade and GNP.

The third world lags behind. The growth of foreign trade there in 2000 was estimated at 5.3 and forecast to be no more than 5 percent in 2001 and only 4.8 percent in 2002. Developing countries have not adequately used the influx of foreign investment capital (which was somewhat higher in 2000 than in the preceding years) to adapt to technological progress. Most important, they have not taken advantage of the opportunity presented by the Internet-Web combination. It is quite likely that the slowdown of the U.S. economy will hit the economies of the Third World harder than other countries because their exports to the United States are higher than the average, as Table 4.6 shows.

As we can see, Mexico is very strongly coupled economically with the United States. The United States absorbs 20 percent of all Asian exports but 28 percent of China's exports—and no country contributed more to opening the doors of the WTO to China than did the United States and its president, Bill Clinton. Owing to its opening to the world market, China could increase its foreign trade in 2000 by one-third: exports have increased by 27.8 percent to $249.2 billion and imports by 35.8 percent to $225.1 billion. In the past two decades, an average increase in foreign trade of 13.4 percent was achieved.[17]

Kofi Annan, secretary general of the United Nations, emphasized that it was Franklin Delano Roosevelt who first recognized the importance of the global engagement of America in world affairs. By entering World War II, he furthered the goals of world civilization in its struggle against Nazi barbarism and toward democracy. In his fourth inaugural address, Roosevelt made a passionate plea for global engagement. He said: "We have learned that we cannot live alone at peace, that our own well-being is dependent on the well-being of other nations, far away. We have learned that we must live as men, and not as ostriches, nor as dogs in the manger. We have learned to be citizens of the world, members of the human community."[18]

With his New Deal, Roosevelt overcame the disastrous world crisis of the 1930s and created the preconditions for the avoidance of such devastating derailments of capitalist economies in the future. The West became stronger in the competition with the Communist superpower, eventually causing the collapse of the latter and the universalization of the capitalist management system. It is perhaps not an accident that on the day of the inauguration of the forty-third president of the United States and the farewell of his predecessor, who had done so much to open China and Vietnam to the Western world, the president of North Korea, Kim Jong Il, returned home and declared, "We hope to begin opening the country's isolated, controlled economy to outside investment and market forces.[19]

Similar signals of opening to the West could be observed in Castro's Cuba. The withdrawal of Soviet subsidies caused the Cuban economy to contract by 35 percent, forcing Fidel Castro to undertake a reform he had long opposed. He "dollarized" the economy, permitting Cubans to receive dollars from abroad; he solicited foreign investment, selling half of the country's cigar export monopoly to Spanish trade organizations. Canada is entering into the nickel sector and European countries into oil. Castro legalized self-employment and small private restaurants and agricultural markets; he opened the doors to tourists as never before, with nearly 2 million visiting in the year 2000. Moreover, Vladimir Putin visited Cuba in December 2000 to revive the old ties, and Castro used this opportunity to make clear to Putin that Cuba could not repay $20 billion it owes the collapsed Soviet Union. The main problem of the negotiations was foreign trade, which declined between 1991 and 1999 from $3.6 billion to $860 million. Both sides declared themselves interested in continuing three large projects started during Soviet times and abandoned thereafter.

This dramatic evolution in former or residual Communist countries is a consequence of the flourishing West, with its third industrial revolution, that of computerization and electronic business, and the shift to capitalism with a human face. The former Communist countries, seared by a deaf and blind bureaucracy, could not keep up. The second half of the twentieth century was unprecedented in the development of living standards. The last decade of the century was even more so. The Clinton presidency was bereft of historic events, such as the New Deal. It is, however, fortunate for humanity that they were not necessary. The policies of the decade paved the way for the United States to go from tremendous budget deficits to surpluses, for NAFTA, and for the prevention of the economic collapse of Southeast Asia in 1997–98. Clinton did exaggerate, however, when he stated in his farewell address that during his presidency America was a force for prosperity in every corner of the globe. As noted, Michel Camdessus, the former Director of the IMF, stated that the number of people who live on $1 or less daily comes to 1.3 billion, and no fewer than 3 billion live on less than $2 a day.

The divide between the rich North and the poor South increased during the last decade of the millennium. Clinton's efforts helped to shield the world economy from the contagion of the Asian crisis. The bailouts, labeled by many a moral hazard because they helped largely big investors to recover their money safely, also had a positive impact on the world economy. A large part of the granted credits was repaid, and the economies previously in recession are now growing at their former rate. But now there is a fear of a contagion of a different kind. This threat emanates from the slowdown of the until now strongest economy in the world—namely, the U.S. economy, which has experienced a slowdown from a 5.2 percent growth rate in 1999 to 2.3 percent in 2000. Policymakers as well as managers know that the lowered U.S. growth is not exclusively a domestic problem. In its boom years, the U.S. economy became the predominant force and engine of global growth.

The question arises whether the new U.S. administration will have the capability to manage the slowdown at home and its effects abroad. Indeed, Asia's government officials doubt that America's slowdown will plunge their countries into a crisis similar to that of 1997–98. The governor of the Bank of Thailand, where that crisis began, was cited as saying that his country was no longer as vulnerable as it once was, Thailand's foreign debt having fallen dramatically.[20] Masahiro Kawai, the World Bank's chief economist for East Asia and the Pacific, claims that many of the countries that were in dire straits two years ago have since accumulated large foreign currency reserves, which should help them during a brief downturn.[21]

There is a fear that investors, pulling back from risk around the world, will make it much more difficult for the developing countries to borrow. The situation will be difficult in Argentina, where $21.8 billion in loans is needed in 2001; the country is now on the IMF list of trouble spots. The contagion effects can be felt by the U.S. NAFTA partner Mexico, 80 percent of whose exports (21 percent of its GNP) are going to the United States. Japan faces the greatest risks in Asia, as it has been unable to recover from its long decline. Yet the most significant problems are in Africa. Colin Powell, immediately after having been designated U.S. secretary of state, chose the Africa Bureau as his first stop on his tour of the State Department and listened to a long litany of ills on the continent, including AIDS, armed conflicts, miserable economies, and drug and arms smuggling. Yet Nigeria and Angola have become important suppliers of oil to the United States. Nigeria is now the fifth largest and Angola the eighth largest supplier of the highly desirable sweet crude oil. Coming from offshore fields, it is relatively easy to drill for by U.S. companies such as Chevron. An expert on the region, Marina Ottaway of the Carnegie Endowment for International Peace, advised in her report, "The Clinton administration tried to pursue a grand vision of what the continent should become rather than developing a policy to address in a realistic manner the problems that exist now." She suggested that the new administration cancel the bilateral debt and push international financial institutions to do the same.[22] One of these recommendations has been fulfilled. The World Bank and the IMF canceled a part of the indebtedness of the twenty-two poorest countries: eighteen African and four South American countries were released in December 2000 from $34 billion in debt. Even this may not be enough.

Faced with the deteriorating economic situation in the United States, the IMF has changed its forecast for 2001. The organization declared on December 4, 2000, that it would dramatically revise the optimistic projections for world economic growth that it had published just a month before. But short-term ups and downs will not be decisive for the precarious situation of the Third World. A long-term strategy is needed to bring its countries closer to the levels of the industrialized world. This is, indeed, a major task of the new American administration, working in tandem with other countries of the world.

5

The European Monetary Union Introduces a New Era: Monetary and Power Relations in the Global Economy

On January 1, 1999, the European Monetary Union (EMU) came into effect, substantially changing international monetary relations. The most industrially developed nations of Western Europe established a common currency, the Euro, and founded the European Central Bank, which is responsible for coordinating EU monetary policy. The Euro has entered the world money market as a new competitive factor. But under certain conditions, it could also serve as a unifying force in worldwide monetary policy. The progress of economic integration in Western Europe has made cooperation among the monetary institutions of the member states both possible and indispensable. In fact, sections 103–107 of the Treaty of Rome dictate that exchange rate regulation and macroeconomic policy are the "common business" of all member states. In order to make this possible, the EU has created a Currency Committee, whose members are made up of representatives of the central banks and finance ministries and include two representatives of the European Commission. In 1964, the Committee of Central Bank Governors was founded, and in 1979 the European Monetary System was established. A European monetary cooperation fund was set up to control currency policy, track credit formalities, and introduce economic uniformity.

Yet the central banks of the EU states were not ready to relinquish their authority. A lack of coordination led to a crisis in 1992–93. Great Britain and Italy distanced themselves from the control mechanism of the exchange rate. But the Maastricht Agreement was reached and the monetary union was created to deepen EU cooperation and perfect the mechanisms of coordination. For instance, section 2 of the European

Monetary System emphasizes price stability as its main goal, and section 9 of the Maastricht Agreement empowers the Council of Ministers to set the "general orientation" of EU monetary policy, though it must also take the exchange rates of nonmembers into consideration. However, section 9 lacks a mechanism to compel the European Central Bank to follow this general orientation. The Maastricht Agreement does not provide a means to coordinate policy between countries inside and outside of the monetary union.

With the United States as its model and the Euro as its common currency, the monetary union will create an integrated economy in Western (and later also Central) Europe. The question now is whether the EMU will help strengthen the worldwide monetary system or spark a new competitive conflict. Furthermore, despite the establishment of the monetary union, the EU states are still members of the IMF and World Bank, and both of these organizations' regulations remain binding. The question in the near future is whether the EMU will be able to agree with the G-7 nations on a common policy for developing markets. Moreover, since the United States and the EU account for 55 percent of the world's economic production and 40 percent of world exports (without counting intra-EU trade), cooperation between the dollar and the Euro will be highly important.

U.S.–EU trade and direct investment have developed dramatically: U.S. exports to the EU rose from $48.3 billion to $127.5 billion between 1985 and 1996, and the increase in EU exports to the United States was even greater, from $67.8 billion to $142.7 billion. Whereas the United States sent 20.4 percent of its exports to the EU in 1996, it took in 18 percent of its imports from the EU. The total volume of bilateral trade ($270 billion in 1996) was only $20 billion less than that between Canada and the United States.[1] Nonetheless, the growth rate of bilateral U.S.–EU trade between 1990 and 1996 (42 percent) was still lower than the total growth rate of US trade (60 percent). Between 1990 and 1995, the United States increased its direct investment in the EU considerably, from $180.9 billion to $315.4 billion; investment in the EU made up 44.3 percent of all U.S. foreign investment. The EU also invested more in the United States: between 1990 and 1995, investment increased by 40 percent, which amounted to $325 billion in 1995, 58 percent of all direct investment in the United States. In contrast, Japan's direct investment in the United States amounted to only 19 percent, and Canada's to only 8 percent.

Although U.S.–EU foreign trade has not been free from conflict, disagreements have never become as hostile as those between the United States and Japan or the United States and China. The United States complains about European agricultural policy, intellectual property legislation, standards, license requests, and investment policy; the EU finds fault with U.S. restrictions on trade and investment in specific services like telecommunications and air transport. In the last three decades, multilateral negotiations have been undertaken to settle these conflicts. For instance, the Kennedy rounds (1963–67) reduced tensions resulting from the EU's Common Agricultural Policy; the Tokyo rounds (1973–79) set new subsidy and antidumping regulations; and the Uruguay rounds (1986–94) introduced an important reform in agricultural subsidies and import restrictions. The establishment of the EMU and a common currency has created an entirely new situation for U.S.–EU relations that will undoubtedly affect trade relations, investment activities, and the future of the global monetary system. "It will mark a turning point comparable to the change when the dollar succeeded sterling during the inter-war years," writes Stefan Collignon.[2]

Two important questions are raised: Will the Euro challenge the U.S. dollar as the world's main currency? And will the EMU stabilize or destabilize the monetary system? Whereas the U.S. dollar makes up 60 percent of the world's currency reserves, European currencies make up only 20 percent, the yen 6 percent, and other currencies 14 percent. Moreover, the U.S. securities market is still twice the size of Europe's, though the establishment of a common EU capital market is expected. Collignon believes that Wall Street and the Federal Reserve will decisively determine worldwide monetary policy for the next five years, but this could change in the future. The United States may not always enjoy the unusual privilege of possessing an international currency that enables it to painlessly finance foreign trade deficits. The stability of the exchange rate and its role as a precondition for an uninterrupted worldwide division of labor will be a high-priority issue. The EMU will ensure such stability in Europe, but it will also want to create worldwide stability through closer relations with the United States. Two currencies, the dollar and the Euro, will dominate the world's currency system and determine the fate of the global monetary system. It lies in the interests of both of these currencies to create the requisite conditions for incorporating developing markets in the world order by coordinating monetary, economic, foreign trade, and investment policy in a competi-

Table 5.1

Worldwide Power Relations in 1997 (in percent)

Country or region	Share of world population	Share of world production	Share of goods and exports	Share of world arms purchases
EU	6.4	27.5	19.7[a]	21.4[a]
United States	4.6	26.5	16.5	34.8
Japan	2.2	14.2	10.1	5.1
Rest of the world	86.8	31.8	53.7	39.5

Source: "Kontinent in neuer Größe," *Der Spiegel*, January 1999 (p. 30).
[a]Does not include trade within the EU.

tive environment. This world order must adapt to the newest stage of universal capitalism. It must take imminent demographic changes into account when creating new jobs, thereby ensuring future security. Finally, this world order must control the enormous amounts of speculative casino capital wandering around the globe. It must utilize this casino capital for economic growth and reducing the growing gap between rich and poor.

Changing Power Relations

The EMU and the creation of the Euro have shifted power relations in favor of Europe, which has become the world's second largest economic power after the United States. The EU's population of 370 million exceeds the United States' 268 million. After the first rounds of EU enlargement in 2004, when Poland, Slovenia, the Czech Republic, Hungary, and Estonia are expected to join, the population of the EU will near 430 million. The $8 trillion EU internal market is the largest in the world. Table 5.1 shows worldwide power relations in 1997.

Although the United States has only 4.6 percent of the world's population, it still accounts for 26.5 percent of world production, making it the world's greatest superpower. It is followed by the fifteen EU states, which make up 6.4 percent of the total world population and exceed the U.S. share of world production by 1 percent and U.S. world exports by 3.2 percent. With only 2.25 percent of the world's population, Japan has an above average share of both world production (14.2 percent) and world exports (10.1 percent). In 1998 the gap between these three regions and the rest of the world was extremely high: the rest of the world's share of the population was 86.6 percent, but its shares of world production and exports were only 31.8 percent and 53.7, respectively. But the rest of the world has been more actively purchasing the world's armaments: 39.5 percent of them, followed by the United States at 34.8 percent and Europe at 21.4 percent.

Europe has ceased to be a continent of war where, according to the philosopher Charles Montesquieu, "a state of tension of all against all" reigned. The desire to unite Europe rose from the ashes of Hitler's war. Germany, fleeing from the terrible atrocities it had committed, became the most active motor of European integration. By agreeing to the establishment of the monetary union and the Euro, Germany significantly advanced EU integration. As noted, Helmut Kohl gave in to Mitterrand's pressure to sacrifice the mark, the strongest currency in Europe, in order to create a new monetary entity. For the first time since World War II, the dollar has a rival. Whereas the dollar accounted for 48 percent of 1997 world trade payments, the EU currencies (i.e., the mark, Franc, British pound, Italian lira, and dutch gulden) made up only 33 percent, the yen 5 percent, and other currencies 14 percent. This payment structure could easily change, however. Central and East European candidates for EU membership have already declared their willingness to conduct their foreign trade in the Euro, link their currencies to it, and hold it as their reserve currency. At a Euro conference in Luxembourg in December 1998, Chinese economist Zhu Rongii reported that his country would consider "cautiously" switching to the Euro as its monetary standard. And Andrei Kortunov, an international expert from Moscow, claimed that Russia intends to substitute the Euro for the dollar as soon as the value of the ruble stabilizes. But the final outcome of this competition between the Euro and the dollar will depend on U.S. economic strength and the progress of European integration.

The United States is still the strongest economic power in the world. The incredible boom of the current growth cycle has lasted almost ten years. U.S. GNP has grown by about 3.9 percent per year, even reaching 5.6 percent in the fourth quarter of 1999. Moreover, for the first time since the end of World War II, the United States has achieved a budget surplus. The EU, on the other hand, had an average growth rate of 2.8 percent in 1998. A year later it founded the currency union and built up an enormous administrative apparatus whose superexecutive, the European Commission, ensures the execution of community agreements, drafts laws for the EU Council, and can mandate costly consultation and research programs. Because commission members, who enjoy ministerial powers, are not elected but sent from the governments of member states, they answer to no one. Nonetheless, they are authorized to make decisions only as a group. Commissioners, who earn about $270,000 a year—more than Germany's chancellor—cannot be forced to resign on an individual basis; instead, the entire commission must resign together. The twenty current EU commissioners and the 21,000 employees working for them in the commission's twenty-four general offices make up "an obscure apparatus filled with French, British, and Spanish EU officials. The commission lacks a unified reference system for documentation, and members cannot help but be influenced by their country's interests and the administrative habits of their native lands."[3] There are also 475 committees and subcommittees working for the commission in advisory and regulatory capacities and an additional 400 committees working with the EU Council. Finally, every commission member can employ up to six confidantes in his or her advisory council. And they are the ones who actually make the deals behind closed doors. This massive system is facetiously referred to in Brussels as "committee-ology," according to Germany's *Der Spiegel*.[4] The commission has no trouble passing the "A points," for which unanimity is required. But the heads of the cabinet, who meet every Monday, have to organize majorities when negotiating the more controversial "B points." "This is accomplished," *Der Spiegel* claims, "only via carping, pressure, and tiny reciprocal favors."

Although the EU has accomplished much in its forty years, it is obviously in need of reform. A few changes have already been made. For instance, each EU state is to be represented by a single commission member. This commissioner will be allowed full voting rights but will not have his or her own department. Germany, France, Great Britain, Italy, and Spain will no longer have two commissioners, as in earlier regulations. Moreover, majority decisions in the EU Council will be carried out only if they represent the will of the majority of the EU population, thereby protecting the larger states from the myriad of smaller states during votes on costly projects. Finally, the authority of the European Parliament and the central governments will be increased. In 80 percent of all legislative processes, the parliament will be placed on an equal footing with the EU Council, the EU's legislative body. The parliament will also have the last word on EU budget affairs, and its representatives will nominate the president of the European Commission.

For the first time in its history, in mid-January 1999 the European Parliament made a confident show of strength by suspending two commissioners, Edith Cresson and Manuel Marín, on suspicion of corruption and nepotism. Since current regulations prohibit the dismissal of any one commissioner, the parliament called for a "no confidence" vote against the entire commission. Although the vote failed, with 232 for and 552 against, this was closer than in previous motions of this type. The commission's high-handedness was thus rebuked, and it was forced to allow independent investigators to examine evidence of fraud, mismanagement, and nepotism. Its internal processes were put under the authority of parliamentary representatives, and the commission was ordered to introduce binding rules of behavior. Finally, the president of the commission vowed to dismiss any commissioner attempting to subvert ethical precepts. The European Parliament will be able to act in the future as the self-confident executor of the will of European voters. An extremely critical commission report, which led to the resignation of the entire European Commission, affirmed this view. A new parliament was elected on June 13, 1999. The scandal had decisively influenced the outcome of these elections, in which conservatives won a majority over the Social Democratic parties.

According to German chancellor Schröder, financial relations in Europe need to be reformed in the coming years (2000–2006), and the EU must tackle problems with its Common Agricultural Policy. Moreover, serious steps need to be taken to reform EU institutions like the European Commission, the EU Council, and the European Parliament. All three tasks, says the chancellor, are contingent upon the progress of EU enlargement. If the EU is unable to rearrange its financial relations and make enlargement a feasible process, then the date for it must be postponed. Will the EU be able to accomplish all this before 2006? Schröder says, "It is an extremely difficult economic and political process. The first five Central and East European candidates for membership must prove their worthiness. This requires them to make an enormous number of internal reforms. The EU must prepare itself for their absorption." It also has to remain financially feasible. According to the German chancellor, "It would make the most sense to use the budget averages from 1993 to 1999 as the basis for the future EU budget, which may not grow faster than the average of all of the national budgets. The uppermost limit should not exceed 1.27 percent of the GNP, and we demand greater fairness for would-be members in favor of those that will be net payers, not just the Germans." Schröder has also made clear his position regarding European competition with the United States. The chancellor does not view European developments as a competitive factor for the U.S.'s status as a world power. However, the Euro, deepening integration, and the expansion of the EU will create a market with more consumers than there are in the United States. The chancellor admits, "Germany has the most to gain from an integrated Europe."

The years 1999 to 2001 are a transitional phase for the EU. National currencies will remain in circulation until 2001 but with set exchange rates that guarantee the stability of the central banks of the member countries. The crises in Southeast Asia and Russia wreaked havoc on financial markets all over the world, including those of several industrialized nations. But Europe remained a safe haven, unaffected by fluctuations in exchange rates. An opinion poll showed that confidence in the EU heightened between 1997 and mid-1998: from 78 to 83 percent in Italy, 58 to 68 percent in France, 40 to 51 percent in Germany, and 44 to 56 percent in Austria; the total EU average rose from 60 to 66 percent. Confidence has also grown in European countries that are not members of the currency union: from 29 to 34 percent in Great Britain, 34 to 39 percent in Sweden, 40 to 51 percent in Denmark, and 59 to 67 percent in Greece, the only country that has yet to fulfill EU criteria.

Although growth rates are lower than in the United States, European economies continue to boom. The head of the pack is Ireland, whose growth rate reached 9.1 percent in 1997, greatly surpassing that of Great Britain (2.7 percent) and the EU's average (3.9 percent) for the same year. Finland's growth rate (4.1 percent), as well as Portugal's (4.0 percent), Spain's (3.8 percent), the Netherlands' (3.8 percent), and Austria's (3.7 percent), were all above average. The EU average growth rate in 1999 was estimated at 2.5 percent, down 0.4 percent from the previous year. Inflation predictions for 1998 and 1999 were low, at 1.3 and 1.4 percent respectively. There are fears, however, that Europe is not "an optimum currency area," as *The Economist* wrote on January 2, 1999. One concern is the large disparity in price formation (in view of exchange rate fluctuations) among the eleven states of the Euro zone; price formation is relatively uniform in the United States. Moreover, Europe's labor force is two-thirds less mobile than its American counterpart. The United States is by far a better area for a common currency than the eleven states of the EU. *The Economist* draws the conclusion that "Europe's monetary union is neither bound to succeed nor doomed to fail. Leadership, circumstances and luck will come together to decide its fate."[5] This conclusion seems quite reasonable. The dollar, on the other hand, as the currency of a unified state, has a much better chance in a struggle with the Euro. For the time being, the Euro will play neither the role of a federal currency, nor the currency of a single federal state. However, under favorable conditions, competition could eventually lead to cooperation between the two monetary units as the key currencies of a global world economy. The United States and the EU, which together make up 11 percent of the world's population and 54 percent of its economic activity, are best suited to creating a worldwide economic center and helping to eliminate the discrepancies between rich industrial states and poor developing countries.

Whereas high technology eliminates more jobs in Europe than it creates, resulting in chronic unemployment, it does just the opposite in the United States. In fact, there are even those in the United States who fear the consequences of full employment. In a hearing before the Economic Committee of the U.S. Congress on June 17, 1999, Alan Greenspan, head of the Federal Reserve, warned that "continued strong growth—fueled in part by booms in the stock market and in housing prices—could soon lead to a shortage of workers, a condition that has historically set off a spiral of rising wages and prices."[6] Greenspan also refuted the view that high technology was a wonder weapon against inflation. In a June 14 hearing he distanced himself from the vision of a "new economy" in which the danger of inflation did not exist. He emphasized that it was still too early to predict the effects of the dynamics of technology. The United States, as leader of the global economy, has an ambitious and thoroughly complicated role to play, and there are many people who often unfairly criticize U.S. economic policy and its results. But Paul Kennedy, Yale professor and best-selling author, is full of praise.[7] The United States, Kennedy begins, has "impressively steered its rudder and today stands as the leader of the world." Yet U.S. industry's share of global GNP, he continues, has decreased considerably. Whereas Great Britain controlled only 25 percent of the world's GNP in the 1850s, "the high point of the British Empire" the United States controlled over 50 percent of the world's GNP in 1950; U.S. economic performance was "simply unprecedented." Kennedy claims that economic conditions have gone downhill since the 1950s. In 1990 the U.S. share of the world's GNP was 23 percent, and the World Bank predicts that by 2010 the United States will account for only one-sixth. Kennedy's gloomy predictions do not end there: "If China does not explode or fall apart, taking all of East Asia with it, America will continue to decline in importance." Yet if one looks more closely at the big picture and the true causes of this rapid drop in the U.S. share of world GNP since 1995, there is no real cause to complain. In 1950 the U.S. was probably the only highly productive economy in the world. Europe's had just been destroyed in the war, and the industrial capacities of China and India were just beginning to grow. Under these conditions, it is no surprise that the United States enjoyed such a massive share of world GNP. Relative decline was unavoidable, and U.S. economic predominance eventually had to abate.

The development of an information and service economy has reduced the role of traditional industry, especially in rapidly developing countries like the United States. However, Kennedy justifiably criticizes America's unfair income practices: twenty years ago, American managers earned forty times as much as their average salaried employee, while today they earn two hundred times as much. U.S. billionaires have more money than the poorest third of the world's population. James Goldsmith, a powerful Anglo-French investor, calculated that an American mechanical engineer earns sixty times more than his colleague in China; a qualified engineer in India earns $10,000 annually, while one in the United States earns $60,000–$80,000. Although there is a huge discrepancy between salaries in developing countries and the United States, productivity remains comparable. For example, a U.S. textile worker finishes a shirt in fourteen minutes; a worker in Bangladesh needs twenty-five minutes. However, while the average wage of a U.S. textile worker is $7.53 per hour, the Bangladeshi worker earns only 25 cents per hour. The production of a ton of steel requires 3.4 hours in the United States and 5.8 hours in Brazil; the wage difference, however, is 10:1.

Capitalism and Democracy: Positive and Negative Aspects

Edward Luttwak, senior fellow at the Center for Strategic and International Studies in Washington, analyzed the tremendous gap between rich and poor in America. During the years of "controlled capitalism," Luttwak writes, the average wage per labor hour rose from $5.34 (1950) to $8.12 (1975). But in the years of "turbo-capitalism," between 1980 and 1997, wages decreased from $7.78 to $7.66 per hour.[8] Yet the earnings of industrial managers continued to grow. In 1992, 800 CEOs earned about $1 million each. Four years later, the CEOs of 365 of the largest concerns in the United States earned $5.8 million and assorted supplements; the 20 best paid chief executives received a salary (plus long-term compensations) of between $102.4 million (Lawrence Coss, Green Tree Financial) and $21.4 million (Drew Lewis, Union Pacific). Despite this incredible wealth, there were approximately 36 million poor in America in 1996—13.7 percent of the entire population. Among them were 14.1 million young people under the age of eighteen, 19.8 percent of all Americans belonging to this age group. Racial differences also played a significant role: among the total number of poor, 24.6 million were white (11.2 percent of the white population), and 9.7 million were black (around 33.3 percent of the African American population). Yet America's unbeatable economy still makes it undoubtedly the most efficient country in the global world economy. Much of this success is due to the entrepreneurial spirit and innovative energy of America's managers, even though they allow themselves to be paid more handsomely for their efforts than anywhere else in the world.

But many aspects of American society are being mercilessly criticized. Norman Birnbaum, professor of social sciences at Georgetown University, revealed his views about the present and future of his country in an article entitled "My Torment over America."[9] What torments the renowned sociologist so terribly? Primarily America's "pathological normality." "Our nation lacks both visions and institutions of solidarity. Not only work, but humans too have now degenerated into pure products." The professor highly praises Roosevelt's New Deal, which renewed the country. But the opponents of the New Deal have returned: "the grumbling defenders of white, Protestant America and the small-minded servants of big capitalism . . . who are obsessed with the fear that somehow history might stop abiding by the rules of Social Darwinism." The professor continues his pessimistic train of thought, which at times sounds somewhat removed from reality: "Why not actually trade the [weakening] dollar for the Euro and settle in a city more lively than Washington?" But the dollar remains strong; half of the world's payments are made in U.S. dollars, and the Euro has already lost about 25 percent of its original value since its establishment at the beginning of 1999. The following comment from Birnbaum also sounds strange: "Half defeated, half triumphant, and in any case with resignation, the Democratic Party has accepted that at best they can give the market a human face, but they will never be able to overcome it." The only alternative to a market economy would be a planned economy, which means a state economy run by an enormous bureaucracy. This alternative has failed everywhere because of its inefficiency. A competitive market economy has been adopted in its place, with the United States as its model. Even in Communist countries like China and Vietnam, private industrial concerns are being established, state concerns privatized, and the economic value of the product–money relationship revived. Although making the market more humane through a fairer distribution of wealth is a desirable aim, the market's virulently competitive nature makes this nearly impossible. The countries of Western Europe, which have succeeded in providing a truly revolutionary distribution of wealth through their present "social market economy," are planning to eliminate costly social services. Professor Birnbaum concludes his critique of America as follows: "If our history does not provide evidence that America belongs to this tradition of the republic of the just that threatened the reigning thrones of Europe at the end of the eighteenth and throughout the nineteenth century, then it will indeed abandon America." But where will it go? Capitalism is the universal social system of the next century, and the American model has brought great prosperity to many Americans. America is still envied and praised as a promised land, and its immigration rate is the highest in the world; many people continue to flock to this promised land, but few leave.

Fareed Zakaria, the former managing editor of *Foreign Affairs*, makes a more serious and sounder critique of the world's current lack of democracy.[10] He interprets the meaning of democracy differently from the generally accepted definition, which is often abused by dictators trying to justify their regimes. For Zakaria, institutions like free elections are not enough to confirm the presence of democracy. In his State of the Union Address in January 1998, Bill Clinton emphasized that the majority of mankind, 54.8 percent, now lives in democratic countries (Arthur Schlesinger, Jr., gives more exact numbers: 3.1 billion people live in democracies; 2.66 billion do not).[11] But "the democracy we see around the world has a distinctly ugly face," says Zakaria. He reminds us of a comment made by Richard Holbrooke, architect of the Dayton peace accords, during the 1996 elections in Bosnia: "Suppose the election was declared free and fair and those elected are racists, separatists who are publicly opposed to [peace and reintegration]. That is the dilemma." This dilemma not only affects former member republics of the Soviet Union or today's Yugoslavia, where entirely democratic elections during the 1990s enabled Slobodan Milošević to stay in power, but many other countries as well. "From Peru to the Palestinian Authority, from Slovakia to Sri Lanka, from Pakistan to the Philippines, we can see the rise of illiberal democracy—plenty of elections, but few individual rights," Zakaria writes. There is no lack of examples to support his view. After the fall of the Soviet Union, the great hope has remained unfulfilled that the successor republics would become an epicenter of freedom and democracy. Although many "democratic" elections have taken place, there can be no talk of democracy in a true sense. Boris Yeltsin and his successor, Vladimir Putin, have always had the final word. Even though Yeltsin spent most of his term in hospitals and sanatoriums, he remained an autocrat. And the Russian people have had other worries, like the mere fight for survival: since Yeltsin's revolution, the standard of living in Russia has declined by 50 percent. People can vote freely, but no one actually believes that the person elected will provide a better future for them or their starving country. Although former general secretaries of the Communist Party are elected president in fully democratic elections in the other successor republics, they continue to practice a dictatorial style of governing.

Zakaria's critique is aimed primarily at the current state of affairs in America. The highest court, he writes, is composed of nine nonelected men and women who are appointed for life. And the U.S. Senate is the most undemocratic upper house in the world, with the exception of the British House of Lords, whose members enjoy life terms. (The British upper house lost much of its power, though, when Tony Blair sent most of the lords packing.) Every American state sends two senators to Washington, regardless of population size. The 481,000 inhabitants of Wyoming have exactly the same number of Senate votes as 31 million Californians. And a single senator can hinder the acceptance of legislation, thwart the will of the majority, and create difficulties for the government. This critique can be supplemented by several other problems, like political apathy and disregard for democratic principles during free elections. For instance, less than a third of all legal voters go to the polls in America. The incumbent president, who is both head of government and the army's commander in chief, was elected by no more than 24 percent of America's eligible voters. Zakaria concludes by commenting that "elections are only a process for creating a fair and law-abiding government; they are not, by themselves, what freedom is all about."

The immortal words of Thomas Jefferson in the Declaration of Independence are worth mentioning here. Jefferson said that governments are established to guarantee "the inalienable rights" of the people to "life, liberty, and the pursuit of happiness." Yet it is also "the right of the people to alter or to abolish" a government that refuses to secure these rights and to build a new government that will realize these goals.[12] The founding fathers were lofty idealists, but their ideas have yet to be realized. During their time, democratic governments existed in only a few places. Today, more than half of the human race lives under democratic regimes, though many of them display what Zakaria called democracy's ugly face. Even in the world's most developed countries, the highly prized ideals of democracy often degenerate into a partiocracy, where the maxim "What's good for the party must be good for the nation" prevails. Naturally, there are elections in which a ruling party loses, thus passing the government to the opposition. It is not the will of the people that plays the deciding role, but the conflict among parties in their fight for power. Such traditions are not changed easily. The election winner does not necessarily come from the party with better policies but the one that can better market its promises with catchy slogans. A winning party possesses a top candidate who is well received by the media, employs a good election manager, and—most important—has plenty of money to fund election campaigns; the Republicans' 2000 election campaign was an excellent example of all three.

Currently the strongest party in the United States, the Republicans ran a campaign directed at capturing votes with pleasant rhetoric, though their actual policies remained similar to those of their opponents. "The Republicans in Congress are currently taking language lessons," writes Greg Hitt.[13] The "steamy days of bomb-throwing rhetoric during the GOP's Contract with America" are over. For instance, the Republicans no longer demand the abolition of the Department of Education since this provided the Democrats with the argument that the Republicans were against education. Instead, the Republicans now call for the control of schools by parents and local communities since polling companies identify such rhetoric as "powerful." The search for a politically convincing vocabulary is a part of the current training program to win back voters who defected to the Democrats in the last two elections. Cathy Chamberlin, a pollster, warns that if politicians are unable to express their intentions strongly enough, they will lose. To rectify this, forty GOP representatives are to receive nine hours of language lessons and media training. The core of this program is to help congressional representatives use words and form sentences that have been shown by polls to be marketable in areas such as education, social security, defense, and tax reduction. According to Wade West, president of the MediaPower Group, Inc., politicians need to be taught how to use "visual" words. In his opinion, words like "good and proper, American, respectable, patriotic, reliable" are the "strongest adjectives which awaken powerful, positive, emotional reactions in every section of the population." Stopgap expressions like "cash flow, feedback" are to be avoided, as are abbreviations and any expression that ends with "ion." And the following rules of thumb for television appearances are effective (among others): no blushing; yawn before the interview in order to relax; the scene should have a calming effect, not cause fear.

The proponents of "the end of history" thesis (notably Francis Fukuyama) provide today's nondemocratic countries with the hope of an imminent "universalization of Western liberal democracy as the perfect, final form of human government," writes Arthur Schlesinger, Jr.,[14] Schlesinger reminds us of the bitter experiences of the last century; for instance, in 1941 there were only a dozen democratic countries left on the planet. Although the majority of the world's population lived under democratic regimes by 1997, it is doubtful, writes Schlesinger, if democracy has really taken root in former totalitarian countries. Between 1991 and 1993 Africa increasingly conducted democratic elections, though analysts have never cited a single case in which the incumbent government lost the election. Schlesinger also condemns the faults of modern democracy, describing it as the "offspring of technology and capitalism." It bears mentioning that in the past the dynamic forces of democracy were abandoned for the initiatives of totalitarianism; history could repeat itself. Schlesinger writes, "Now the democratic adventure must confront tremendous pent-up energies threatening to blow it off course and even drive it on to the rocks."

A partiocracy is definitely not the best means for the realization of democracy. And yet there are no alternatives to the competitive contest among political parties wrangling for power. This competition is just as important as economic competition in a profitable market. Populist movements are not any worse in the United States than elsewhere. However, one thing that is worse in the United States than in Western Europe is the extremely low voter turnout for both legislative and presidential elections—especially surprising given the president's array of powers. Nonetheless, the causes of low voter participation are not necessarily negative or related to undemocratic behavior. Americans have more confidence in the existing, thoroughly progressive, established and functioning social and economic institutions than in "big government" or in a legislature that produces more sweet-sounding rhetoric than decent legislation.

Absence of a Real Challenger to the United States

Building a truly effective democracy requires a fair property structure that works to eliminate the deep gap between rich and poor, an income distribution that guarantees general prosperity, and economic policies that protect the environment and prevent unemployment. This is an economic–political basis that, as the eighteenth century British philosopher Jeremy Bentham wrote, guarantees "the greatest happiness as a fundamental and self-evident principle of morality." Without a well-ordered democratic foundation, the best institutions, like free elections, degenerate into a paper democracy in which elected officials often resort to authoritarian means of government. The United States has a well-ordered democratic foundation, especially in areas such as health insurance (the most expensive despite its inefficiency) and the use of its strength and reputation. Thus the United States continues to play its role as the only true superpower in the world. Democracy has had and continues to have many enemies, though its sympathizers have grown more numerous. One adamant supporter of the United States was the British elder statesman Winston Churchill. "His belief in and predilection for the American democracy are the foundation of his political outlook," writes Isaiah Berlin.[15] The United States was able to lead a successful Western alliance to victory in the Cold War thanks to its rich intellectual and social potential and the steadfast power of America's democratic society. This victory brought with it the implosion of the Soviet Union, the world's second most powerful superpower, and rang in a new era that enabled America to become the world's principal leader.

Josef Joffe, an eminent German journalist and formerly an associate member of the Olin Institute for Strategic Studies at Harvard, writes: "The principal paradox of the post–Cold War era is the unchallenged primacy of the United States," which need fear neither an "existential enemy nor a foreseeable danger of being besieged."[16] The Warsaw Pact is defunct, but NATO continues to grow. Three former members of the Soviet-led Warsaw Pact defected to NATO on NATO's fiftieth birthday; six other former members are waiting to do the same. NATO promised Russia, which vehemently opposed NATO expansion on its western border, that it would not spread its operations into Central and Eastern Europe. But in a May 1997 agreement, NATO awarded Russia a seat in the permanent NATO Unified Council. Although this gave the former Warsaw Pact leader the right to take a position in problems being discussed, it did not give Russia veto rights. Nevertheless, Russia's voice was not taken into account when NATO decided to bomb Yugoslavia, one of Moscow's allies. The prime minister at the time, Yevgeny Primakov, who happened to be on his way to Washington, D.C., was unable to protest because his airplane was diverted back to Moscow. NATO's representative in Moscow was held in custody, and other NATO personnel were expelled from the country. Yet the bombing of Yugoslavia continued with increasing intensity. As NATO began to run out of targets and diplomatic efforts failed, Russia's ambivalent relationship with NATO—and, more important, its friendly relationship with Yugoslavia—took center stage. Viktor Chernomyrdin, former head of government, was sent to Belgrade, where he spent many hours with Slobodan Milošević trying to convince him to concede. Chernomyrdin, however, was not responsible for the peace agreement. It was former Finnish president Martti Ahtissari who finally forced the Yugoslav president to yield. Chernomyrdin then returned to Moscow, where many Russians received him with indignation and contempt. Nevertheless, Boris Yeltsin handsomely rewarded Chernomyrdin by making him chairman of Gazprom, which he had also led prior to Yeltsin's 1991 revolution. At the time of the writing of this book (the end of July 2000), neither NATO's personnel in Moscow nor Russia's NATO representatives in Brussels have returned.

America, the only remaining superpower, does not consider territorial conquest one of its foreign policy goals. More than one hundred years have passed since the United States invaded Spanish Cuba and the Philippines, and American participation in both world wars was not motivated by any territorial ambitions. America's goal was to help its troubled European allies free themselves from the hegemony of the Kaiser and Hitler's Germany. Since World War II and the end of the Cold War, America's foreign policy aim has been to guarantee security for entire regions of the globe—the Near and Middle East, Europe, the Pacific, and elsewhere. America attempts to protect democratic values, the only true guarantee of freedom in the world, wherever they are endangered. Josef Joffe defines U.S. foreign policy as a "hub and spoke" strategy, in which the hub is Washington and the spokes are Western Europe, Japan, China, Russia, and the Middle East. Good relations with Washington, the center, were more important for the "spoke" states than relations with each other. The main emphasis of U.S. foreign policy lies in the organization of trade and credit relations as a precondition for world-wide economic growth, which is the decisive condition for the country's own economic expansion. Thanks to American initiatives, global institutions like the IMF and World Bank, GATT (now the WTO), the OECD, and others have been founded. And U.S. influence, while often the target of criticism, has enabled the realization of many important international ventures. The economic rescue operations for Southeast Asia, Mexico, and Brazil, initiated with U.S. assistance, though denounced as a "moral hazard," helped relieve the crises in these regions and stopped them from spreading to other countries.

After the triumph of the U.S.-led Western allies in the Cold War (made possible by a containment policy), the convincing superiority of democratic values, regulation of the market economy, the contrast between Western prosperity and the stagnant planned economy in the East, and the decline of socialism's ideological attractiveness, it seemed as if any danger of military confrontation had finally disappeared. Even China and Vietnam, which still define themselves as Communist, have recognized the inefficiency of planned economic control by an unwieldy state bureaucracy. They are renewing traditional commodity–money relations and permitting ever more private economic activity and profit-making services. The basic justification for the continuation of a dominant one-party system is crumbling as China's economy becomes more and more decentralized. Although communism still remains the official state ideology, it is no longer the *spiritus movens*. Traditional Confucian values are returning with undiminished strength and displacing the hollow, empty dogma of communism. But memories of the ideologically inspired wars of the last decade remain fresh, especially in Vietnam. The Vietnam War resulted in the deaths of fifty-seven thousand U.S. soldiers and nearly 3 million Vietnamese, though it did not hinder the unification of South and North Vietnam under Communist rule. The Korean War also resulted in the deaths of thousands of U.S. and Korean soldiers. The country remains divided into a communist north and a capitalist south; thirty-seven thousand U.S. soldiers have been defending that delicate peace for over fifty years. And finally, there was the failed invasion of Cuba at the Bay of Pigs.

Thus the question is raised: Does the United States have enemies that are really strong enough to threaten its security? Richard Pipes, former head of the East European and Soviet department in the American National Security Council and Harvard professor emeritus, recalls that in the three hundred years before the Bolshevik seizure of power, tsarist Russia was exceptionally friendly with the United States. The argument over the northwestern territories of North America was settled peacefully in a treaty in 1824. In 1867, the weary tsarist government, which had to bear Alaska's administrative and defense costs, convinced the hesitant U.S. Congress to take over the region at a merely symbolic price. During the U.S. Civil War, units of the Russian fleet sailed to New York and San Francisco to strengthen the morale of the northern states. Moreover, Pipes reminds us of the words of Secretary of State William Henry Seward when he voiced his preference for Russia over any other East European state since "she always wishes us well." Following the Yeltsin revolution, Russia's military doctrine proclaimed that it "does not regard any state to be its adversary."[17] Former Gorbachev adviser Georgiy Arbatov described U.S.–Russian relations after the Cold War: "We are doing something really terrible to you—we are depriving you of an enemy."[18] Russia was and is dependent upon U.S. economic assistance, both directly and via worldwide credit and trade organizations. This U.S. tactic is fully justified. It has bound Russia in a net of international connections and is trying to pull Russia out of its economic misery; it is also helping to accelerate Russia's democratization. Even the tension surrounding NATO's unpopular expansion appears to have been settled by granting Russia a seat in the permanent NATO Unified Council. Though Yeltsin's successor, Vladimir Putin, wants to stop further expansion at any price, nothing points to a renewal of hostile U.S.–Russian relations.

U.S. relations with China are also on the way to improvement. Despite strong opposition, Clinton initiated an appeasement strategy of "integration, not exclusion." America cannot express its dissatisfaction with China's human rights record through a Cold War containment policy. Instead, the U.S. must pursue its goals through foreign trade and active political, economic, and cultural contact. It must try to integrate China into world civilization—which would also open one of the largest markets in the world. Of course, this would require the United States to accept a steadily increasing foreign trade deficit, which reached over $4 billion in 1998—the second largest U.S. trade deficit after its deficit with Japan. With U.S. support, China's acceptance in the WTO is to be expected. Zbigniew Brzezinski, former U.S. national security adviser, writes that there was a possibility of developing a trans-European security system that could include not only the Eastern states of an enlarged NATO (depending upon a cooperative security agreement with Russia), but also China and Japan.[19] Professor Brzezinski states that the U.S. status as the world's superior power has not been challenged for more than a generation. Bernhard Wrabetz, a member of the Austrian representation at the United Nations, writes, and rightly so: "The traditional conflicts between states are tending to become exceptions. The classic war of conquest, as in the case of the Kuwait crisis, is increasingly being substituted by conflicts that arise from the implosion of states (Yugoslavia), tensions between ethnic, religious, or social groups within a state (Bosnia, Rwanda)."[20] Josef Joffe correctly points out that there are powerful competitors that might challenge America's superpower status—if not alone, then in a coalition with others. He mentions the EU, with its two nuclear states and an economy even bigger than that of the United States; Russia, which possesses powerful nuclear potential; Japan, which has the world's second strongest economy; and China, with its nuclear capability and the world's largest population. Joffe recalls how in April 1997 Boris Yeltsin and Jiang Zemin signed a "strategic partnership," designed to foil the plans of powers that wanted to force a "unipolar order" on the world. One month later, the presidents of France and China made a joint, clearly antihegemonist declaration in which a new world order with "power centers other than the United States" was called for.[21] The air war against Yugoslavia heightened tensions with Russia and China, destroying lengthy U.S. efforts to normalize relations and accelerate the disarmament talks already under way. Did the United States simply accept this situation and other disastrous complications in order to carry out the carefully planned action against Yugoslavia? A historical retrospective of Yugoslavia is necessary to truly explain the tragic developments of the last decade and the destructive collapse of the Balkans.

America was the father of the idea of Yugoslavia as a multicultural state, but it was also America that led the devastating air war and assumed the bulk of the costs. Steven R. Weisman writes: "At the Versailles peace conference following World War I Wilson arrived after reviewing European history and then helped to establish a new Southern Slavic state to fill the vacuum created by the collapse of the Ottoman and Austrian empires."[22] Woodrow Wilson, America's twenty-eighth president and architect of the Versailles Treaty, did not miss the opportunity to proclaim that "it is the most serious game ever undertaken." At first, history seemed to confirm this view. Yugoslavia remained a multiracial state in the interwar period and during World War II, though not without conflict. One can say without exaggeration that no other occupied country during World War II resisted Nazi Germany more actively than Tito's Partisans. The view that Tito's opposition contributed to the disintegration of the Soviet empire is also true. Fifty years ago, at a meeting of the Cominform in June 1949, a decision was made to liquidate the renegade Yugoslav "Trotskyist," Tito. Stalin threatened to annihilate him with his finger but in truth did not dare to send his troops into the turbulent country. He was all too familiar with the powers of resistance of the Serbian and Croatian people. Thus Yugoslavia continued its economic policy of decentralization. Although Stalin's successor, Nikita Khrushchev, crushed the heroic revolt of the Hungarian people in 1956 with brute force, and Leonid Brezhnev sent Soviet tanks into Czechoslovakia to suppress the Prague Spring in 1968, neither ever dared to order their troops into Yugoslavia to return the renegade Serbs and Croats to the fold of the communist community. Yugoslavia, ruled by a Communist party, became totalitarian but increasingly distanced itself from Soviet communism. Slobodan Milošević, who was elected president of the Serbian Republic in free elections and later president of the remainder of Yugoslavia, followed the example of other East and Central European leaders by renaming his ruling party a socialist party. A post-Communist regime was introduced, with several political parties, relatively free media, and an ever-broader market economy.

6

The Global World Economy Tends Toward Universalization of Economic Policymaking

The majority of Europe's Social Democratic governments have hitherto refused to pattern themselves after the U.S. economy's "torpedo capitalism." Instead, as discussed in chapter 3 above, they have striven to develop a "third way" in which the failures of both a planned economy and American capitalism can be avoided. Yet U.S. policy has produced one of the longest economic booms in history while curbing the growth of unemployment and inflation. The rapid development of high technology has raised U.S. competitive power to a level scarcely to be excelled, yet without having to make 10 percent of the employed population redundant, as has been the case in Europe. The situation in Europe has taken a different direction.

The Middle Ground Does Not Lead to Success

During the boom period in Germany, Konrad Adenauer and Ludwig Erhard were able to establish a diversified state welfare system that covered citizens "from cradle to grave." But Germany's short working hours and long vacations, strong labor unions, inflexible labor market, and wage rates, as well as the highest state participation in the national income and the highest taxes, undermined European competitiveness. Modern technology has forced an ever-growing proportion of the population out of the labor process, overtaxing the already enormous system of state welfare handouts. The Kosovo conflict not only revealed technological gaps in weaponry, but also exposed the weakness of the European economy in world competition.

The global economy has demonstrated that a planned economy run by state bureaucracy cannot compete with America's torpedo capitalism. But it has also demonstrated the inferiority of a welfare-oriented market economy overburdened by the costs of an expansive state welfare system. The monetary union, which came into effect in early 1999, showed the weakness of the eleven participating EU states in competition with the strong American economy: Only a few months after its introduction, the Euro lost more than 25 percent of its value against the U.S. dollar. The "Third Way" seemed impassable. Even Europe's Social Democrats, the most zealous proponents of a social market economy, have come to realize that the "Third Way" has no chance of successfully competing with the flexible labor market of America's robust capitalism. The SPD's Bad Godesberg program made it the first Social Democratic party in Europe to distance itself from the traditional path between plan and market (i.e., between state-run and private enterprise). But the SPD was unable to mount a resistance to the class-struggle strategy of the labor unions, whose influence grew steadily. State welfare benefits continued to rise unabated, and wages, as well as the wide range of ancillary benefits and subsidies, reached the highest levels in the world.

It was not the SPD but the British Labour Party under Tony Blair that was the first to realize that the strategy of the "Third Way" was inadequate to cope with the ever more intense market competition, that the election could not be won with its traditional but shrinking base of blue-collar voters, and that the Tories could not be pushed out of the government. Tony Blair did not win the 1998 election with a welfare program, as is Labour's tradition, but rather with a promise to renew British society and strengthen Britain's competitiveness and role in the world. Several months later, the SPD under Gerhard Schröder won the elections in Germany after a bitter campaign against the CDU led by Helmut Kohl. In both cases, the conservative opponents were exhausted from their long years in power. The CDU, which had governed democratic Germany uninterrupted for sixteen years, had succeeded in reuniting divided Germany and had done much to develop the EU into a monetary union. Moreover—and this is especially important for this study—during Helmut Kohl's reign the CDU notably increased welfare benefits and raised real wages substantially. Unlike in Great Britain, where Margaret Thatcher reduced the omnipotence of the strike-happy unions to a tolerable level, in Germany the influence of the unions within the cooperative social partner system grew and the welfare component of the modern market economy expanded. Further increases in taxes, already the highest in the world, were unable to compensate for the even higher levels of welfare expenditures (and the costs of integrating bankrupt East Germany). Thus the competitiveness of Europe's economically strongest country was significantly weakened.

The Social Democrats inherited a difficult legacy in their victory in Germany's September 1998 elections. The Geneva World Economic Forum in June 1999 ranked Germany in twenty-fifth place, one spot lower than in the previous year. The rival IDM Institute in Lausanne, ranked Germany ninth, somewhat better than the year before. But Germany continued to rank in third or fourth place after the United States, Japan, Singapore, or Switzerland. The analyses of both institutes put the following states in the upper ranks: Singapore, the United States, and Hong Kong, followed by Taiwan, Canada, Switzerland, Luxembourg, Great Britain, Finland, Ireland, and the Netherlands. Japan's position dropped two places in both lists, to fourteenth and eighteenth respectively. The World Economic Forum cited high taxes, an inflexible labor market, and deficient customer care on the part of businesses as the reasons for Germany's poor showing. The IDM, on the other hand, underscored the progress made by Germany's managers and the restructuring of business through a merger process already under way.[1] Gerhard Schröder was aware that Germany's once dynamic economy would stagnate and that the high unemployment rate could not be combated if there were no radical reforms. Schröder's finance minister and former head of the SPD, Oskar Lafontaine, suggested that unemployment be combated by raising wages and increasing buying power. The chancellor refused to take this path since it would have increased production costs, which were already high, further weakening Germany's ability to compete. But Lafontaine was unwilling to accept Schröder's housecleaning program and resigned. Schröder had been flirting for some time with the renewal program of the British Labour Party and Tony Blair, whose sights were set on creating a "New Labour" and on economic reforms that would bring Britain's economic system closer to America's torpedo capitalism. Mid-June 1999 marked the turning point. The two heads of party and government issued a joint declaration that was decisive for the continued development of social democracy toward a centrist position.

The days of the Marxist theory of revolution, of Eduard Bernstein reformism ("The end is nothing, the movement is all"), and of the Willy Brandt–inspired Bad Godesberg program were over. The new Social

Democratic position was far removed from a planned or state economy. In their joint declaration Blair and Schröder outlined the basic principles of a "Third Way," which *New York Times* columnist Roger Cohen described as "a Clintonian updating of Social Democratic values that attempts to place political movements formerly regarded as of the left firmly in the center of the political spectrum of modern societies."[2] Here are several selections from the declaration: "The demand for social justice was sometimes equated with income equality. Yet this neglects the importance of reward in accordance with the measure of responsibility and the effort expended." Further, according to the declaration, "The weakness of the market was overestimated, its strength underestimated." Blair and Schröder criticized left-wing Social Democratic values and blamed overblown state subsidies for high unemployment. Social justice was equated with a "higher level of public spending" without consideration of how many taxes had to be raised to finance that spending or of the effects on competitiveness and employment. Whereas in Britain Margaret Thatcher had already laid the groundwork for the realization of these principles, Schröder's reforms were at this point still in *statu nascendi.* But in July the chancellor introduced his housecleaning program to the German public. At its basis were the theses of the declaration outlined above. The program called for a $16 billion cut in state welfare benefits, and retirement packages and pensions were to be frozen at their current levels. Further, corporate taxes were to be reduced to a level lower than in the United States, and a previously proposed inheritance tax was dropped from the agenda.

The chancellor justified dropping the inheritance tax by citing the opinion of several economists who had concluded that "it is so difficult to draw a line between a business tax and an inheritance tax that it would require the intercession of a bureaucracy that would in turn eat up any revenues that would come from lawful taxation."[3] It bears mentioning that in 1906, when Teddy Roosevelt, a Republican, demanded approval of his proposed inheritance tax, he justified his proposal with the argument that the bestowal of enormous wealth upon young people "does not do them any real service and is of great and genuine detriment to the community at large." The president warned, "If ever our people become too sordid as to feel that all that counts is moneyed property, ignoble well-being, effortless ease and comfort, then this nation shall perish, as it will deserve to perish, from the earth."[4] The inheritance tax took effect in 1916—eight years after Roosevelt left office. Democratic president

Franklin Roosevelt railed against the untaxed transfer of assets, just like his great conservative predecessor had done. He claimed that the inheritance or gift, is not consistent with the ideals and sentiments of the American people. In letting his inheritance tax initiative fall by the wayside, Social Democrat Gerhard Schröder stands in contradiction to both the conservative views of "Teddy" and the democratic views of Franklin Roosevelt. His policy is, however, in agreement with that of the present American Republican legislature, which is calling for a repeal of the 1916 inheritance tax. Just like the conservatives in the United States, Germany's Social Democratic chancellor ignores both the moral aspects of this form of taxation and his own lauded ideals of social justice.

The proposed pension reforms, however, could be quite advantageous. The current "pay-as-you-go" system requires employees to make regular payments toward pension accrual, instead of saving or investing money so that they can later draw on the it in retirement, as is the practice in the United States. But this system seems no longer adequate, given that people are living much longer. Thus there is broad support for a proposal by the minister of labor and union politicians to establish private funds earmarked for employees in addition to the state-subsidized welfare fund.

As expected, Schröder's somewhat conservative housecleaning program has met with little enthusiasm from the left wing of the SPD. After the resignation of Lafontaine, Saarland's prime minister, Reinhard Klimmt, moved into the leadership position of the left-wing opposition within the party. Several union leaders have already given their support to Klimmt's platform. Schröder's "modernization strategy," they say, may be at the cost of social justice. Furthermore, they strongly criticize the chancellor's abandonment of the inheritance tax. Reinhard Höppner, the Social Democratic prime minister of Sachsen-Anhalt, also supports Schröder's challenger. In Höppner's opinion, the citizens of the former East Germany consider it a party duty—the party at issue is the Party of Democratic Socialism (PDS), successor to the German Socialist Party (SED)—to think in categories of social justice, and this must not be forgotten in any debate on modernization. The chancellor, however, supported by business managers, is firmly convinced that only greater flexibility, less state intervention, and a "revamping of the welfare state" can create the preconditions necessary for a reduction in unemployment. Schröder is determined to carry his reforms out to the end, and he assures the public that the advantages of his policy will become visible in fall 2002, just before the next parliamentary elections.

Whereas Gerhard Schröder is only in the initial stages of his efforts to boost the stagnating economy and reduce unemployment, his like-minded British colleague has already been in power for two years. *The Economist* describes a seminar on "Third Way" policies attended by Bill Clinton and Tony Blair at which the U.S. president remarked that he would go down in history as a great election winner.[5] Blair replied, "I hope I can do more than that." *The Economist* recalled that in his first speech after his election victory the prime minister promised to create "one of the great radical reforming governments of our history." *The Economist* then takes stock of Blair's work after two years in power. The prime minister has no reason to be embarrassed, it said, about the work that he has done during that time; the British economy has fared well—thanks especially to the measures Blair initiated shortly after the election, such as giving full independence to the Bank of England and the introduction of several impressive heath care and education reforms. Still, there have hardly been the kind of fundamental reforms that would mark a turning point in Great Britain's history. At least there have been no reforms in the same sense as the 1945–51 Labour Party's introduction of health insurance or Margaret Thatcher's privatization of countless industrial businesses and curbing of the trade unions.

It is not that Blair and his team have disregarded the chance to be the architects of a historical turning point, but the great results expected have not come about. Blair's efforts, regardless of how remarkable they might be, have failed to create lasting peace or stability in Northern Ireland or to consolidate Great Britain's role in the EU. Moreover, Labour's poor election showing was a disappointment to Blair—the party lost over half of its seats in the European Parliament. But he reaffirmed his government's determination to become a member of the European Monetary Union. "It would be incorrect," he said on June 14 after the election setback, "to exclude the possibility of participation in the monetary union when all of the economic conditions are met." However, the "Business for Sterling" lobby thinks that Blair will distance himself further from the Euro. And Tory leader William Hague, insists that the conservative party "will fight for the pound." "We want to be in Europe, but not ruled from Europe," says Hague. American Investment Bank economist Michael Saunders maintains that "Labour cannot afford to run the next election with a pro-Euro strategy when the majority of the British are against participation in the monetary union."[6] The skeptical attitude of the British population toward the Euro has intensified according to the survey institute ICM, where opinion polls are published in cooperation with *The Guardian.* The number of people opposing Great Britain's entrance into the monetary union in June 1999 rose from 8 percent to 61 percent, a record high. The number of people who support British participation in the EMU decreased from 34 percent in May to 27 percent in June. Political observers explain that the swing in opinion is a result of the Euro's weakness and the failure of the European mainland to initiate structural reforms. Salomon Smith Barney suggested that "The people probably have more faith that Great Britain's economy will be able to develop well outside of the monetary union."[7] Tony Blair is well aware of his citizens' aversion to the Euro and will therefore most likely not set a date for a referendum during the current legislative period.

The polls list health insurance and improvement of the school system as two of the most important concerns for the British. But the promises to initiate a "revolution" in these two areas, which would mean a fundamental reform of the welfare state, are far from being fulfilled. The money New Labour would like to release for such objectives is far too modest a sum to finance a real reform, and other sources of money (e.g., the levying of taxes) are not an option for New Labour's leader. Social services have also not been privatized to such a degree as to effect a "revolution" in health care and in the school system. Though there is talk of a "Third Way," there have been no clarifications as to what that could mean concretely. In a few cases, Blair has allowed private concerns to take bankrupt schools under their wing, but these measures, important though they may be, are not enough to accomplish the urgently needed reform of Great Britain's educational system.

After a successful parliamentary election in December 1995, Austria's socialist leader, Franz Vranitzky, spoke of the "emancipation of the underprivileged" and emphasized that the "megatrends of the century are Social Democratic." But Tony Blair and Gerhard Schröder have taken an enormous step in shifting social democracy and its left-wing traditions to the right. This trend is also a part of the globalization of the world economy. The Social Democratic leaders have come to the conclusion that the opening and internationalization of markets intensify competition and that the only national economies with a chance to succeed are the ones that can cheaply produce and better market high-quality goods. José Luis Rodríguez Zapatero's election as party leader of Spain's SD at the end of July 2000 marked the shift to a Tony Blair–style reform program. The welfare market economy, originally supported by the Social Democrats, is in danger of losing its "welfare" element. Sir Karl Popper warned that the greatest political achievement of humankind, the welfare state, could become the victim of this new economic orientation. The competitive challenge of globalization caused the implosion of the Soviet empire and the worldwide Communist movement, the remnants of which turned in droves to the path of Social Democracy. Social democracy, however, is no longer the movement that it was when the world was divided. The leaders of both the former Soviet Union and the Social Democrats have accepted capitalism as the universal social order. They have acknowledged the rules of its game and accepted the competitive challenges that the late twentieth century poses.

Monetary Union: A Milestone in European History

"Historians may well count January 4th 1999 as an epic moment," claimed Britain's *The Economist.*[8] For the first time in history, it said, had so many countries of such a wide territory and of such overall economic strength joined together to create a common currency and reduce their monetary sovereignty to a single entity. *The Economist*, a renowned British publication, still hesitates to support British participation in the monetary union. Nonetheless, it came to the conclusion that this monumental innovation could be as important as the establishment of the U.S. dollar in 1792.

The monetary union is made up of eleven members of the fifteen member EU. Great Britain, Denmark, Sweden, and Greece still remain outside of the monetary union—Greece because of its inability to fulfill membership requirements. The eleven members of the monetary union have relinquished their right to relieve budget deficits by issuing money or to boost exports via currency devaluation and have handed over control to the European Central Bank (ECB) in Frankfurt. The European System of Central Banks (ESCB) is now responsible for all EU monetary policies. Yet the ESCB is not a legal person in its own right but is made up of the ECB and the national central banks of the member states. Money policy decisions are made in the ECB Council, in which the national central banks have one vote, regardless of size. The central banks are basically independent. They conduct the ESCB's operations and are fundamentally obligated to keep price stability as their primary goal.

The eleven members of the monetary union had an economic clout in 1999 comparable to that of the United States: the Euro zone has nearly

Table 6.1

Economic Strength of EMU, EU, United States, and Japan

Country or region	Total GDP (in billions of dollars)	Per capita GDP (in billions of dollars)	Population (in millions)	Unemployment (in percent)
EMU–11	6,297	21,700	290.8	12.3
EU–15	8,150	21,800	374.5	10.9
United States	8,085	30,100	268.2	4.9
Japan	4,230	3,500	126.4	3.4

Source: OECD.

Table 6.2

Comparison of Stock Values for Selected Countries and Regions

Country or region	Businesses listed on stock market at end of 1997	Market capitalization at end of 1997 (in billions of dollars)	(in percent of GDP)
United States	8,559	10,879	139
Japan	2,334	2,069	50
EMU-11	2,769	2,712	44
Germany	699	783	38
EU-15	5,926	5,218	66
Great Britain	2,456	2,120	163

Source: Federation of European Stock Exchanges and Deutsche Bank estimates.

300 million inhabitants, and it accounts for 19.4 percent of the world's GDP and 18.6 percent of world trade. Table 6.1 shows the monetary union's economic strength in comparison to other large powers.

Although the EMU has a larger population than the United States, its economic potential is around one-fourth less. But after the integration of the four remaining EU countries, which may choose to join the currency union later, Europe's economic potential will be even larger than that of the United States. The monetary union is expected to cause a notable boom in capital markets, which have much catching up to do since the stock markets in EU countries are relatively small and continental Europe's stock market culture is rather underdeveloped. Table 6.2 shows the disparities between the stock values for the United States and other countries.

It is expected that most businesses in the EMU will direct their finan-

Table 6.3

Investment in Government Bonds for Seven EMU Countries at End of 1996

Country	Total volume (in billions of dollars)	Domestic investors (in percent)	Foreign investors (in percent)
Germany	793.0	52	48
France	660.4	90	10
Italy	1,164.5	85	15
Spain	275.2	82	18
Belgium	252.4	94	6
Netherlands	183.9	76	24
Austria	70.6	83	17

Source: Bank for International Settlements.

cial strategies toward the currency region as a whole. Thus not only will the stock culture change, but so will the investment structure, which has hitherto been primarily concentrated in each domestic market, especially in government bonds. A restructuring of portfolios is expected that will induce large movements of capital. Table 6.3 displays the structure of investment in government bonds for seven EMU countries.

The table shows that Italy had the largest investment volume. This is a result of the considerable budget deficit in 1995, which is normally financed with government bonds. Whereas in Germany the percentage of foreign investors was exceptionally high (48 percent), the number of foreign investors in France was only 10 and in Belgium 6 percent. EMU members are expected to restructure their investments because of intensifying competition. Investors will begin to invest more in business loans and stocks and less in government bonds. The experts at the Deutsche Bank believe that the EMU will dramatically change the European financial markets. The Euro capital markets will grow at a considerable rate, and their volume and diversification could create serious competition for U.S. markets.

The Euro: A Challenge to the U.S. Dollar?

The Euro performed rather disappointingly during its first year. It lost between 10 and 25 percent of its value against the U.S. dollar. Nonetheless, most experts are convinced that the Euro can become a stable, competitive currency whose influence will spread beyond the Euro region. In his essay "Will the Euro Challenge the Dollar?," Norbert Walter, head economist of the Deutsche Bank, expresses his conviction that the Euro will be used increasingly as an invoicing, reserve, and anchor currency.[9] According to Walter, the Euro has been brought into circulation in a reliable economic region, in which prices are generally more stable and interest rates lower than elsewhere. Foreign investors have confidence in the Euro and the European Central Bank, and they believe that price stability will be guaranteed in the Euro region. Thanks to the Euro, a considerable part of what used to be foreign trade has become domestic trade. Half of all trade carried out in the Euro region and 12 percent of trade with the EU countries that will join the EMU in a second phase is settled entirely in Euros, and around 13 percent of all trade with the United States is settled in Euros. Professor Walter, a currency expert, is convinced that the Euro will spread to neighboring states in Central and Eastern Europe within a few years. Several of these countries, such as Poland, already conduct 70 percent of their foreign trade with the Euro region. Countries in the Middle East and North Africa will also increasingly use the Euro as their trade currency in the next decade. The difference between the U.S. and European share of Asian foreign trade, 20 percent and 15 percent respectively, is not that large. One-half of Asian trade is internal to that continent, and it is primarily conducted in U.S. dollars. If Europe is able to increase Asian confidence in the Euro, the Euro could gradually take over the U.S. dollar's position as the currency of choice for trade there. Yet it is hard to imagine, argues Professor Walter, that the foreign trade of goods like crude oil will be conducted in Euros rather than dollars in the near future. It is conceivable, however, that the Euro's 20 percent share of the world's currency reserves could rise to more than 30 percent in the course of the coming years. The U.S. dollar is expected to reach around 50 percent. Nonetheless, the EU cannot become the world's leading power because it lacks common foreign and security policies as well as its own constitution. Thus the EU cannot become a United States of Europe. At present, the United States and the U.S. dollar have no real fear of a serious European challenge. According to Professor Walter, "The United States is the only true world power—economic and political, thus the U.S. dollar will remain the number one reserve currency." But he does claim that the Euro could, in addition to the dollar, become an anchor currency for the setting of exchange rates in regions like the Middle East, Asia, and Latin America.

Professor Walter does not seem to exaggerate the potential role of the Euro. After a transition phase, a relationship could develop between the

U.S. dollar and the Euro that would be similar to the relationship between Airbus and Boeing. Like Airbus–Boeing relations, which may lead to the perfection of the airplane, the two key currencies could together lead to the further development of the world monetary system. The establishment of the Euro market will change the dollar's standing—the EU currency is already number two in international world markets, well ahead of the yen. If Great Britain joins the EMU, it could pose a serious challenge for the United States, though the danger of this seems unlikely at present. Britain's top politicians have declared that they will participate in the EMU only if the economic conditions are advantageous and if a referendum, which is to be held after the May 2002 parliamentary elections, enables Britain's participation. On September 6, 1999, British foreign minister Robin Cook said to Japanese investors, "I assure you that if the Euro proves a stable, successful currency, Tony Blair's government will make sure that Britain is ready to take part, subject to the support of the British people in a referendum."[10] A change in attitude toward the Euro is to be expected only when its relation to the U.S. dollar substantially improves. The concluding sentence of Professor Walter's essay concisely expresses the opinion of Europe's politicians: "The Euro is a good catalyst, but it is not the end of the hard work to be done to achieve a prosperous and united Europe."

Austria's currency expert, Fritz Breuss, thoroughly analyzed the external aspects of the monetary union in a series of reports for the Research Institute for European Questions in 1999.[11] In his opinion, "the EMU is the most ambitious project in the history of European integration . . . a project with historical dimensions." Breuss suggests that if this project succeeds, the new Euro zone will be more attractive for potential foreign investors and could eventually become the largest market for public borrowing in the world. However, European integration can occur only however, through the establishment of a cross-border target payment system, the harmonization of financial instruments, and the elimination of exchange rate risks. A major restructuring of private portfolios could be the result, strengthening tendencies that have been evident for some time, such as the decrease in dollar deposits from 67 to 40 percent in the last ten years. The internal market, which will be more integrated as a result of the single currency, will reduce the EU members' need for currency reserves. The EU presently holds a total currency reserve six times larger than that of the United States and twice as large as Japan's. This will be gradually reduced and converted into dollars. In the end, Breuss claims, the EU will need to hold currency reserves only as large as those held in the United States.

The special report from the Deutsche Bank, issued in July 1999 and entitled "The Euro: First Six Months," maintains that the EMU financial market was completely converted to the Euro on January 4, 1999, the first trading day. The establishment of the EMU has "made for the issuing of more stocks and securities." The transformation during the first half of the year was more noticeable in the fixed-interest securities market, especially in business loans, than in the stock market. The Euro zone has a 24 percent share of fixed-interest securities, making it the second largest fixed-interest securities market in the world. Half of all European bonds issued during the first half of 1999 were in Euros, while only 40 percent were issued in U.S. dollars. The volume of business loans doubled, whereby the share of lower ratings grew considerably. The expected shift from country-specific to branch-specific strategies already began to manifest itself during the first half of the year.

The Euro's Weakness

The Euro's tendency to devaluate, especially against the U.S. dollar, dominated discussion during the first six months of the currency's existence. On January 4, 1999, the day of the Euro's introduction and the first day of trading, one Euro was valued at $1.1789. By July 19 it fell to its lowest level, at $1.0146 Euros, a total loss of 14 percent against the dollar and 6 percent against the yen. In the following three months the Euro stabilized for a while at an exchange rate of 1.05–1.06 Euro against the U.S. dollar. During the course of 2000, its value decreased substantially below dollar parity. The main reason for the Euro's weakness was the economic divide between Euro zone and the United States. Doubts about the resumption of economic growth plague Euroland and hurt the Euro's performance on foreign exchange markets. Moreover, skepticism over the resolve of certain member states, especially Italy, to keep stability and growth agreements have further undermined confidence in the Euro.

Four renowned German academics have stepped up their criticism of the Euro's negative start.[12] The Euro's foreign purchasing power, the professors say, has gone from being "strong as a bear" in the beginning of the experiment to "soft as butter." The most important preconditions for Europe's economic development have been weakened, it is stated in a declaration published on March 24, 1999. Germany's debt has almost doubled in the last eight years and is so high that it no longer corresponds to Maastricht Treaty regulations. The federal government alone paid around DM 82 billion in interest in 1999, 22 percent of its tax income (it was only 12.4 percent in 1982). Interest payments are the second largest part of the federal budget, after social spending. According to the Finance Ministry, the federal government will have to borrow between DM 80 and 90 billion a year for the next three years—more than 2 percent of the GNP—without the planned austerity package.[13] The experts warn against intervention on foreign exchange markets since it would further hinder the growth of confidence. They also criticize the goal of the ECB to set a unified interest rate for the entire Euro zone that would ignore structural and economic disparities. A unified interest rate would act like a straitjacket, hindering rational policymaking.

Hans Tietmeyer, the former president of the German Federal Bank (who resigned on September 1, 1999), pressed for the EU to adopt a more competitive economic policy. The Euro, Tietmeyer said in an interview, has changed both Europe's mind-set and its political situation.[14] According to him, there must be competition between the tax and welfare systems of individual member states; the entire welfare system must accommodate to competition. "It is forever. . . . There is no going back," Tietmeyer claims. For him, the Euro is not the main problem but rather the lack of dynamic competition. He sees no substantial danger for the monetary union in the foreseeable future but adds that "the real test . . . will come later."

"One must give the Euro more time," U.S. experts argued at a seminar in Konstanz at the beginning of June 1999. "They [the U.S. experts] follow the agitated European debate over the weakness of the Euro with amazement," writes *Frankfurter Allgemeine Zeitung*.[15] "It is way too early to pass judgment on the quality of the Euro today," maintains Bennet McCallum of Carnegie Mellon University. "One should not begin to worry unless the Euro remains weak over a period of several years," the currency expert says. His colleague at Carnegie Mellon, Allan Meltzer, expresses a similar opinion: "The lamentations over the Euro are just the reverse of the overoptimism that reigned at its introduction." Meltzer suggests that monetary policies should be geared to controlling inflation, rather than focusing on exchange rates. In Meltzer's opinion, if the European economy picks up, the Euro will begin to gain value. He is convinced that the key to a healthy European economy is not so much active monetary and financial policies as the stabilization of the labor markets. Michael Parkin, professor at the University of Western Ontario, suggests that Europeans should use American and British method to fight unemployment and worry less about the Euro's exchange rate.

Heinz Kienzl, vice president of Austria's Society for European Policy, also admits that Europe's economic policies are a more important factor in the EU's success than the Euro's exchange rate. Kienzl, a renowned union politician, writes in his essay, "Welfare State And Casino Capitalism," that "It is definitely wrong to expect huge economic advantages from the Euro, and its introduction is unlikely to lead to an increase in employment."[16] The Euro, Kienzl claims, should make it impossible to use changes in the exchange rate to eliminate balance of payments deficits The Austrian policy of competitive devaluation against the Italian lira, the Swedish krone, and the Finnish mark cost the Austrian economy forty thousand jobs in the 1990s. (In the 1960s one lira was worth twenty Austrian groschen, but it was worth just one groschen in 1998. And while one Swedish krone was worth five schillings in the 1960s, it was worth only two in 1998.) Nevertheless, Kienzl is convinced that the common currency offers enormous possibilities: "If it succeeds in making the EU's economy more attractive for investors and in keeping interest rates low, then important advantages will develop for the real economic sector over the finance sector."

U.S. Experts Predict a Positive Future for the Euro

In an interview with the Austrian magazine *Trend*, Michael Mussa, former economic adviser and head economist at the IMF, said that "The common currency policy will be excellent for Europe and will therefore be a successful venture."[17] But he also remarked that the EMU has a limited range of movement that restricts problem-solving options. Currency policy, according to Mussa, is not responsible for high unemployment levels or the lack of flexibility in the national economies of member states. The EU's currency policy cannot prevent the problems caused by an aging population in the pension system and health care sector. Mussa says that in the next two or three years, the economic climate in Europe will be relatively friendly and growth rates will be above average, thereby allowing governments to reduce their budget deficits. Mussa warns that the main focus should be on increasing economic flexibility, not on the Maastricht Agreement, since the need for increased flexibility would exist regardless of the monetary union. In Mussa's opinion, the large tax-evading "shadow economy" is putting enormous pressure on the national budgets. Mussa, like many others, believes that constricting exchange rate flexibility will endanger the adaptability of the EU to the changing world economy—though eliminating exchange rates may be a definite advantage for hard currency countries. The eleven members of the monetary union, Mussa says, will represent the second largest currency community in the world. The Euro will assert itself internationally and establish itself as second only to the dollar. Yet there is no desire on either side of the Atlantic to adjust the U.S.–Euro exchange rate. In comparison to the dollar, the Euro will continue to fluctuate. And the strong dollar, claims Mussa, not a problem at present, could become one if the U.S. trade deficit grows substantially.

William J. McDonough, president of the Federal Reserve Bank of New York, also assesses the Euro positively in his article, "Dollar and Euro—A View from the Federal Reserve."[18] The United States, he claims, has profited from the deepening of world economic integration and will also profit from the establishment of the Euro. Europe's growing participation in international capital markets, which promote a successful European monetary system, will stimulate the transfer of savings and investments from Europe to America and vice versa. The Euro already functions as an important international currency alongside the dollar. It would be a mistake, McDonough warns, to think that the United States is worried that the Euro will restrict its ability to conduct trade and investments with the rest of the world. The U.S. dollar is the exchange currency of 50 percent of world trade and 80 percent of world financial transactions. The Fed manager argues plausibly that the new currency, which could accelerate foreign trade and invigorate global financial markets, will benefit all countries of the world—including the United States, the world's most active participant in markets and trade. McDonough claims that the Euro could extend its importance outside the EU's borders into world trade and rise to the level of a reserve currency just like the U.S. dollar and the pound sterling before it, provided the financial world remains convinced of the Euro's stability. McDonough concludes that the establishment of a currency that could compete with the U.S. dollar would force the United States to adopt a stricter market discipline and help it to address a few of its own domestic problems.

Paul Krugman, professor of economics at Princeton University, discusses in depth the problem of the dollar as a reserve currency and the Euro's potential difficulties in taking on that function.[19] Krugman plays down the role of the U.S. dollar as a reserve currency and suggests that there would be little change in the worldwide monetary system if the Euro assumed the same function. According to him, the dominance of the dollar is often overstated and its advantages for the U.S. are exaggerated. Admittedly, the Americans owe dollar holders nearly $5 trillion as a result of the foreign trade deficit accumulated over the last thirty years. But other countries, whose currencies have no reserve functions, import more than they export, creating even greater deficits than those of the United States. Since 1980, the balance of payments deficit has been an average of 1.5 percent of the U.S.'s GNP, as is Britain's, but it is less than Canada's (2.2 percent) and much less than Australia's (4.2 percent). These countries finance their trade deficits, as the Americans do, through the issue of bonds, the sale of foreign stocks, real estate, and the like. America's total debt is not that large. Whereas Americans owe $5 trillion in foreign debt, foreign debtors owe the United States more than $4 trillion. The difference amounts to around $800 billion, or about 10 percent of the GNP. The dollar's international role, Krugman writes, is a result of its function as a measure of value—oil trade, for example, is conducted in dollars. But America's advantage does not lie in these transactions. Naturally, the Fed profits from interest-free foreign deposits, but the profit in this case is just several billion dollars—a negligible quantity in comparison with the United States' $8 trillion GNP. The United States enjoys a certain flexibility, Krugman claims, because foreigners are willing to accept U.S. banknotes—they possess more than $200 billion. The dollar is also the preferred currency for illegal businesses. Foreigners receive $15 billion in cash—around 0.2 percent of the GNP—for various goods and services every year, though Krugman warns that one "better not ask what kind." In around five years, hundred-Euro notes may replace the $100 bill as the currency of choice for dealers from (say) Vladivostok, causing an approximately 0.1 percent loss in the GNP for the U.S. economy. "Somehow, I think we can live with that," Krugman concludes.

Europe's solid balance of payments surplus does offer one important advantage for the Euro in competition with the dollar. Whereas the United States suffered a balance of payments deficit of over $250 billion in 1999, the Euro zone is expected to earn a 60 billion Euro surplus.[20] Whereas Europe earned a surplus of 67 billion Euros in 1998 (or 1.2 percent of its GNP), the U.S. deficit was as high as 2.7 percent of its

GNP. Nonetheless, this favorable balance of payments did not save the Euro from devaluation against the dollar. The robust U.S. economy and the skepticism surrounding medium-term economic dynamics in the Euro zone are important causes for the Euro's devaluation.

The U.S. lead in economic growth, if one believes the multitude of prognoses, will probably continue for the foreseeable future. But there is also an optimistic outlook for the Euro zone. After the slowing of economic growth from 2.8 percent in 1998 to 1.9 percent in 1999, the OECD estimated that the EU's GNP would grow at 2.4 percent in 2000. Unemployment, however, will decline at a slower rate, from 10.1 percent in 1999 to 9.8 percent in 2000. And the gap between the rich and poor will continue to grow larger. In 1983 the richest 1 percent of U.S. households possessed around 68.2 percent of U.S. wealth. In 1997 that had risen to over 73.2 percent of U.S. wealth and 51.4 percent of stock capital. The wealthiest 10 percent of U.S. households possessed 90 percent of capital in stocks and shares, with the 1 percent superrich possessing 51.4 percent.[21] It bears mentioning that 77 percent of U.S. college students expect to become millionaires within their lifetimes. The gap between rich and poor is also great in Europe. According to calculations by Eurostat, 18 percent of all EU citizens live under the poverty line (have incomes less than 60 percent of the national average).

Despite the still young yet already tired Euro, which has not been able to recover from its July 1999 devaluation, several Euro bankers are still convinced that the it will expand its influence outside of the EU. The common currency has an especially good chance to "develop the status of a popular parallel currency and to wear down the U.S. dollar's status" in Central and East European countries, as well as in regions of the Mediterranean, writes Alexander Schrader, economist at the Hypo-Vereinsbank.[22] The Euro notes that will come into circulation in 2002, could compete with the greenback and secure a part of the foreign circulation of dollars (around $12–15 billion annually) for the Euro zone if the Euro establishes itself as a stable price and exchange rate currency. The printing of Euro notes started in July 1999—13 billion banknotes with a total value of 600 billion Euros (610 billion) and $56 billion worth of coinage.[23] The Balkan and CIS countries are especially important circulation regions for the parallel currency. The "Euroization" of those regions could offer the EU's neighbors a chance to discipline their money and financial policies and provide an impulse for economic growth. Many countries neighboring the EU are linking their currencies

Table 6.4

Exchange Rate System in Euro Region

Country	Exchange rate system	Orientation (currency/currency basket)
Albania	Free floating	—
Bosnia–Herzegovina	Currency board	Euro
Bulgaria	Currency board	Euro
Croatia	Managed floating[b]	Euro
Czech Republic	Managed floating	—
Estonia	Currency board	Euro[d]
Hungary	Sliding peg[c]	70% Euro,[d] 30% U.S. dollar
Latvia	Fixed linkage	Special drawing rights
Lithuania	Currency board	U.S. dollar
Macedonia	Managed floating	De facto link to Euro
Poland	Sliding Peg	45% U.S. dollar, 40% Euro,[e] 10% pound, 5% Swiss franc
Romania	Free floating	—
Slovakia	Fixed linkage	60% Euro,[d] 40% U.S. dollar
Slovenia	Managed floating	De facto link to Euro[d]
Cyprus	Fixed linkage	Euro[f]
Israel	Sliding peg	54% U.S. dollar, 32% Euro,[g] 8% pound, 7% yen
Malta	Fixed linkage	67% Euro,[f] 21% U.S. dollar, 12% pound
Turkey	Managed floating	U.S. dollar
Algeria	Managed floating	U.S. dollar
Iran	Fixed linkage	U.S. dollar
Jordan	Fixed linkage	U.S. dollar
Lebanon	Managed floating	U.S. dollar
Morocco	Fixed linkage	Currency basket
Saudi Arabia	Fixed linkage	U.S. dollar
Syria	Fixed linkage	U.S. dollar
Tunisia	Managed floating	U.S. dollar
ACP countries[a]	Fixed linkage	Euro[h]

Source: International Currency Funds, World Economic Outlook, *The Economist*, 1998.

[a]Benin, Burkina Faso, Cameroon, Central African Republic, Chad, Comoros, Republic of Congo, Ivory Coast, Equatorial Guinea, Gabon, Mali, Niger, Senegal, and Togo.

[b]The monetary policymakers decide at their discretion about revaluation and devaluation.

[c]Revaluation and devaluation according to fixed, not quantitative, methods.

[d]Hitherto DM.

[e]Hitherto 35% DM.

[f]Hitherto Ecu.

[g]Hitherto 26% DM.

[h]Hitherto French franc.

to the Euro either directly or over a currency board. Table 6.4 shows the linkage of the Euro with other countries' currencies.

Wim Duisenberg, the president of the ECB, has an interesting view concerning the Euro and European monetary policy: "The governing council believes that the Euro is firmly based on internal price stability, and it therefore has the clear potential to achieve a stronger external value." The Euro system's monetary policy will secure the internal buying power of the Euro, thereby strengthening its international value.[24] But economic growth is the necessary precondition for the Euro's recovery, and the forecast is optimistic. In its meeting at the end of September 1999, the IMF raised the estimates for worldwide economic growth from 2.5 to 2.8 percent. The basis of this rosy projection is not only the unabated health of the U.S. economy, but also the signs of an economic boom in Europe in 2000, the improvement of the situation in Japan, and the doubling of oil prices in Russia.

7

The Eastern Enlargement of the European Union as a Precondition for the Continent's Economic and Political Unity

The term "European Union" denotes more of a goal than a reality. Although nearly every free market democracy in Western Europe (with the exception of Norway and Switzerland) belongs to the EU, the countries of Central and Eastern Europe are still far from being members. It will be a while before the first five candidates—Poland, the Czech Republic, Hungary, Slovenia, and Estonia—are admitted. Bulgaria, Romania, Latvia, and Lithuania have an even longer wait. And the admission of Russia, Belarus, and Ukraine is not even on the EU's agenda.

The EU agreement states that "every European state can apply to become a member of the Union." But "conditions for admission and the necessary adaptation to the treaties on which the EU rests are set by an agreement between the member states and the state making its membership application." The admission criteria have become much stricter. In addition to acceptance of the *acquis* (position of legal property), political and economic conditions play a decisive role in the admission process. European heads of state established new criteria for admission negotiations at the 1993 Copenhagen summit. Applicants must now ensure institutional stability as a guarantee for democracy and the rule of law, as well as the protection of human rights and minorities. Furthermore, they must develop a functioning market economy that is capable of holding its own against the pressures of competition and EU market forces. Applicants must adhere to the legal regulations accompanying membership and accept the EU's political goals, as well as the EU and EMU's economic goals, as their own. The 1999 Vienna summit added an emphasis on the union's achievement of social goals to the agenda. In addition to efforts aimed at growth, new applicants are now required to take the social goals of the union into account.

The Gap Between the EU and Eastern Europe

The gap between the EU's output and that of its East European applicants continues to grow. With a population of approximately 100 million, the new members would potentially constitute one-fifth of the EU's total population, though the economic strength of the union would grow by only 5 percent.[1] The per capita GDPs of the East European countries applying for EU membership are only one-third of the Austrian GDP, and salaries are but one-tenth of Austria's.[2] The Czech Republic's per capita GDP decreased from 64 percent of the EU average in 1996 to 60 percent in 1998. The most economically efficient applicant, Slovenia, has a per capita GDP of 72 percent of the EU average. Poland's was a mere 41 percent of the EU average. Until 1998, the Polish economy grew more dynamically than any other state in Central or Eastern Europe, but its ten-year growth rate (17 percent) was still lower than the EU's (19 percent).[3]

In 1995, Franz Fischler, the EU minister of agriculture, presented a study on the agricultural prospects of the ten East European countries that have completed their association agreements with the EU. In his study, Fischler described the enormous gaps that exist between the agricultural sector of these countries and that of the EU. Whereas in Eastern Europe 25 percent of those employed work in the agricultural sector, agriculture comprises only 6 percent of total employment in EU countries. Nevertheless, the Eastern countries remain net importers of agricultural products, with the exception of Hungary, Bulgaria, and Estonia. There is uncertainty about property rights in Eastern Europe, and the capital needed for privatization and investment in the East European food industry is scant. Fischler concludes that it will take decades before the average per capita income in Eastern Europe reaches 75 percent of the EU average. Regardless of the strong desire for rapid enlargement to the east, Fischler says, the consequences must not be underestimated.[4]

The *Wall Street Journal for Europe* ranked the first five candidates for EU membership on a scale from zero to ten according to ten differ-

Table 7.1

Rankings for Five EU Candidates, 1998

	Hungary	Poland	Slovenia	Czech Republic	Estonia
Overall ranking[a]	1.0	2.0	3.0	4.0	5.0
Average score of worthiness	8.0	7.8	7.7	7.2	7.2
Ranking in 1997	5.0	3.0	2.0	1.0	4.0
Economic growth	6.4	8.0	6.2	5.2	7.0
Price stability	6.0	6.4	2.2	7.7	6.4
Integration in the world economy	9.2	9.1	8.4	9.0	8.3
Currency stability	7.4	6.6	8.8	6.9	7.4
Rule of law	9.3	9.0	8.6	8.7	7.8
Portfolio strategy	9.4	9.2	7.4	9.0	8.1
Productivity	8.7	8.5	8.3	6.4	7.0
Payment balance	7.0	5.2	8.9	4.2	4.4
Political stability	8.7	8.4	9.3	6.6	7.3
Corruption	8.6	8.2	8.6	7.9	7.4

Source: CEER Risk Assessment, January 1998.
Note: Scores are based on a range of 1 to 10.
[a]Ranking is from 1 to 10, with 1 being the highest.

ent criteria (see Table 7.1).[5] Hungary moved up from fifth place to first (the Czech Republic dropped to fourth) and appears to be leading the pack among the five candidates. Hungary's GDP has grown dramatically: 4.6 percent in 1997 and 5.1 percent in 1998. It surpassed Poland to attain the strongest economic growth among the Central European reform countries, most of which suffered a significant setback from Russia's economic crisis. Hungary's industrial and construction sectors—the driving forces of economic growth—grew by about 12 percent. Its agricultural sector, however, had a –1.5 percent growth rate, by far the worst showing among the candidates. Exports increased by 16 percent and investments by 11.4 percent. Private consumption grew at a slower rate, from 2 percent (1997) to 3 percent (1998). Imports (+22 percent) continued to increase more than exports, and signs of weakness appeared in the last quarter of 1998. Investments fell in the third quarter, from 18.1 percent to 8.2 percent. Exports also declined, from 28.3 percent in the first month of 1998 to 9.5 percent in the last three months. Pressures on the balance of payments also increased. But the prognosis for 1999 remained optimistic. The GDP was expected to rise, as in the previous year, by 5 percent. And while the budget revenues increased by 5 percent, spending increased by only 4 percent. According to Hungary's prime minister, Viktor Orbán, the budget surplus should create a reserve for possible hard times on world markets in the future. But he hopes that the EU, with which Hungary conducts 75 percent of its foreign trade, will remain strong enough not to cause any undue difficulties. In Orbán's opinion, Hungary is politically stable. It is the only country in the region whose government has held power for its entire four-year term.[6]

Assessment of the Central and East European Economies

The Czech Republic, which fell to fourth place in the *Wall Street Journal's* ranking, has not climbed out of its recession, and there are no signs of an economic boom on the way. A 1 percent decrease in the GDP was predicted for 1999. Whereas real salaries increased by several percentage points, labor productivity dropped and unemployment grew from 8.8 percent to 9 percent, or 465,454 persons, in August 1999 alone. The greatest problems lay in coal production and heavy industry in northern Bohemia and northern Moravia, where unemployment rates have reached more than 16 percent. Drastic setbacks were expected in foreign trade. According to estimates by the Czech Statistics Office (CSU), exports were expected to drop from 17.7 percent in 1998 to 4.1 percent in 1999, and imports were to decrease from 7.9 to 3.4 percent.

This recession was no accident. Prior to World War II, Czechoslovakia was a highly developed industrial country, and during the Soviet period it was even considered the "Prussia of Eastern Europe." There were great hopes that Czechoslovakia's transition to a market economy and Western democracy would be successful. In the first years of reform, it appeared that these hopes for an economic miracle would come true. Václav Klaus, the father of Czech reform, understood how to reawaken the slumbering *homo economicus* in the Czech population and return to the market traditions of the prewar era. Private initiatives quickly displaced the planned economy, and privatization progressed rapidly. The focus of foreign trade shifted from East to West, and the economy, which offered every willing citizen a job, grew dynamically. But by 1997 the euphoric boom period was over. The Czech Republic, once praised as the ideal model for a transition to capitalism, hit rock bottom.

The success of the Czech Republic's rapid privatization has been unduly praised: 72 percent of the privatized businesses came to be owned by 353 investment funds, most of which were controlled by state banks.

The majority of citizens entrusted their privatization coupons to these funds: 6.17 million, or 60 percent of the population, participated in the countrywide operation; 820,000 Czechs sold their coupons to Viktor Kozeny, an expatriate Czech from the United States, whose experience as an adviser to the state's privatization officials enabled him to found a successful firm called Harvard Capital and Consulting with twenty-three investment funds. He promised to pay his customers ten times the value of their coupons within ten years. During that time, however, the nimble robber baron fled to the Bahamas, where he now administers his enormous fortune with American tycoon Michael Dingman, his partner. Most of the small proprietors who entrusted Kozeny with their coupons lost everything. Corruption grew: Jaroslav Lizner, director of the central privatization office, was caught accepting a $300,000 bribe in October 1994 as the privatization operation was coming to an end. Several months later, another case shocked the public. The private Bohemia bank in which Lizner had deposited privatization funds went bankrupt, and its director, Jiri Cadek, fled abroad. Duŝan Triska, the former acting minister of finance, said at the time: "We're living in the wild East. Honesty will not reign until the rise of the second generation."

Klaus's successor, the Social Democrat Miloŝ Zeman, admitted to the *New York Times* that voucher privatization had done more harm than good.[7] In its wake, said Zeman, millions of small stockholders emerged who could neither influence their companies' fate nor expect an adequate income from them. "The country is left with local entrepreneurs without sufficient capital, resulting in a high number of bankruptcies, inefficiency, low competitiveness and declining GDP." The Czech Republic, which had been praised by the OECD and the IMF as a model reform country, fell deeper and deeper into recession.

The Czech banking system also suffered. In 1998 the banks could not cover 263.4 billion crowns in credit, and in 1999 they defaulted on almost one-third of all bank credit, about 311.9 billion crowns (around $9 billion). Czech finance experts pointed out that the situation was much worse than in Poland and Hungary, where problem credit amounted to only 16 or 17 percent. After his "successful" program of privatization, Václav Klaus had proudly declared that "business is not our business," thereby presenting himself as a true proponent of the principles of laissez-faire. However, in early 1997 he was forced to introduce a strict austerity program, which required painful cuts in wages and state social services. Klaus and his center-right party lost their parliamentary majority in early elections; Zeman won a relative majority and built a minority government. In accordance with their "opposition pact," Klaus's liberal-conservative party supported Zeman. The "opposition pact" made Zeman head of the government and Klaus head of parliament. Strategically important industries and the banking system were readied for privatization. The head of government announced an ambitious restructuring project, although he was aware that it would increase unemployment from 7.5 percent to more than 9 percent (it was only 4.5 percent in 1997).

The head of government failed to mention another, more decisive element of his program for economic recovery: the goal of raising people's buying power. It is strange that he failed to emphasize this in light of the thoroughly unpleasant nature of his other reforms. The Czech Republic's per capita GDP is about 40 percent lower than the EU average, and according to the Austrian labor association, a Czech employee earns no more than 40 percent of the average Austrian salary. But prior to World War II, Czechoslovakia's standard of living was higher than Austria's. Although the Czech Republic has been a NATO member since March 12, 1999, and wants to join the EU as soon as possible, it is still unable to meet the admission criteria.

Poland is also finding it difficult to reform. In an analysis accompanying Table 7.1, the *Wall Street Journal* wrote the following: "Of all the region's countries, Poland is a good bellwether. Nearly a decade into the transition, it remains Central Europe's 'tiger economy' whose recipe for growth of monetarist policies and grass-roots entrepreneurship subsequently became the regional standard."[8] On the sixtieth anniversary of Hitler's September 1, 1939, invasion of Poland, Germany's top politicians—President Johannes Rau, Chancellor Gerhard Schröder, and Foreign Minister Joschka Fischer—visited Poland in order to express their peaceful sentiments and goodwill toward the Polish people. They vowed to integrate their neighbors across the Oder–Neisse border into the EU. But Poland's agricultural sector fears competition from the EU. Prime Minister Jerzy Buzek announced a September 7, 1999, referendum on joining the EU; apparently, the excitement over the prospect of membership has waned. A transition period in which subsidies are cut or entirely withheld will not satisfy the Poles. Farmers fear that EU membership will trigger a massive sellout of Polish farmland, especially in the western part of the country bordering Germany. EU officials refused Poland's demand for a twenty-five-year moratorium on land purchases. Germany also fears that opening borders will trigger a massive influx of guest workers, and this at a time when unemployment in Germany has risen above 10 percent. The Austrian Institute for Economic Research (WIFO) estimated that the lack of economic productivity would cause an annual migration of 0.3 percent of the populations of Poland, Slovakia, the Czech Republic, Hungary, and Slovenia to the "golden West." That would amount to about two hundred thousand people, in addition to the approximately one hundred and fifth thousand commuters that already work in the West. WIFO warns that it will take a decade to raise the standard of living and halt migration of the workforce.

A serious obstacle to Poland's admission into the EU is its antiquated agricultural sector. According to Poland's minister of agriculture, although a veritable revolution in agriculture is needed, the "organization and structure of Poland's agricultural economy" are not in themselves an obstacle to joining the EU.[9] The goal is to reduce the proportion of citizens working in agriculture from 27 percent to between 5 and 7 percent, and to raise the average farm size from seven to sixteen hectares. This restructuring would allow a quarter of Poland's farmers to aggressively participate in the EU agricultural market. But this revolution will require a great deal of money—money that does not exist since the mining industry and the antiquated iron and steel works will also require government aid. World Bank experts have estimated that without a change in subsidy strategy and a reduction in the minimal price for agricultural products, Polish agriculture will need to collect $5 billion in EU subsidies annually. Poland has plenty of farmland; in fact, after Russia, Ukraine, France, and Spain, it ranks fifth in all of Europe. But only 16 percent of farmers own their piece of land. Poland has more people per one hundred hectares of farmland than any other country in Europe; there are twenty-three people per one hundred hectares in Poland and only five in the EU. One-half of Polish farmers—one million people—have nothing to offer the agricultural market. Whereas the average value creation per laborer in Poland was $1,752 between 1996 and 1998, the other EU candidates had higher averages: Slovenia had $6,116, Hungary $4,770, and Estonia $3,519.[10] Every tenth Polish farmer collects an income equal to the average EU income. Considering the constantly increasing competition and the superiority of the Western farmers' modern agrotechnology, Poland's backward, splintered agricultural sector will not find life easy in the EU. The minister of agriculture's revolution must be completed before Poland becomes an EU member, and the needed money must be acquired in the form of long-term credit.

But the agricultural sector is not the only branch of the economy in need of urgent reform. If Poland wants to stay competitive in the demanding EU market, then it needs to fundamentally alter property relations and the means of production. Several days before the Pope's visit in June 1991, miners from the coal region of Silesia besieged the government in order to protest a plan to cut coal production (due to a drop in demand) and reduce government subsidies by 20 percent to finance the growing losses. The plan called for a reduction in the number of miners from 230,000 to 138,000 by the year 2002, the year in which Poland originally intended to join the EU. This is an unavoidable reform called for by EU admission criteria. Apart from reforms in agriculture and the coal industry, the Solidarity government considers its austerity program a precondition for EU membership. This program, which calls for the reduction of already shrinking social services, the restructuring of antiquated industrial businesses with their artificially elevated employment rates, and cuts in school and health care expenditures, is meeting increasing resistance from workers and farmers. On September 14, 1999, thousands marched to the slogan "Hands off, thieves" through the streets of the capital. The leader of the farmers, Andrzej Lepper, demanded the government's resignation since, in his opinion, it follows the "orders of the rotten West." The angry demonstrators burned the blue flag of the EU and the head of government's image in effigy. While workers demanded job security and an increase in their miserable wages, farmers clamored for an increase in subsidies and higher prices for agricultural products. The government was cheating them, they claimed, promising much but delivering nothing. As far as they were concerned, it had brought only poverty since the beginning of the 1990s. On the evening of the protest, Prime Minister Buzek appeared on television and promised to take measures against unemployment, which had reached 12 percent, and to offer more aid to farmers. One thing seems sure: Poland's adaptation to the requirements of the Maastricht Treaty, the precondition for EU membership, will require the poverty-stricken population to make many sacrifices that it is obviously unwilling to make.

Foreign investors have noticeably reduced their holdings in Poland. Direct investments in July 1999 were only 48 percent of the amount invested in the same period during the previous year. If this trend continues, the influx of foreign money will be enough to finance only 50 percent of the 1999 balance of payments deficit; in 1998, it had covered 75 percent. The escalating tension has led to a government crisis. The junior partner in the coalition, the Unia Wolnosci (Freedom Union), left the government. And Solidarnosc has been reduced to the status of a minority government, with no chance of holding on until the next elections. Thus negotiations with the EU will only become more complicated.

In contrast, Slovenia's integration into the EU would not result in serious economic difficulty, at least with regard to the country's GDP. Slovenia's population of 1.9 million has a per capita GDP of 72 percent of the EU average, making it the wealthiest country in Central and Eastern Europe. The average monthly income grew from 57 to 67 percent of Austria's average between 1992 and 1998. Yet even in Slovenia, signs of wear and tear are beginning to show. The tiny country does not want to be lumped with its Balkan neighbors. It considers itself a part of Central Europe and would like to be quickly integrated into the EU. But there are signs of imminent political crisis: the reformed Communists of the liberal–democratic party (LDS), who have yet to make a real break with their past, have been in power with their small coalition partner, the Slovenian People's Party (SLG), since 1996. The transformation of the social elite is slowly advancing. Slovenia has always been the most progressive and Europe-friendly part of the Balkans, both between the two world wars and under Communist rule in Yugoslavia. As a result of its better economic situation, it does appear likely that Slovenia will be the first of the five candidates to make the leap into the EU.

Economic and political problems, though surmountable, have also surfaced in Estonia, the fifth candidate for membership. Productivity dropped by more than 5 percent between early 1998 and early 1999, and an economic growth rate of only 0.4 percent was predicted for 1999. But the share of foreign trade with the EU has risen to over 50 percent, and Estonian dependency on the Russian market has thus dropped from over 25 percent to 10 percent in the last five years. Today, Sweden and Finland are Estonia's leading markets.

Although all three Baltic countries—Estonia, Latvia, and Lithuania—have chalked up considerable balance of payments deficits, Estonia's is the largest. The cause appears to be its overvalued currency. Since 1992, the ratio of the Estonian kroon to the German mark has been 8:1, though inflation has certainly made this obsolete. Extreme reforms are needed to rectify this imbalance and to tackle other economic woes. After independence, Estonia's radical reformers concentrated mainly on macroeconomic reforms. They liberalized prices, examined tax levels, linked the currency to the mark, sold a large number of state businesses to foreign investors, and thus created the basis for an economic upswing. But all of this was done without drastically changing Estonia's antiquated industrial structures. The reformers governed for just two years and lost power to a coalition government, which focused on modernizing the administration of the state; these attempts were in vain. Estonia's courts, police, and bureaucracy are in a sorrier state than those of the other northern countries, which serve as Estonia's model.[11] "Government offices often seem to be run more for the convenience of civil servants than citizens," *The Economist* writes. A leading conservative politician, Tunne Kelam, was quoted as saying, "So far, only the skeleton of the Estonian Republic has been restored." The center–right government of Mart Siimann suffered a bad loss in parliamentary elections on March 7, 1999. Just 7 of the 37 representatives of Siimann's government retained their seats. The left-leaning center party, on the other hand, picked up 28 of the 101 seats. If the new government, which made many promises during the campaign, really wants to fulfill EU membership criteria, then it will have to undertake the reforms necessary to rehabilitate Estonia's economy. Moreover, it must put an end to growing corruption and provide the population with more security. If these goals are accomplished, Estonia, with its 2.3 million citizens, could be the first Baltic nation to join the EU.

Bulgaria and Romania are hapless latecomers to the Central and Eastern European reform process. Unlike Poland, the Czech Republic, and Hungary, they were not invited to join NATO on March 3, 1999. However, they began to draw more attention during NATO's extensive bombardment of Yugoslavia. Romania sent peacekeeping troops to Albania, and Bulgaria promised to send police units into Kosovo. In turn, France and Italy supported Romania's aspiration to join NATO and the EU. The United Nations and EU then promised to include the two countries in the reconstruction of the war-torn Balkan region. Furthermore, Madeleine Albright declared that Romania was already a "part of the NATO family." And Tony Blair, the first British prime minister to visit Bulgaria, promised to support the start of negotiations for Bulgaria's and Romania's admission to the EU at the Helsinki summit in December 1999. So far, so good, but neither country is unprepared for membership in the EU, and they will be unable to surmount their economic problems and backwardness in the near future. "Their civil services are pretty feeble: bloated, corrupt, short of cash and talent, and patently ill-equipped to rewrite the laws of their countries to fit the complex EU rulebook," wrote *The Econo-*

mist.[12] Their economies could not even compete with the weakest among the EU countries.

Nevertheless, it would be a mistake to consider the situations in Bulgaria and Romania as identical. Bulgaria has had a much harder time with reforms, though it now seems as if it will be able to overcome the long economic crisis that has been plaguing the country. In the past, Bulgaria conducted most of its foreign trade with Council for Mutual Economic Assistance (CMEA) states; they accounted for 80 percent of its income. The collapse of this economic pact dramatically shrank turnover from trade. Exports dropped from $13.4 billion (1990) to $3.4 billion (1991), and imports decreased from $13.12 billion to $2.7 billion. It was only in 1994 that a meager part of Bulgaria's foreign trade was shifted to the West; exports increased by $4.0 billion, and imports increased by $4.3 billion. The government inherited an $8.5 billion foreign debt from the former regime, and it climbed to $12.5 billion in just a few years. In 1997, a wave of protests began against corruption, the illegal transfer of deposits abroad—estimated at about $70 billion between 1995 and 1996—and the unemployment rate of 12 percent. The massive demonstrations forced Zhan Videnov's post-Communist government to resign. In the elections that followed on April 20, 1997, the Union of Democratic Forces (UDF) won 52 percent of the votes, while the ex-Communists could gather only 22 percent. The post-Communist government had driven its country to economic ruin, just as its communist stepfathers had done in the days of real socialism, when the apparatchiks subscribed to the motto "Bulgaria and the Soviet Union should make up a single organism with a shared circulatory system."

Though the post-Communist successor regime started a transition to democracy and a market economy, its leaders also grabbed the best parts of the state's meager fortune for themselves. They took over the most lucrative businesses in the country and deposited export profits abroad. Thus the post-Communists left behind a terrible economic legacy: in 1998, the country's GDP was only 78 percent and the industrial production 50 percent of 1984 levels.[13] Ivan Kostov's democratic government did not have an easy time bringing order to Bulgaria's chaotic economy. But Kostov did what he could to stop corrupt firms and help revive sluggish reforms. Inflation was reduced to a tolerable level, reserve deposits reached a once unthinkable level of $2.6 billion, and privatization accelerated. The head of the World Bank's department for Bulgaria and Romania has described Bulgaria as a credible place for investment; in fact, it could jump from last place to the head of the region in regard to credit worthiness. Bulgaria is an associate EU member, striving to join the EU, but it still belongs to the second wave of admission candidates.

Romania's political and economic situation is significantly worse. In the ranking by the *Wall Street Journal*, Romania received 5.7 out of 10 possible points, landing it in nineteenth place out of twenty-six. Romania had been unable to free itself from the ex-Communists, led by former apparatchik Ion Iliescu, until liberal politician Emil Constantinescu was elected president. But the economic situation did not improve. The most optimistic moment occurred when the minister of finance, Daniel Daianu, announced a successful reduction of inflation rates at the eighteenth Munich talks on Eastern Europe. And it was a truly significant drop: from 130 percent in 1997 down to 30 percent in 1998. But in 1999 inflation again increased at a monthly rate of 5 percent, and the leu has lost 50 percent of its value against the U.S. dollar since the end of 1998. The IMF froze a planned credit transfer of $475 million in July 1999, and the unemployment rate was hovering between 10 and 12 percent. The minister of finance said, quite accurately, in Munich: "Romania has a long way ahead of it before reaching a significantly better situation." He pointed to two major difficulties: the fragile banking system and the enormous number of unprofitable businesses. Yet the government refuses to shut these businesses down since that would only further increase the unemployment rate. Romania, like Bulgaria, belongs to the second wave of admissions to the EU.

The Costs of Admission to the EU

The German Institute for Economic Research in Halle (IWH) estimated that the second wave of admissions to the EU would be more costly than the first wave, planned for 2006, when Poland, the Czech Republic, Hungary, Slovenia, and Estonia will join the EU. It has been estimated that the first five applicants will require between 4.5 and 6.5 billion Euros annually; the admission of Romania, Bulgaria, Slovakia, Latvia, and Lithuania would require up to 26 billion Euros a year. EU officials are even more cautious. The chief economist of the ECB, Otmar Issing, announced on September 20, 1999, that expansion to as many as thirty states "in the perhaps not too distant future" could overly increase the heterogeneity of the EU. It could thus threaten to transform the earlier goal of a political union into an illusion. Issing warned of the dangers of moving too fast and of developing a "social union" in Europe. In his opinion, attempting to change the original idea of the EMU as a "Europe of money and finance" will lead the EU in the wrong direction. Issing's advice: instead of harmonizing social standards at the highest level possible and establishing Europe-wide unified salary agreements, the EU should set salaries that "take the differences in productivity and the labor situation into account."[14]

The European Economic Community was established with the intention of integrating the entire continent. The collapse of the Soviet Union made this vision a real possibility. But no East European state has become an EU member yet. These countries' histories and economic structures are so different, the discrepancies in productivity (especially in agriculture) so enormous, that integrating them into the highly advanced European community would endanger the fundamental objectives of the EU. Until now, every expansion of the EU has been accompanied by an increase in cooperation among the member states. The number of members increased from six to twelve, and then to fifteen. The steel and coal community developed into a West European domestic market without customs or transfer borders for capital and labor, and then later into a currency union. Even when economically underdeveloped countries like Greece and Portugal became members, the community's profile did not change, and progress continued. But the countries now preparing to join the EU have 100 million inhabitants and a level of productivity two-thirds lower than the EU average. Every new member, without exception, will require subsidies, especially to finance the hopelessly backward agricultural sectors. In just a few years, the admission criteria set at the Copenhagen summit—institutional stability as "a guarantee for democratic order and the rule of law, the protection of human rights"; the establishment of "a functioning market economy" capable of holding its own under the "competitive pressures of market forces"—will be obsolete. A lengthy period of adaptation is necessary to at least partially reduce the discrepancies in productivity, thus increasing competitiveness, and to narrow the huge gap in income structures, which would thereby ease the flow of migrant laborers from the East. According to Eurostat, labor costs in Poland for the production of goods were 16.6 percent of the Austrian level; the Czech Republic's labor costs amounted to 14.3 percent of the Austrian level; Slovakia's 13.9 percent; Hungary's 13.7 percent; Romania's 6.5 percent; and Bulgaria's 5.5 percent (figures for 1998). In the "richest" reform country, Slovenia, labor costs were 32 percent of the Austrian level.[15]

Table 7.2 shows an international comparison of labor costs for the production of goods in 1998 (using the Austrian schilling as a basis). Germany is at the top. Its labor costs are about 27.2 percent higher than Austria's; it is followed by Switzerland, with 21.4 percent higher labor costs. In the United States, labor costs are 9.9 percent lower than in Austria; in France, they are 10.1 percent lower, and in Italy, 14.2 percent lower.

To significantly reduce the migration of Eastern workers, economic structures in the East must be modernized and made more European; salaries must be increased. The expected five-to-seven-year period for negotiations between the applicants and EU officials will not be long enough. Even if they had three times as long, it would not be enough time to eliminate the problems plaguing EU expansion. The EU has recognized that expansion is not financially feasible under the current subsidy system. Its 2000 agenda calls for fundamental reforms in agricultural and budget policies and institutions; these reforms are the necessary precondition for expansion to the East. The EU warns that watering down the union to its lowest common denominator, instead of deepening relations among the fifteen member states and the applicants, would be of no use to anyone. There is another alternative: the introduction of longer adaptation periods, in which the migration of cheap labor and the purchase of land would be delayed. But this would treat the newcomers like impoverished stepchildren, something they would surely not accept. There are no shortcut solutions for complicated long-term problems. No matter how desirable a speedy economic and political integration of Europe may be, at least from a political point of view, it seems clear that this will not be possible without removing the considerable remains of the Soviet Union's Asiatic mode of production. Moreover, the colossal military–industrial complex, which was created to satisfy the needs of the Soviet superpower, must be dismantled. The establishment of a modern (European) humane capitalism is necessary for the expanded EU—otherwise heterogeneity within the EU will increase, considerably weakening its ability to function.

A further solution comes to mind: the preparation of long-term credit through international finance and credit institutions like the World Bank or the London-based European Bank for Reconstruction and Development, which could help these countries build growth-friendly, export-oriented, and competitive economies. The preconditions for the establishment of a civil society would thus be created, allowing the EU to welcome the applicants as equal partners. The EU commissioner responsible for expansion, Günter Verheugen, said during a visit to Slovenia

Table 7.2

International Comparison of Labor Costs for the Production of Goods, 1998 (Austria = 100%)

Germany	127.2
Switzerland	121.4
Denmark	116.7
Norway	114.7
Belgium	112.8
Sweden	107.0
Finland	107.0
Netherlands	102.0
Austria	100.0
EU	96.5
United States	90.1
France	89.9
Italy	85.8
Japan	85.7
Great Britain	84.8
Australia[a]	77.9
Canada	76.1
Ireland	69.8
Spain	62.7
Israel[a]	58.6
New Zealand[a]	53.6
Greece	42.4
Singapore[a]	40.1
Korea[a]	35.1
Slovenia	32.0
Taiwan[a]	28.7
Hong Kong[a]	26.4
Portugal	25.1
Poland	16.6
Czech Republic	14.3
Slovakia	13.9
Hungary	13.7
Mexico[a]	8.5
Romania	6.5
Russia	5.7
Bulgaria	5.5
Sri Lanka[b]	2.1

Source: Eurostat, "*Der Standard*," September 22, 1999.
[a]1997.
[b]1996.

in July 2000 that the conclusion of negotiations for the first five EU applicants would not take place until 2003 at the earliest. Ratification would require a further two years. Thus the earliest probable date of admission will be January 1, 2005.

8

The Countries of the Former Soviet Union

Crisis-Ridden Russia and Its Ambitions to Be a World Power

Russia was a world power under both the tsars and the Communists. No military defeat could shake its position. Through its victory over Hitler's Germany, Soviet Russia was able to amass unprecedented power and establish an "outer ring" empire in Central and Eastern Europe and the Baltic states that challenged the world's greatest power, the United States, in the Cold War. While Boris Yeltsin, Russia's freely elected president, broke apart the Soviet Union in order to remove the last of the general secretaries, he had no intention of relinquishing Russia's position of international power. The Soviet Union's permanent seat in the UN Security Council, including its veto rights, was transferred to Russia with Western agreement. Yeltsin also intended to retain the imperial institutions: on December 8, 1991, he created the CIS in cooperation with the president of Ukraine, Leonid Kravchuk, and the president of Belarus, Stanislav Shushkevich. The former Soviet republics of Central Asia and Armenia joined the commonwealth on December 21, 1991.

Russia's foreign policy is not, as it was in the past, anti-Western, although a considerable part of its society is vehemently critical of the wealthy West. Everyone is aware that effective economic aid can come only from the "decadent" West, and the West *has* offered substantial amounts of aid. Apart from the $70 billion in credit inherited from the collapsed Soviet Union, the period of haplessly organized economic transformation required new credits, amounting to at least $150 billion. A large portion of that credit became stuck in Western banks as a result of illegal money transfers and money laundering. The creditors, especially the currency funds, lost control. Russia is like a bottomless barrel. Yet Russia, with its weapons arsenal, simply cannot be allowed to collapse. The need for money is growing, and the economy continues to decline. Economic productivity has dropped by 40 percent as a result of Russia's transformation to capitalism. No other reform country has experienced a catastrophe of this magnitude. Asked if Russia should still be viewed as the enemy, Richard Pipes says, "It is official: Russia no longer considers the Western democracies antagonists. The military doctrine that the government of the Russian Federation adopted in 1993 declares that Russia does not regard any state to be its adversary."[1] In fact, the West helps Russia, investing a great deal of capital and modern technology there, and it does not want to see the unique form of capitalism that it has helped establish fall. Mistrust is growing, and there is a danger that this broken-down state, which lacks a solid foundation and a real middle class, could collapse. The political establishment is more shaken by the crisis than the devastated economy. Relations are tense. The West suspiciously watches the superpower ambitions of this enormous, heavily armed, yet paralyzed and helpless country. But Russia feels that it has been snubbed in regard to some of the most important political decisions in recent years. The most recent examples are the expansion of NATO and the war in Kosovo. Although Russia openly expressed its opposition, the first three candidates for admission to NATO—Poland, the Czech Republic, and Hungary—joined on March 12, 1999. It was just one month prior to the NATO bombardment of Kosovo, which was also vehemently opposed by Russia. There were also Western opponents of NATO's expansion to the east. The most renowned expert on Russian affairs, George Kennan, expressed his opposition as follows: "I have never seen the evidence that the recent NATO enlargement was necessary or desirable. . . . I agree that NATO, as we now know it, has no intention of attacking Russia. But NATO remains, in concept and in much of its substance, a military alliance." Moreover, and even clearer: "If there is any country at all against which it is conceived as being directed, that is Russia."[2]

Russia's Western- and democracy-oriented politicians and intellectuals agree with Kennan, as well as with Strobe Talbott, former U.S. deputy secretary of state, who wrote, "Russia today is part of the world to an extent and in a way that it never was in the past. Counteracting the old temptations of autarky and regression are new and powerful forces pulling Russia outward and forward, toward integration, not just with the global market but also with the global network. . . . Russia is now plugged into the rest of the world through cellular telephones, fax machines, modems and PC's."[3] If other U.S. policymakers agree with the logical and well-founded arguments of Kennan and Talbott, then there is no reason to include former Warsaw Pact members in NATO—especially if the brunt of NATO's power, as Kennan claims, is directed toward Russia. Though NATO provided Russia with a seat in its security council, it proved of little value when NATO ordered the bombardment of the former Yugoslavia, Russia's Slavic ally, just a month after Russia accepted its seat. The bombardment went ahead without even taking Russian opposition into account. The seat in the NATO council was as meaningless as Russia's permanent seat in the UN Security Council since NATO never asked the United Nations for approval, a move that would have allowed Russia and China to use their veto rights.

Non-Russian Republics of the Former Soviet Union

Russia's future is contingent on how it forms its state, which is made up of eighty-nine autonomous areas, many of which, like Chechnya, Tatarstan, Ingushetia, Kalmykia, North Ossetia-Alania, and Moldova, do not have much in common with Russia's culture, religion, or language. The development of relations between Russia and its "near neighbors," the former Soviet republics, within the CIS framework will also play an important role. Yevgeny Primakov, who was a former presidential candidate and also served a short term as prime minister, proclaimed to the Duma upon entering office that his main priority was Russia's territorial integrity. This was after the first, unsuccessful war against Chechnya. Shortly thereafter, the war flamed up again with renewed vigor. Airports and various objects, mostly civilian, were ruthlessly bombarded. For a time, it was feared that the military conflict could spread to the entire northern Caucasus, which would have had disastrous results for the entire country. The generally held belief that Yeltsin had used the conflict to expand his power proved unfounded. In fact, in hindsight, the war in Chechnya actually served as the mechanism for the rise to power of a new strongman, Vladimir Putin. Yeltsin could certainly fire a prime minister in order to install a new one, which he often did, but he could hardly restrict the powers of the state governors. Four of them, including the governor of oil-rich Tatarstan, declared in their constitutions that the laws of their states take precedence over those of the federal government. The majority of governors wanted to extend the autonomy they had enjoyed in the Yeltsin era. But this began to lead to an erosion of central power, especially in the form of a drop in the tax base, which Putin was intent on fighting. The hapless architect of the new market economy and democratic Russia, Boris Yeltsin, intended to realize his dream of a renaissance of imperial proportions with the help of the CIS. This would bring back the former Soviet republics to the Russian fold. But the republics, finally free of Soviet control, had no intention of returning to anybody's umbrella rule. They instead made contacts with the outer world in order to secure their independence. Though several did seek Russia's assistance, like Armenia in its conflict with Azerbaijan over Nagorno–Karabakh, they had no intention of subjecting themselves to Russian control. The authority of the former superpower had dwindled so much as a result of mismanagement, corruption, and the power of the Mafia that it would have been pointless.

It seems doubtful that Putin will be able to alter this situation. The harsh memory of the colonial rule of the Soviet empire, which broke apart as a result of its overexpansion, is still too fresh for the former republics. The Soviet Union was an involuntary assemblage of countries with extraordinarily different traditions, cultures, and religions, which were heavily restricted by Russian colonial power. No state wanted to voluntarily join the Soviet Union. The vast majority, like Ukraine or the Central Asian republics, fought bitter battles for their independence. Just as Soviet Russia, upon renaming itself the Soviet Union, refused to do without any piece of "holy Russian earth," Yeltsin intended to preserve Russia's imperial greatness by binding the former Soviet republics to the CIS. But Russia's methods of colonial rule, like Soviet Russia's, were infamous. Not a single member republic was allowed to develop its own economic profile with control mechanisms that corresponded to national traditions. None were able to develop a modern industrial state. Even Ukraine, the second strongest republic, blessed with raw materials and fuel, was forced to rely on agricultural exports to other republics. The third largest republic, Uzbekistan, was reduced to the status of a cotton colony, in which the farming culture ruined a land rich in minerals and lowered the standard of living to that of a developing country. The Soviets forced Kazakhstan, the fourth largest republic and the richest in oil resources, to spend exorbitant amounts of money to transform desert into farmland. However, the costs for such a project were extreme and the benefits minimal. It would have been better for Kazakhstan to explore its rich oil resources, which is what the independent republic is now doing with the help of the American firm Chevron.

Every member republic was molded to participate in the Soviet superpower's monstrous military–industrial complex, which made up more than 70 percent of the Soviet GDP. This took place, of course, at the cost of the people's needs. Russia's predominance was overwhelming: It had 52 percent of the entire population, 84.6 percent of total exports, 68.4 percent of the electricity demand, 89.7 percent of oil requirements, and 85.4 percent of the gas needs of the country. Ukraine had 18.2 percent of the population, 7.4 percent of the exports, 14.3 percent of the electricity demand, 1.1 percent of oil requirements, and 2.3 percent of the natural gas needs. Uzbekistan had 7.9 percent of the population, 1.7 percent of the exports, 3.7 percent of the electricity demand, 1.6 percent of oil requirements, and 6.6 percent of the natural gas needs. The republic in the union with the largest oil and gas deposits, Turkmenistan, needed a mere 1.2 percent of the crude oil and 5.0 percent natural gas. According to fuel experts, Turkmenistan could become as wealthy as Kuwait in the foreseeable future.

Immediately after the establishment of the CIS, unforeseen difficulties emerged. At first the Commonwealth included only Slavic states, but several days later the rest of the republics joined, with the exception of the Baltic states. Ukraine was cofounder of the commonwealth. However, it later became the center of opposition to any long-term integration plans, primarily as a result of pressure from the ultranationalist Ruch movement in the western part of the republic. Memories of old Soviet colonial practices were still too fresh to allow even the tiniest relinquishment of sovereignty. Although Ukraine ratified its commonwealth status, it insisted upon twelve special conditions. The main points of controversy surrounded the establishment of a common currency and a unified defense and foreign policy, the lack of which would reduce the commonwealth to an institution without any effective functions. Ukraine, as well as other commonwealth members, resisted the proposed common defense policy, afraid that a unified Russian army would help make it possible for Russia to revive its imperial strength. Russia would be allowed to conclude agreements with each republic concerning the defense of the outer borders, but the option of unified military leadership was rejected in June 1993. Ukraine was the first CIS country to found its own national army, among other reasons because of Russia's unyielding position on the Crimean Peninsula. Nikita Khrushchev gave the peninsula to Ukraine in 1954, on the three hundredth anniversary of the Ukrainian–Russian union, which had started with the treaty of Pereyaslav in 1654. Other important conflicts centered on the Black Sea fleet and the rights of 11 million ethnic Russians living in Ukraine.

Ukraine was the first CIS country to establish its own national currency, the grivna, primarily because of the continuing devaluation of the ruble. The attempt to create cooperative institutions and pass a new charter evoked major resistance from Ukraine. Paul Kubicek writes, "We don't want to have any supra-state structure playing the role of a drill sergeant who would give orders to the Commonwealth countries."[4] Ukraine puts increasing importance on the improvement of relations with the West. In 1997 it acquired $3.5 billion in IMF credit and became the third largest recipient of U.S. aid after Israel and Egypt. Although it concluded an agreement of friendship, cooperation, and partnership with Russia in May 1997, Ukraine also joined NATO's Partnership for Peace program. It welcomed NATO expansion and has even considered joining the organization if conditions permit. But since Ukraine formed a union with other CIS dissidents, the "GUAM group" (Georgia, Ukraine, Azerbaijan, Moldova in October 1997), relations with the CIS have worsened. The GUAM group wants to build oil and gas pipelines outside of Russian territory, as well as to construct refineries and harbors without Russian participation. Ukraine is increasingly being viewed as an outsider or mere CIS observer. Yet it is more dependent upon Russia and other CIS members than any other republic of the former Soviet Union. While it imports 80 percent of its oil and gas from Russia, 57 percent of its exports and 55 percent of its imports either go to or come from CIS states. The demand for Ukrainian export goods like coal, pig iron, and steel is rather low, though the demand for grain is considerable. The former granary of Europe is itself forced to import grain as a result of outdated farming methods. The young, independent republic is unable to pay its debts to Russia. Gazprom, which supplied around $4 billion worth of credit, making it the country's largest creditor, demanded a 35–50 percent share in some of the larger Ukrainian companies in order to at least partially recover some of the debt. In the end, it agreed to change the terms of the debt to $3 billion.

The Ukrainian economy continues to decline; the production of consumer goods fell 19 percent in 1997. The transformation to a market economy is progressing at a snail's pace. Of the eight thousand state businesses to be privatized, only 10–15 percent have been denationalized. Only a few companies have the necessary capital. And the government is not prepared to introduce voucher privatization, which would result in the concentration of state property in the hands of robber barons, as happened in Russia. Foreign investors have no interest in this European poorhouse: between 1992 and 1997 no more than $2.7 billion of foreign investment flowed into Ukraine, a negligible amount when one considers what is needed to modernize the country's hopelessly outdated technology. And corruption is growing. Former prime minister Pavlo Lazarenko spoke at a World Bank investors' conference about the inadequacy of the country's managerial class. Now even he is under arrest in the United States on suspicion of cheating and money laundering. In the *Wall Street Journal* evaluation discussed in chapter 7, Ukraine was given 3.9 out of 10 possible points and ranked the last of among the twenty-six reform countries of Central and Eastern Europe and Central Asia. Naturally, Ukraine could achieve more by cooperating more closely with the CIS, but the fear of Russian hegemony is so great that it is prepared to avoid this at any cost.

Relations between the third Slavic cofounder of the CIS, Belarus, and both Russia and the commonwealth developed quite differently after the election of Belarus's former kolkhoz leader Aleksandr Lukashenko on October 7, 1994. Lukashenko replaced the first democratically elected president, Stanislav Shushkevich, who was a member of the Academy of Sciences and had signed the CIS agreement on December 8, 1991. The economic situation was extremely precarious. In 1993, the inflation rate reached 1,290 percent; in 1994, it increased to 2,220 percent. It was only in 1995 that Belarus could push inflation down to 1,000 percent. Real control was not possible until 1998, when inflation was reduced to 57 percent. Economic decline seemed unavoidable.

Belarus had a closer connection to the Soviet economy than any other republic. And this was one of the main reasons for its acute transition crisis. Whereas Belarus exported 69.6 percent of its national product to other Soviet republics, only 8 percent went to foreign countries. The *Wall Street Journal* ranked Belarus twenty-fourth among the reform countries, giving it 2.6 out of 10 possible points. As Belarussian dependency on Russia grew, fuel debt rose to $740 million. Former president Shushkevich's reforms were practically canceled by a parliament decision on January 25, 1993 in which 53 percent of the price of consumer goods was made subject to state control. In light of the increasingly difficult economic situation, Lukashenko saw no other choice but to initiate a union with Russia. He undertook a "pilgrimage" to Moscow in September 1995 to speak with then prime minister Viktor Chernomyrdin. The talks began with the suggestion of establishing a customs union and ended with the desire to form a federation with Russia as quickly as possible. The first step toward a union was the creation of a common army. Russia's head of government was surprised, suggesting that the Belarussian president travel to Sochi, where the Russian president was on vacation, to meet with Yeltsin and discuss the issue. Yeltsin then suggested that Lukashenko travel to Kiev to discuss the December 8, 1991 Slavic commonwealth and its possible reactivation with Ukraine. The Ukrainian leader did not want to hear any more about a possible union or commonwealth. And even Russia seemed unenthusiastic about a possible fusion with the two economically troubled states. Moreover, there was fear that a union of this nature could exert an unwanted influence on other CIS members. But Lukashenko was untiring in his pursuit. In the end he was able to convince influential Russian politicians, especially those in the Duma's Communist faction, of the validity of his cause. The Duma, dominated by Communists and nationalists, passed a bill in 1996 that proclaimed the dissolution of the Soviet Union illegal. It thereby made it possible to politically reactivate the union in the future. On September 27, 1999, the time had come. On that day, Yeltsin approved the draft of a treaty for the possible union of Russia and Belarus. He then ordered Vladimir Putin, then head of government, to initiate a public discussion of the draft treaty. It bears mentioning that the shape of the union sketched in 1999 foresaw no serious restrictions in the authority of either government. Among other things, Yeltsin's draft treaty called for the creation of a future common economic area in which a common currency and budget would be introduced. By 2005, a common money issuing policy was to be introduced.[5] However, Putin announced after these efforts that a possible union of the two states could be decided only by referendum.

The Central Asian Republics Want Closer Contacts with Foreign Powers

The republics of Central Asia joined the CIS thirteen days after its establishment. The republics had feared that they would be left out of the progressive cooperative pact. However, they have since become convinced that neither the former superpower nor the newly founded substitute union has much to offer them. Instead, they have established closer political and economic contacts with each other and with neighboring states—especially Islamic countries such as Turkey and Iran. But their economic situation is precarious; until 1995 the rate of economic development was stuck in the negative numbers. The worst hit was Kazakhstan, though it also possesses the richest raw materials and fuel resources. It showed negative growth rates of –13 percent, –12.9 percent, –25.5 percent, and –8.9 percent from 1992 to 1995. Turkmenistan, with its rich raw materials resources, followed Kazakhstan with a GDP that declined no less than 35.7 percent in 1992, the first year of reforms. Although the situation improved to –10 percent in 1993, productivity fell to –18 percent in the following year, and by 1995 economic growth was still in the negative figures at –7.5 percent. Tajikistan, shaken by civil war, also suffered negative rates of economic growth between 1992 and 1995: –30.1 percent, –17.3 percent, –12.7 percent, and –12.6 percent. Kyrgyzstan's economy, with growth rates over the same period of –13.9 percent, –15.5 percent, –20.1 percent, and –6.2 percent, did not fare much better. The situation in Uzbekistan was somewhat better, though it still chalked up rates of –11.1 percent, –2.4 percent, –3.5 percent, and –1 percent.[6] All the Central Asian countries first achieved positive economic growth in 1998: Kazakhstan at 3.7 percent, Kyrgyzstan 4.9 percent, Tajikistan 1.6 percent, Turkmenistan 0.6 percent, and Uzbekistan 4.3 percent (estimates). Turkmenistan, with the most fuel resources in the region, earned only 2.5 out of 10 possible points, putting it twenty-fifth in the *Wall Street Journal*'s ranking. Tajikistan, which earned just 2.2 points, came in last.

Kazakhstan, with its per capita GDP of $3,510, is the richest republic in Central Asia; Turkmenistan follows at $3,330, Kyrgyzstan at $2,440, and Uzbekistan at $2,430. The poorest republic is Tajikistan, which has a per capita GDP of $1,100. The republic with the largest population is Uzbekistan, with 22.6 million inhabitants. Kazakhstan follows with a population of 17.3 million. Whereas Turkmenistan, with an area of 448,000 square kilometers (a territory the size of France) has only 4 million inhabitants, Kyrgyzstan has a population of 4.7 million and Tajikistan 6.4 million.

Confidence in Russia's true intentions plummeted as the former superpower increased pressure on the heavily indebted republics through sanctions in the form of halted oil and gas deliveries. The first victim was Kazakhstan, whose president, Nursultan Nazarbayev, had been the most active proponent of the reintegration of the former Soviet republics under the umbrella rule of the CIS. As the debt for oil and gas soared to almost $1 billion, Russia threatened to interrupt further deliveries and demanded wide concessions in oil and gas production and their transportation abroad. Nazarbayev gave in and approved Russian participation in the stock capital from oil and gas fields. He also promised to protect the Russian minority inhabiting the north of his country.

The Kazakh president did not entrust oil development to the Russians, however, but rather to the U.S. concern Chevron. Nazarbayev signed the joint venture agreement of the century with the U.S. oil giant in April 1993. Tengizchevroil will explore the giant Tengiz fields, in which an estimated 6 billion barrels of oil lie. Within six years, the output is expected to reach 35 million tons. The total production of oil at the beginning of the 1990s amounted to no more than 27 million tons, of which 10 million were exported abroad. Chevron will invest $10 billion and receive a 19.6 percent share of the stock capital. But development has been delayed as a result of disagreements surrounding the construction of the oil pipeline. Russia insists upon participation and is capable of exerting pressure to achieve this goal. On April 21, 1996, an agreement was signed among Russia, Kazakhstan, and Oman concerning the construction of a pipeline that would connect the Tengiz fields with the Russian port of Novosibirsk. Russia's share, which also includes the shares of Russian oil firms Lukoil and Rosneft, should amount to 44 percent. Nazarbayev demonstrated his desire to further support the integration of the CIS states; in mid-1996 he signed an agreement on the establishment of a customs union among Kazakhstan, Kyrgyzstan, Russia, and Belarus. Efforts to include Ukraine in this union failed. Details concerning the modus operandi of this long-term project were drawn up in an additional agreement in January 1998. But in the first half of 1997, the exports of CIS states to Russia decreased by 14 percent, and imports from Russia declined by 5 percent. In contrast, foreign imports increased by 16.8 percent in 1996 and 18 percent in the first half of 1997, and exports increased by 35.2 percent and 16.2 percent.[7] Yet Kazakhstan's economic situation has not improved. The development of the oil fields has been postponed, and the financial situation has worsened. Kazakhstan was forced to request as much as $400 million in IMF credits at the beginning of October 1999 to replenish its scarce foreign currency reserves. Nurlan Balgimbayev, Kazakhstan's prime minister, resigned under the pressure of the continuing economic crisis in early October 1999. The foreign minister was made acting head of government.

Russia has also attempted to pressure Turkmenistan, which has its own oil and gas resources. "Russia," writes Martha Brill Olcott, "demands participation in all energy resources on the Caspian Sea, and demands that all gas and oil pipelines be routed through Russian territory in order to enable it to share in the output."[8] Russia blocked the only gas pipeline running through its territory from Turkmenistan to the West in an attempt to increase its own gas exports. In 1996, Turkmenistan's pipeline construction was cut back to one-fourth of its 1989 level. Thus the republic with the richest gas resources in the region has been reduced to the poorest member of the CIS. However, a possible solution has been found to this seemingly hopeless situation. Unocal, a Los Angeles-based oil and gas company, and Delta Oil of Saudi Arabia have agreed to build a 1,400–kilometer-long gas pipeline via Afghanistan. But Russia's Gazprom, which has a 46 percent share of the joint venture with Turkmenistan, has refused to approve the already negotiated pipeline construction. Russian resistance also put an end to Iran's suggestion of a gas pipeline that would transport 27 billion cubic meters of gas via Turkey and Iran to Western Europe. Russia simply insists on being a part of every transport pipeline. Nevertheless, several republics have succeeded in avoiding Moscow's grip. Azerbaijan and Georgia have built an oil pipeline from Baku to Suspa that bypasses Russian territory. Opened at the end of 1998, it is the first part of a larger pipeline that would transfer oil and gas deposits in Kazakhstan and Turkmenistan via underwater routes to the Turkish Mediterranean coast.

Russia's demand to participate in the transport of oil and gas in other CIS member states has met heavy resistance from the countries involved. The greatest challenge and the most vigorous resistance to Russian hegemony come from the GUAM group. These countries along the Caspian and Black Sea coasts have adamantly expressed their desire to develop their deposits without Russian intervention. According to Paul Kubicek, these states "are all drawing up a Western-leaning security agenda, pushing for more involvement in the region by NATO and the Organization for Security and Cooperation in Europe at the clear expense of Russia."[9] Russia has good reason to fear that Kazakhstan and Uzbekistan will join NATO since this would further decrease Russia's already dwindling influence on CIS activities.

The CIS was established without really clarifying its competencies or providing for an effective executive that could turn the organization's decisions into action. The practice of allowing interested member states to take part in a planned project was carried over from the dissolved CMEA, the former economic community of the Eastern bloc. The CMEA had a powerful executive that had been shaped by the Soviet Union. The division of tasks among the member states was planned in great detail, and it functioned efficiently because each member state had agreed to specialize in a particular economic branch. For instance, Czechoslovakia specialized in mechanical engineering, the Soviet Union in raw materials and fuel resources, Poland in coal and chemical production, and so forth. In this way, mutual foreign trade was planned and primarily conducted among the Eastern bloc countries. In the end, there was little left over for trade with countries outside the bloc. Poland and Hungary were exceptions to this rule; they had developed active credit and economic relations with Western Europe and other developing countries in the final years before the dissolution of the Eastern bloc.

Eastern trade was fundamentally based on the exchange of Soviet raw materials and fuel resources for the finished products of the satellite states. The Soviet functionaries in the CMEA liked to describe themselves as the representatives of the Eastern bloc's raw materials colony. Delivery costs were much lower than in the West, even up to the collapse of the Soviet Union. But the USSR often complained that while the quality of its raw materials met all generally accepted criteria, the goods it received from its trading partners were of such low quality that they would not interest a buyer on the world market. Yet the Soviet empire had created this situation by forcing a planned economic system upon its satellite states. It was responsible for the introduction of dysfunctional mechanisms like nonexchangeable money, a uniform price bases that was unexposed to international competition, and the like.

The Soviet superpower could achieve its economic aims neither in the CMEA (which it fully controlled), nor with its ominous doctrine of "restricted sovereignty" in the GDR (1953), Hungary (1956), and Czechoslovakia (1968). In its present state, Russia, which is economically and politically devastated (productivity has declined by 40 percent), will hardly be able to make any significant economic advances within the CIS. Russia may still deliver oil and gas to its "near neighbors" but at world market prices and for U.S. dollars, as is routine in the international oil trade. Though Russia may overlook the CIS members' debts now and then, it will always find an adequate means of recouping those debts—usually by coercing states into allowing the Russians to participate in the development, extraction, and transport of newly discovered oil or gas. But the republics that gained their freedom in 1991 will not allow Russia to restrict their sovereignty.

The Central Asian republics have returned in the meantime to a seemingly feudal political structure. The former party general secretaries have been elected presidents, and they have made useful contacts with capitalists abroad, from which they will acquire advanced technology and credit under good conditions. They have been able to exploit the similarities between Islam and Soviet communism to their benefit and the benefit of clan members. In the meantime, they have further expanded their personality cults among the population and now look down from on high upon Russia's impoverished and powerless functionaries. The republics will not allow any unacceptable CIS regulations to be forced upon them. On November 22, 1995, the *New York Times* ran an article about the governing style of Turkmenistan's president, Saparmurad Niyazov ("Ex-Communist Rules Turkmenistan Like a Sultan"). His people call him "Turkenbashi"—the leader of the Turkmens—and in order to extol the president's glory, a French consortium was given the task of building a palace in the center of the capital. The cost—$100 million—would not have seemed too extreme if one did not take into account that the president's fellow citizens earn just $40 a month. Although his colleagues in the other republics are perhaps more modest, their rule is hardly less authoritarian. Turkmenistan's president claims that his people are not ready for "a civilized, pluralistic system." Islam Karimov, the ex-general secretary and current president of the region's most populous republic, Uzbekistan, shares this opinion and has eliminated any organized opposition. Reforms that were started at the beginning of the transition to a market economy will not be completed. The majority of businesses are still in the hands of the state; the former "red directors" have bought the most lucrative companies for a price much lower than their actual value; and Kyrgyzstan and Tajikistan have become the center of Asia's drug trade.

The outlook for an effective integration of the Central Asian republics into the CIS is not positive. Russia is too weak to control them, and its resources are too limited to offer any constructive aid. Russia's functionaries also recognize that an integration of such dissimilar participants will do little to help Russia recapture its former imperial greatness. But the smaller countries' hopes for effective economic aid are dwindling. The majority of CIS decisions are not put into effect due to the disinterest of its members, who are increasingly escaping common decisions by calling upon the fixed rule that allows each state to refuse to participate in a venture if it does not interest it.

Any important measures are introduced through bilateral and multilateral agreements among interested CIS members. Proposals on general integration are understood to be empty declarations. There is no authoritative executive body to ensure the fulfillment of such declarations. The January 1993 Minsk summit was called with the intention of bringing order to CIS activities. A charter was to be passed similar to the organizational documents of the European Economic Community (EEC). But from the beginning, Ukraine refused to discuss the draft charter. President Niyazov of Turkmenistan pointed out that the document did not clearly express its intentions, nor did it adequately explain the duties of the members—so he refused to sign. Belarus and Uzbekistan also voiced their reservations. The agreement, already watered down, also foresaw the coordination of domestic and foreign policy. The fulfillment of this point, however, was impossible from the start since another point of the agreement explicitly prohibited member states from intervening in the internal affairs of other members. Not much remains of this highly praised integration document.

The agreement on the creation of an economic union in September 1993, which was to lead to the establishment of a common market, and the declaration of a "free trade zone" in April 1994 hardly advanced the CIS cause. But in October 1994 an international economic committee was created and hailed as a breakthrough. The committee was to act as the first supranational CIS organ, and it was conceived as the CIS equivalent of the EEC. But the actual economic policy of each CIS member stood in crass contradiction to the common decisions made by the CIS. The proposed payments union was never initiated, and the idea of a "ruble zone" fell by the wayside. The CIS members put their own national currencies into circulation and distanced themselves from the idea of a common currency policy. The member states increasingly drifted apart, foreign trade among them declined, and talk of an economic union was forgotten.

A December 8, 1996, proposal of the architects of the Slavic CIS for a common defense policy was condemned to failure. Above all, Ukraine, which had played a significant role in creating the CIS, vehemently opposed the establishment of a common army. The escalating conflict surrounding the Crimean Peninsula and the division of the Black Sea fleet were the main reasons for this opposition. But the other member states also realized that they had more to fear from Russia's power ambitions than from any foreign enemy. Meanwhile, under pressure from the United States, Kazakhstan and Ukraine transported their missile arsenals to Russia. The smaller states recognized that the creation of a common command with a large army, which would have twenty thousand nuclear missiles at its disposal (among them six thousand long-range missiles), would be useless to the smaller states and would serve only Russia's interests.

An agreement on stationing peacekeeping troops in areas troubled by armed conflict has a better chance of realization. Ten member states signed an agreement on collective units in March 1992. Such troops, which only Russia could assemble, were created outside of the CIS's jurisdiction. But in contrast to international regulations, in which the troops were to be neutral and approved by both conflicting parties after the end of an armed conflict, Russia supported one of the conflicting parties in each case, thereby strengthening its power position. This abuse of power can be seen most clearly in the conflict over Nagorno-Karabakh. The president of Azerbaijan, Abulfaz Elchibey, was toppled with the help of Moscow since he refused to accept Moscow's suggested solution to the conflict with Armenia over Nagorno-Karabakh, an area annexed by Azerbaijan but mainly populated by Armenians. Elchibey had withdrawn his country from the CIS pact in October 1992 and sought the assistance of Turkey in the conflict. The unruly president was replaced with a former Politburo member and Soviet KGB official, Geydar Aliyev, who had already declared his intention to return Azerbaijan to the CIS. Aliyev took on an appeasing tone concerning the conflict in Nagorno-Karabakh, and he further promised to halt all talks with Western firms about the development of oil resources.

The president of Georgia, the former Soviet foreign minister Eduard Shevardnadze, also opposed joining the CIS for a long time. Russia broke his resistance in another way. The country was entangled in a bloody civil war with the troops of former president Zviad Gamsakhurdia, and in July 1993 the Georgian republic of Abkhazia seceded. In order to avoid an imminent military disaster, Shevardnadze turned to Russia for help. His request for aid was approved, and the Abhkazian rebels were butchered. But Georgia was forced to make certain concessions in regard to the Black Sea, and it was required to join the CIS. Russian peacekeeping troops have also pursued their own interests by supporting one of the warring parties in conflicts in Moldova, South Ossetia, and Tajikistan. It bears mentioning that the civil war in Tajikistan continues with undiminished brutality. "In Tajikistan a normal life is not possible. The government is Mafia-like and criminal," says Shodmon Yusuf, former head of the Democratic Party, which is currently operating underground.[10] The country is bankrupt; the civil war, planned in Moscow, has cost it $7 billion in damages, and this in a country with an annual budget of $110 million. The majority of Tajikistan's 6 million inhabitants, Yusuf claims, no longer have any hope for the future, and 80 percent live below the poverty line.

Western influence is spreading in the former Soviet republics. The Organization for Security and Cooperation in Europe (OSCE) disavowed the "Pax Russia" in Nagorno-Karabakh and ordered its observers out of the region in 1994. The United States is also making efforts to find a political solution to this extraordinarily difficult problem. Shevardnadze, very troubled by the stationing of Russian "peace troops" in Azerbaijan, has begun to look to the West and to rethink his decision at the beginning of the conflict to join the CIS.[11] The announcement of Georgia's membership in the WTO is a step in the direction of closer cooperation with the West. The WTO approved Georgia's membership at its Geneva meeting on October 7, 1999, and on May 15, 2000, Georgia became its 137th member.

Though it may sound too strange to be true, even Azerbaijan's president Geydar Aliyev, who rose to power with Moscow's help, is deeply disappointed by Russian imperial ambitions. He thoroughly surprised Russia by announcing in mid-1999 that he intended to join NATO, while at the same time seeking U.S. aid in the development of the enormous oil resources on the Caspian coast. Several Central Asian republics had intensified foreign cooperation and raked in the money prior to the collapse of the Soviet empire. Even in his role as Turkmenistan's party general secretary, Saparmurad Niyazov signed new bilateral trade and cooperation agreements with Iran in mid-1989. In the beginning phase of the fall of the Soviet Union, Niyazov ordered the profits from oil and gas exports (10 percent of total Soviet exports) to be deposited in U.S. banks. The Central Asian members of the CIS consider the intensification of international cooperation outside the commonwealth increasingly important. With this objective in mind, the Central Asian Union (CAU) was formed, with Kazakhstan, Kyrgyzstan, Tajikistan, and Uzbekistan as members. This union has accomplished tasks in a short period that stand in stark contrast to the increasingly inefficient CIS. Moscow's strategists are also following the activities of GUAM with growing concern. GUAM's activities are particularly dangerous for Russia since it is GUAM's proclaimed intention to develop oil resources and pipelines without Russian participation and to strengthen the influence of NATO and the OSCE in the region, naturally at the expense of Russian power. The five Central Asian states have also joined the Economic Organization for Cooperation, of which Iran, Pakistan, and Turkey are members. Russia's declaration that it was unwilling to tolerate the intervention of Iran or Turkey in the internal affairs of the CIS fell upon deaf ears.

Centrifugal forces in the Central Asian republics are growing stronger, and Moscow's influence is diminishing rapidly. Russia simply has nothing left to offer. The country, rocked by crisis, refuses to give up its ambitions of imperial power in the region, though it no longer has the power to enforce them. The republics want to develop their oil resources with the help of wealthy Western firms, and they intend to build oil pipelines outside of Russian territory. The corrupt, inflexible Russian firms no longer inspire confidence, and the financial crisis of 1998 destroyed once and for all any remaining sliver of trust. Whereas cooperation with NATO, the IMF, the World Bank, and the EU brings fruitful results, cooperation with Russia brings only disappointment. Even Moscow recognizes the futility of membership in the CIS for the Central Asian republics. Its influence, which increasingly weakened as the Yeltsin era reached an end, can no longer motivate anyone. Although Russia will not give up its imperial methods of rule, it can no longer force its will upon the independent states. Putin will not move too quickly to alter this state of affairs. One no longer trusts Russia's corrupt, inflexible firms—whether private or state-owned. Even Moscow admits that the prospect of useful cooperation with the ex-republics of the Soviet Union seems bleak. Yet it is difficult for Russia to do without the appearance of solidarity with its former republics; it still believes in a possible renaissance of the totally destitute empire. The CIS crisis is but a pale copy of the crisis in Russia, which has lost nearly one-half of its economic power in the transition to a capitalistic social system. Never has Willy Brandt's description of the former Soviet Russia as an "Upper Volta with missiles" been more correct than in the case of Russia at the end of the twentieth century. The Central Asian republics no longer want to be Russian allies. They suffered greatly under the bankruptcy of the

Soviet Union, and they certainly do not want to help Russia's bankrupt politicians reconstruct their country's lost and unrecoverable imperial greatness. The Central Asian republics will increasingly cooperate among themselves and with neighboring Islamic countries like Iran or Turkey. They will not allow Russia to entangle them in an integrated community in which it plays the leading role. The CIS exists in name only. True, tiny, bankrupt Belarus is prepared to create a union with Russia, and the Ukraine is willing to bilaterally cooperate with Russia on economic affairs, but it will not accept a multilateral, integrated community, not only because of its terrible experience with the former Soviet Union, but also because of Russia's ineffective policy during its transformation into a market economy and modern democracy. In the end, Russia, Belarus, and Ukraine could join the Western community and help contribute to the union of the European continent. However, this could occur only if they establish themselves as democratic, civil societies; a goal they are currently far from achieving.

Prospects in the Post-Soviet Region

Russia's main worry is not so much cooperation within the CIS since the members no longer have common interests, and, despite their common past, cannot speak of a common future. Rather its main concern is guaranteeing the territorial unity of its eighty-nine autonomous territories. Many of them, like Chechnya, Tatarstan, Dagestan, and Yakutia, have nothing in common with Russia. Yevgeny Primakov is not alone in the opinion he expressed upon taking office as head of government (he was fired on May 12, 1999) concerning the difficulties of coexistence among the federal states. The governor of the Russian region of Krasnoyarsk, Aleksandr Lebed, said in a *Spiegel* interview, "I prove to the bandits that it isn't they who govern this land, but rather people like me." And further: "Soon the entire Northern Caucasus will be caught up in war."[12] The war against Chechnya, which appeared to have been settled in 1996, rages on with undiminished force. Obviously, it has not only served as a means to establish Putin's popularity as president, but also as a warning to other potentially separatist regions.

Russia has another equally difficult problem: the insurmountable transition crisis exacerbated by its financial collapse on August 17, 1998. This extreme crisis pervades the entire society. The state, which can no longer perform its functions, is stuck in an even more difficult situation.

At the end of Yeltsin's rule, chaos reigned in whole regions of civil life. There was official talk of the erosion of central power. One-half of the economy fled underground in order to avoid paying taxes. Profits were deposited abroad since businessmen, suspicious of the jungle of Russian law, did not dare invest money in their homeland. Russia's strategy for the transition from a planned economy to a market economy and from state property to private property resulted in a dramatic situation that one would normally encounter during conditions of war. Primakov argued with IMF representatives who refused to give the bankrupt state new credit. They refused to "throw good money at poorly managed countries," even though Russia "had followed their advice." Yet it is true that although President Yeltsin gathered together excellent advisers from the West, their advice was not always good. The local officials in charge of putting this advice into action were not any better. Indeed, it was the domestic advisers who were responsible for the choice of a reform strategy and for its fatal results: the successive erosion of central power, the threatening danger of territorial collapse, and decline of Russian authority in the Central Asian republics.

The first wave of reforms, price liberalization, was conducted with Poland as a model; the second wave, voucher privatization, was conducted with Czechoslovakia as a model. Yet the ancient Latin saying rang true: *Si duo faciunt idem non est idem* (When two do the same thing, the results are not exactly the same). Russia's social structures, political class, and traditions were totally different from those of its Central and East European neighbors, which had been forced by the bayonets of triumphant Soviet soldiers to accept a foreign, collectivist social system. The collective economic system was alien to these states, and it was fought with all possible means until it was finally swept away, be it by a ten-year-long resistance movement by 10 million Solidarity members in Poland or by the 1989 "Velvet Revolution" in Czechoslovakia.

In Russia the situation was different: collective property relations had a long tradition. The freeing of the serfs in 1863, a full hundred years later than in Western Europe, did not transfer land to the farmers as elsewhere, but rather to the *Obshchina*, or farming community. It was only under the Stolypin government in 1907 that the majority of farmable land was given to the farmers, but this lasted for only a short while. The Bolshevik October Revolution in 1917 gave all the land to the farmers, only to later force collectivization of farms into kolkhoz property in the 1930s—a policy that caused the deaths of millions. The deeply ingrained collectivist traditions were integrated by the farmers' sons—later the country's elite—into the state structures of real socialism, where they lasted for seven decades. "Private initiative" was first introduced as a part of General Secretary Mikhail S. Gorbachev's *perestroika* and *glasnost* reforms, which were never carried to their final conclusion. Instead, Gorbachev's reforms led to the infamous Tocqueville effect. Alexis de Tocqueville, the acute nineteenth century observer, claimed in his epochal work, *L'Ancien régime et la Révolution*, that the true threat to a government in crisis starts when that government begins to reform. Indeed, the reform of the fossilized, inefficient, uncompetitive social system was indispensable, but its realization was limited because of the lack of a clear vision for the future. Boris Yeltsin overthrew the hapless architect of *perestroika* and put his country on the thorny road to capitalism. The only true democracy in Russian history existed for a mere eight months between March and November 1917, after the overthrow of the tsar, before it made way for a totalitarian Bolshevik regime. And once again, the disaster began with the wrong path of transformation. Unlike in Eastern Europe, the collective mentality and bureaucratic methods of control were deeply ingrained in Russia. They had been a part of the country's history for a long time. The world famous philosopher Bertrand Russell recognized this during a trip to Russia in 1920. He came to the conclusion that despite the brutality of Bolshevik rule, the regime appeared adequate for the country. There was no other elite than the Communist elite and no other experience than the totalitarian Bolshevik regime, which had subjected the entirety of social activity to its merciless control. And it was this political class that was supposed to initiate the transition from unrealized socialism, which is unrealizable because of its utopian nature, to capitalism: feared yet longed for by many. "Many of those who had been responsible for the old order are now shaping the new one," writes Strobe Talbott.[13] And this would occur in a shock-like way, as in Poland: "Russia's problems were actually caused by reforms that were too slow and partial," writes Anders Åslund, a top Yeltsin adviser.[14]

The largest oil and gas concerns, automobile factories, and banks fell into the hands of a powerful oligarchy whose members had been small and large state and party functionaries and became multibillionaires. Occasionally, as noted, these robber barons have been compared to the money barons of the early days of American or German capitalism. However, this is inaccurate. Although the Rockefellers, Fords, Carnegies, and Krupps did not always use honest methods to acquire their fortunes, they were distinguished by their uncompromising competence in creating the foundations of a modern, highly productive industrial society. In contrast, the present captains of the Russian economy are true robber barons. They have taken hold of entire businesses, thanks to good relationships with the establishment, and failed to make them competitive. And just as they stole this enormous wealth through immoral, illegal means, so do they manage their wealth. They disavow any traditional ethical codes of business conduct; they evade taxes, deposit their profits in foreign banks, and opulently consume in order to show off their newly acquired wealth.

Strobe Talbott emphasizes the need to intensify Russia's investments and designate where these investments should be directed. "The Russian energy sector," Talbott says, "needs $15 billion a year in investment for each of the next seven or eight years just to get back to 1988 production levels."[15] Talbott compares the developments in Russia to a scene in Russian–Ukrainian author Nikolai Gogol's unforgettable work, *Dead Souls*: a three-horse carriage (troika) tears through the snow-covered steppes, while other nations observe, outraged, and ask themselves where this wild ride can lead. The ride is financed by enormous amounts from the IMF, the World Bank, the London East Bank, and others, without any knowledge of whether the money invested will ever be returned. It can be confidently said that as things in Russia now stand, no repayment should be expected. The prevalent argument—that one cannot allow this paralyzed giant, heavily armed with long-range missiles, to fall—no longer seems reasonable. Reform is demanded as a precondition, yet no one knows which reforms are necessary to bring the country out of its crisis. Privatization methods used in the past will only further enrich the small gang of oligarchs and help them to transfer their borrowed money to the West. It appears that a reform of the present reforms is necessary, and the direction must be set by the Russian people and their democratically elected representatives.

Whether or not Putin's election victory and his "party conjured from nothing" will relieve the situation remains unclear since the present party constellation is quite weakly structured. It is also reasonable to assume that the West needs to drastically change its current method of providing assistance to Russia. It has not helped Russia but rather piled up a mountain of credit that Russia will not be able to repay. This could eventually lead to the exhaustion of IMF resources needed for economic bailouts in other countries. An end must be put to the constant practice of throwing good money at Russia in order to recover money that has somehow disappeared into black holes. In its transition period, Russia distinguishes itself from every other borrower. Thus the credit relations with this declining country must be formed differently, without abandoning or restricting them. Joint ventures in promising areas like the energy sector, with the participation of qualified local and foreign management, cofinanced by national and international money institutions, could be the best way to bring about self-help.

Europe must consider overcoming the crisis in Russia and Ukraine as a major priority. The three Slavic republics of the fallen Soviet Union must associate more closely with the EU, which will play an important role in their reconstruction. Further integration will finally put an end to the still divided continent and lead to the establishment of a common European home. The globalization of the world economy could thereby become more complete and efficient.

Putin is intensifying his efforts to subject the Central Asian republics to his influence. The newly elected president's first trip abroad was to Uzbekistan and Turkmenistan. Speed is of the essence since Central Asia is also of strategic importance to the United States due to its proximity to China and its unexplored but enormous gas and oil resources. In April 2000, just a month before Putin's trip, American secretary of state Madeleine Albright visited Kazakhstan, Kyrgyzstan, and Uzbekistan. It was announced that the United States was merely interested in fighting the reawakening of Islamic fundamentalism. In order to emphasize this matter of concern, Albright left behind generous sums of "immediate aid" to Kazakhstan ($10 million) and Kyrgyzstan ($100 million). Putin also wants to convince the pubic that his primary interest lies in the fight against Islamic terrorism.

The question of whether a rebirth of terrorism had occurred since the collapse of the Soviet Union was the theme of a conference in June 2000 in Vienna on "Central Asia and Islam." A German expert on the Orient, Uwe Halbach, addressed this question in his opening speech, which divided the effects of Islam in the Central Asian successor republics into two fundamental aspects. He emphasized that one can hardly speak of a rebirth of the "practice of . . . everyday Islam." Even during the Soviet era, despite the officially atheist ideology, this tradition never really disappeared. However, Halbach claims that the spread of what he calls "educational Islam"—the theological, juridical, and philosophical fundamentals of Islam—has "experienced a revival from above, as well as a renaissance from below."[16] The supporters of this revival have been the post-Soviet governments and the religious authorities, which were intent on integrating Islam into the body of the nation-state. Islamic parties and cultural associations—movements that are cofinanced by Saudi Arabia—are also active proponents of this Islamic revival. Halbach called for calm, appealing to the conference participants "not to allow the theme of Islam in Central Asia to be perceived in a close-minded manner, as is often the case when one hears of the frequently mentioned Islamic threat."

Other experts, however, point to the flames of instability that the fundamentalists are fanning. They have infiltrated Kyrgyzstan and Uzbekistan from Afghanistan, where a civil war has been raging for twenty years. Fundamentalists killed over one hundred people in a terrorist bombing in Tashkent, the capital of Uzbekistan, in February 1999, and in the summer they terrorized the Fergana Valley with kidnappings and the occupation of villages. The valley, which lies in Uzbekistan's border region, is considered a terrorist stronghold. The terrorists are supported by the Tajiks, which make up one-fourth of Uzbekistan's population. Islamic fundamentalists are also responsible for the continuing civil war in Tajikistan. This problem surfaced unexpectedly at the CIS summit on June 21, 2000. Islam Karimov, the Uzbek president, appealed to the conference participants for a combined preventive strike against Afghanistan, the cause of so much trouble in the region. But Putin was not eager to accept the proposal, especially considering Russia's bitter experiences in its war in Afghanistan in the first half of the 1980s. Nonetheless, Russia's president could chalk up a partial victory at that summit; on June 22, 2000, the CIS members announced their opposition to U.S. plans to build a missile defense system and the demand for a change in the ABM treaty of 1972. At the conference, Russian defense minister Igor Sergeyev said, "With this [missile defense] project the United States is endangering the security of the world and will trigger a new arms race."[17]

However, observers of the region believe that "Islamic terrorism" is not the most important concern for U.S. and Russian policy. In reality, the United States, which wants to expand its influence in Central Asia, and powerless Russia, which wants to restore its lost influence despite its economic destitution, are both more interested in substantial economic and geostrategic interests than "terrorism." The goal is not a partner-like cooperation between the American superpower and economically devastated Russia, but influence and power in a newly independent region that is trying to forge new foreign relations. Madeleine Albright wanted to make it clear to the governments of Central Asia that there is an alternative to Russia, especially when it comes to the development of energy resources and the construction of pipelines. The United States wants to transport energy resources through Turkey without crossing Russian territory, building an oil pipeline from the Caspian Sea via Azerbaijan and Georgia, right through Turkey to the Mediterranean: the Baku–Ceyhan line. In the first conflicts over influence in Central Asia, Putin was able to chalk up a victory; he defeated the "energy corridor project," as Russia describes the planned pipeline that is to steer clear of Russian territory, by substantially increasing Turkmen gas deliveries to Russia, which had previously traveled over Russian territory to Ukraine, where they were illegally tapped. Romania and Bulgaria are also connected to this natural gas network. By purchasing this gas from Turkmenistan, Putin has put into question the necessity of a gas pipeline leading into Turkey. The U.S.-sponsored construction of the Baku–Ceyhan line is also in danger. When it was discovered that the oil reserves were smaller than expected, negotiations were postponed at a meeting between Turkmenistan and Turkey, which now seem to be leaning toward the original, cheaper project that would put the end station in Novorossisk.

The CIS summit in June 2000 did little to deepen the economic cooperation among its members. But strengthened by CIS support for Russia's position against U.S. plans to build a national missile defense system, Putin traveled to China and North Korea in mid-July 2000. There he secured the support of their leaders for his condemnation of the U.S. plan.

9

The Bretton Woods Institutions: Better Division of Labor But No Real Reform

Those expecting radical reforms of the heavily criticized IMF and World Bank at their April 2000 summit were disappointed. The summit brought a reflection of the basic elements of the Bretton Woods conference of July 1944 rather than an attempt at major change. At the founding meeting of the new international G–20 group, there were clear signs of irreconcilable differences between industrialized and industrializing countries concerning reforms of the finance market and the Bretton Woods institutions. The members of the G–20 group are the G–7 states, the G–8 member, Russia, plus Argentina, Australia, Brazil, China, India, Indonesia, Mexico, Saudi Arabia, South Africa, South Korea, and Turkey. The chair of the EU (held by Finland at the December 1999 summit, the president of the ECB, and representatives of the World Bank and IMF also participated. Members of the G–20 account for over 85 percent of the gross world product and almost two-thirds of the world's population.

In the December 1999 summit U.S. treasury secretary Larry Summers initiated a discussion about necessary reforms. "We believe," he said, "that the time has come to rethink the role of the IMF in the long-term financing of its members." Summers thinks that private capital needs to play a greater role in the long-term and mid-term financing of industrializing and developing countries. This is already beginning to happen. In the past few years, the share of financing from public sources like the World Bank and IMF has sunk to just $60 billion. Private sources of capital, on the other hand, have grown noticeably and amount to more than $200 billion.[1] The IMF, Summers continued, should concentrate on "macroeconomic stabilization and the temporary financing of member countries with balance of payments difficulties." The line between

Table 9.1

Changes in World Bank Credit Allocations Between 1980 and 1999

Area receiving financing	Change in credit allocation (in percent)
Education, health care, food aid, and social programs	+20
Economic policy and reforms	+11
Finance policy	+17
Administrative reforms	+ 4
Transport and telecommunications	− 3
Water and urban development	− 4
Industry, oil, gas, and mining	− 8
Energy industry	−19
Agriculture and environment	−20

Source: New York Times, April 16, 2000.

the two Bretton Woods institutions would thus be clarified. The World Bank would primarily focus on the "tasks of structural development and long-term financing in developing regions." The IMF, Summers added, should concentrate more on crisis prevention and a quick-response plan for surmounting difficulties in the case of a crisis than on long-term development aid. According to the United States, the IMF should stop acting like a "weak credit business, with low-interest, long-term loans." Summers claims, "The IMF does not need to ensure countries long-term access to the capital markets, nor does it need to lavishly support bad habits and bad policies."[2]

The World Bank was heavily criticized for its policy of giving credit to wealthier countries rather than poor ones and for freezing money in long-term projects. James D. Wolfensohn, its president, denied these accusations and presented his balance sheet, which showed that large investment projects, previously about 25 percent of the bank's credit, have been reduced to a level of just 2 percent. Wolfensohn also contested the accusation that the World Bank was not adequately concentrating on the financing of education, health care, and other social programs by presenting information (shown in Table 9.1) on changes in the bank's programs between 1980 and 1999 (during which the volume of credits rose from $11.5 to $29 billion).

Table 9.1 undoubtedly proves that World Bank credit allocations for industry, energy, and agriculture have all decreased significantly over the last two decades, while credit for education, food, and social programs has increased. The bank also disputes the claim of Professor Allan Meltzer, chairman of the U.S. Congressional committee researching World Bank and IMF activities, that 70 percent of World Bank–financed projects have failed. In fact, according to the bank, 81 percent of allocated credit has led to "satisfying results" in the last two fiscal years.[3]

The IMF refused to accept Professor Meltzer's suggestion to lend members on the verge of liquidation credit for a 120–day period, with a chance for extension in certain cases. IMF experts argue that the repayment deadline would approach before the debtor was in a position to even begin the process of economic rehabilitation. Nancy Birdsall, an expert at the Carnegie Endowment for International Peace, appealed to the two Bretton Woods institutions to return to their original objectives: The IMF should support poor countries, though on a short-term basis, in order to avoid freezing money in long-term projects that may be needed for other purposes. Poverty relief, she claims, should be the task of the World Bank and crisis management the IMF's main objective.[4] Stanley Fischer, the second most powerful person in the IMF hierarchy, admitted that IMF policies have not improved the situation but have made a bad situation worse. Sometimes IMF help is required, though mainly when private capital decides to withdraw. Joseph E. Stiglitz, former economic adviser to President Clinton and later head economist at the World Bank, wrote the following about the two institutions: "The protesters in the streets would say that the IMF's economic aid makes things worse, and actually turns minor recessions into depressions. In many cases they would be right; primarily in those cases where the IMF undermines the democratic process by providing emergency cash in contradiction to its own basic policies." Rudiger Dornbusch, MIT professor and IMF critic, replied that "a drastic policy is required to be able to avoid the loss of blood, the imminent currency collapse, and irreparable damage."[5]

A recent article in the *Frankfurter Allgemeine Zeitung* noted that the Meltzer commission had triggered passionate discussions about the future of the Bretton Woods institutions.[6] Yet none of the 182 member states were prepared to follow Meltzer's suggestion and transfer the IMF and World Bank responsibilities to the private markets. The IMF's main tasks are still macroeconomic monitoring, the provision of technical aid, and bridging loans in case of payment difficulties. Several days before the April 2000 conference, the IMF board of directors approved a suggestion aimed at preventing member states from constantly acquiring loans when they were unable to pay the borrowed money back in a timely fashion. The G–7 resolved to take into account the demands of both parliaments and protesters. The IMF should concentrate on crisis management and not long-term development problems; it should be concerned with short-term emergency loans, as the IMF founders in 1944 had intended. The seven powerful industrialized countries have resolved to allow for differentiated interest rates, which will be determined by how often the debtor applies for loans, how much economic aid is desired, and the length of the repayment period. Lower interest rates will be available to countries that want a smaller amount of money for a shorter period of time. The IMF's practice until now has been unsatisfactory since many developing countries acquired long-term credit, made an agreement with the IMF on interest rates, and then, after the payment deadline had passed, acquired more loans.

Shortly before the April 2000 meeting, the IMF board of directors listed the measures it would take to halt the misuse of IMF resources, especially in countries like Russia and Ukraine. For example, the IMF intended to thin out its current credit instruments and to modify the few acceptable ones that remained. The private economy's role in the prevention and surmounting of economic crises is still an area of contention. There are differences of opinion on how private loan providers will be able to concretely participate. There is, however, agreement that the IMF should set the direction of crisis management, though it should not become actively involved in negotiations between an affected country and its private creditor. It is also agreed that the IMF should cancel 100 percent of the debts of the world's poorest countries. Japan, which originally wanted to cancel only 90 percent, supports this decision. Concrete, binding decisions would materialize only at the fall summit since there was an interregnum at the time of the April summit; the newly elected director, Horst Köhler, was to take office in May. Germany was strictly opposed to Allan Meltzer's suggestion that IMF and World Bank responsibilities be transferred to private markets. Heidemarie Wieczorek-Zeul, Germany's development minister, with colleagues from Britain, the Netherlands, and Norway, presented a position paper opposed to Meltzer's suggestion entitled "The World Needs Strong Multilateral Development Institutions." It called for the IMF to continue providing short and mid-term loans to help rectify temporary payment problems and finance structural reform. The IMF should also remain active in the poorest member states, while retaining the credit line that was accepted in the fall of 1999 to help reduce poverty and spur economic growth. Meltzer had also suggested an end to IMF activity in Africa and to subsidized loans to poor countries, and he also wanted to halt the World Bank's work in industrializing nations in order to concentrate on aiding truly impoverished countries. According to Meltzer, the World Bank should not provide loans but rather grants that are linked to concrete indicators of success. The bank should transform itself into a world development agent. But the ministers' counterpaper concludes that "many of these suggestions would be more likely to hurt the poor than help."[7] They suggest that the role of the Bretton Woods institutions needs to be "reevaluated after half a century," but they do not accept the suggestion of completely restructuring their objectives. Their paper calls for closer cooperation between the IMF and World Bank, suggesting that the IMF develop a better understanding of the relations among "stabilization, poverty, and growth." They refuse to accept Meltzer's opinion that "access to credit from Bretton Woods institutions should be taken away from countries with higher per capita social products." The world needs multilateral development organizations that can transcend inequality and the massive changes wrought by globalization and its uncontrolled market forces.[8]

The 182 member states that participated in the spring 2000 summit did not agree to the Meltzer commission's suggestion that they conduct a comprehensive structural reform of the Bretton Woods institutions but instead supported U.S. treasury secretary Summers's more cautious recommendations. The integration of the private sector into international financial activity must be at the top of the list of measures to be taken. Köhler should accomplish what his predecessor (Michel Camdessus) could not—that is, the establishment of a widespread network of contacts among the world's top banks. The Institute of International Finance (IIF), which contains more than three hundred banks and financial concerns, is the most important partner for the integration of the private sector into the work of multilateral financial institutions like the IMF and World Bank. The "big player" wants more influence on the IMF and World Bank reform agendas, primarily a right to help set the world finance system's agenda. It would like a quicker and more comprehensive division of the burden from banks and borrowers. "The 'Big Player' and the Basel Bank for International Settlements (BIS) and its Committee for Bank Supervision have found an important partner for cooperation."[9] Caio Koch-Weser, Germany's finance secretary and former candidate for the director's chair of the IMF, claims, "By establishing the principles of when and how to conduct the future integration of the private sector in the IMF and World Bank's program, we have taken a big step on the route to a new international financial architecture."[10] Former U.S. treasury secretary Nicholas Brady commented succinctly on this issue at the convention of large banks in The Hague prior to the conference on Bretton Woods institutions. Brady said that Köhler has "an incredible chance to adapt his institution to the realities of global private capital markets." Moreover, Brady "hopes that Köhler understands just how divorced the current IMF is from the reality of development on the global finance market. International financial institutions hardly function any more as capital providers in the world financial system. They must adapt their operations to take into account the fact that 90 percent of capital is streaming in from private markets."[11]

This message should be understood as follows: The influence of the large credit providers on worldwide financial activity should be made dependent on the amount of money they provide. In other words, the Bretton Woods institutions must realize that there are more powerful institutions that have authority over them than the G–7 industrialized states—for instance, the large banks and financial concerns of the IIF. In the era of globalization, it is not the economic middlemen that make the important decisions, but the moneymaking institutions.

How Does Horst Köhler View His Role as the Head of the IMF?

The Americans refused to accept Germany's first choice for the directorship of the IMF, Caio Koch-Weser. Even Köhler, who was head of the East European Bank in London, was told privately by a U.S. negotiator to drop his candidacy. According to Köhler, "I said in a calm and friendly manner that I believed it was in America's interests to support my candidacy." Köhler received U.S. support (the United States accounts for the largest share of the IMF and enjoys a veto right). The new IMF director's views do not deviate much from those of U.S. treasury secretary Summers, who recently said, "Today, threats to America come just as much from states that are too weak as from states that are too strong." Köhler commented on this statement: "That is simply the acknowledgment that even the superpowers have become entangled and are aware of the difficulties of this network. These difficulties range from terror to

AIDS to manifold forms of environmental catastrophe. Hence, the poorer countries must be helped—in our own interest."[12] The new head of the IMF views IMF aid as follows: The rich countries must finally fulfill two old promises. First, they must give 0.7 percent of their GDP in the form of public development aid to poor countries in order to fund reconstruction. Second, they must open up their markets to products from poorer countries. According to Köhler, the main task of the IMF is to "concentrate on the macroeconomic stability of the world economy and on the ability of the finance and currency systems to fend off crisis." There must be a common understanding between the World Bank and IMF on a global strategy, but the responsibilities for the realization of this strategy should be divided among different organizations. Thus the fight against poverty should be the World Bank's primary function. The IMF's task, on the other hand, should be to intensify "politico-economic surveillance" and make the system more transparent. But, Köhler says, the IMF is not an omnipotent god. As far as the exchange rate is concerned, the IMF director supports a floating policy, though a fixed linkage to the dollar, for instance, is not taboo since it helps "build confidence, which is borrowed from the world power, the United States." He also believes that rules for capital markets are necessary—not the outflow of capital, but at least its inflow should follow certain regulations. If a country cannot manage the flood of incoming capital, then that incoming capital should be stopped. Köhler considers the strategy of "They have to open their countries; the rest is not important to us" too risky. We must work, he added, on a market economic framework for the global economy. "I will try to do a good job," he said, concluding, "Whether or not it really is a good job, we will see at the end of the period."

Köhler is right that the conditions for IMF activities will become more complicated than they were previously. The member states, and especially the U.S. Congress, are increasingly unwilling to support the IMF and want to bring in the private sector to handle temporary liquidation difficulties among the member states. Recent bailouts, which were primarily concerned with the interests of incautious lenders, have had little appeal. Professor Meltzer has even suggested the elimination of the IMF as an international financial institution. The IMF and its director will have to fight harder than ever to maintain its main objectives: the support of macroeconomic stability and the prevention of crises in the financial and currency systems.

The Colorful Mix of Protesters Against the Bretton Woods Institutions

The protest strategy against the IMF and World Bank meeting in April 2000 was similar to the November 1999 protests against the WTO in Seattle. Under the umbrella organization Mobilization for Global Justice, thousands of people gathered in Washington, D.C., with the goal of obstructing the meeting. But the Washington police were better prepared than their colleagues in Seattle. On the evening before the meeting, six hundred protesters were arrested and their staging area was closed off. On the following day, fifteen hundred police officers maintained peace on the streets and provided security for representatives of the member states participating in the meeting. The protesters were unable to cause any great damage, and the meetings began as usual. As in Seattle, the protesters were a jumbled assortment of causes: environmentalists, defenders of the rights of developing countries, student organizations, religious groups, etc., which gathered to protest against all forms of capitalism. The presence of labor unions was greater than it had been in Seattle. They were primarily protesting against the liberalization of U.S. foreign trade and against the expansion of trade relations with China. The unions argued that the Clinton administration's policy and the entrance of China into the WTO cost U.S. workers hundreds of thousands of jobs.

George Becker, president of the unionized steel workers of America and an active opponent of expanding trade relations with China, claims that globalization helps only multinational concerns and not U.S. workers. Becker emphasized that many unions have found a common voice with student groups and nongovernmental organizations that demand a restructuring of globalization to better protect the environment, improve working conditions, and relieve poverty. The United Auto Workers, the International Association of Machine Tool Industries, and the textile workers' union brought about twenty thousand members to protest against the Bretton Woods institutions and trade with China. It bears mentioning that imports from China to the U.S. are five times greater than U.S. exports to China, which will result in a trade deficit of around $80 billion by the end of 2001.

The comments of several politicians at the Group of 77 Havana summit, which was attended by forty-two heads of government from various developing countries in April of 2000, were much harsher than those of the Washington demonstrators. Fidel Castro demanded the "destruction of the IMF," which he described as a "sinister institution." "It is essential for the Third World," Cuba's leader said, "that the IMF and its philosophy disappear." Castro called the Third World a "bomb that could explode at any time." Olusegun Obasanjo, Nigeria's head of state, reproached the wealthy nations for not keeping their promises of economic aid and debt relief. "This summit," Obasanjo said, "sends a clear message to the industrialized states. Their refusal to reform the international financial institutions is a great threat to international peace and security."[13]

Kofi Annan, UN secretary general, called for the world's financial leaders to listen to the demonstrators who protested in Washington against worldwide poverty and against the exclusion of many nations from the benefits of new technology. "We must transform this discontent, this ferment of confrontational energy, into constructive behavior that benefits all mankind, and which can be supported by all people."[14] Annan thus commented at the common meeting of the UN Economic and Social Council with the finance ministers and central bank governors who took part in the IMF and World Bank meeting in Washington. Annan repeated his hope that by 2015 more than a billion people would be free of oppressive poverty. The demand to write off the debt of the poorest developing countries was also repeated. Cuba emphasized that of the thirty-three states only four would be affected by debt remission.

Experts Engage in Charged Debates with the Opponents of Globalization

Gregg Easterbrook, senior editor of the *New Republic*, claims that in the past, it was the conservatives who feared economic changes.[15] Conservative authors railed against factories that forced workers out of their agricultural communities and into the city, worrying that this would separate the worker from his customary existence in small settlements and alter the role of women in society, family structures, and sexual morality (among other things). However, Easterbrook writes, it is now the Left that fears change. The antiglobalization bloc decries the way the modern economy drives citizens in developing countries from their traditional agricultural roots into the city. This resentment has its origins, Easterbrooks claims, in the "romantic idea" that developing countries would be better off if they were left untouched by the West. But, according to Easterbrook, only those people who enjoy a comfortable life in a wealthy nation can come up with such notions. Easterbrook, a Pakistani by birth, is convinced that 99.9 percent of the non-Western population longs for a Western lifestyle, education, and democracy. Contact with the West is not ideal, the author admits, but relationships with the West are and will remain the only hope of developing countries. The fear surrounding globalization is based on the fact that no government carries responsibility for developments.

Lori Wallach, a leader of the anti-WTO movement, says that she "fears big government as much as she fears big business." Wallach's other comments sound equally convincing: the changes wrought by globalization, though accompanied by stress and confusion, have hitherto benefited humankind and raised income and life expectancy. Food production has grown faster than population, thereby refuting Malthus's prediction of starvation; education levels are increasing; and communications technology undermines the rule of dictators. Wallach points out the noticeably improved conditions of life in the United States, the low unemployment rates and high growth rates, and the fact that developing countries that accept the WTO's trade policy have three times as much economic growth as those with more restrictive trade regulations. Easterbrook claims to understand the concern of globalization opponents about growing inequality (the income of CEOs has increased to 420 times that of workers). But he is convinced that trade restrictions will only further reduce the workers' share of the pie and are not an adequate means to fight inequality. Other means must be used. Easterbrook does believe that one should listen to the protesters in Washington since not all of their complaints are groundless. For instance, they are correct in demanding inclusions in trade agreements that enforce the improvement of working conditions. This demand is primarily concerned with agreements with developing countries that are supposed to guarantee better health care and wages above the mere subsistence level. Although Easterbrook's arguments sound convincing, it bears mentioning that the advance of globalization has brought no significant improvement in the situation in developing countries, where the gap between rich and poor remains especially large. And the UN secretary general certainly did not aim too high when he demanded that one billion people be lifted out of the depths of poverty by 2015.

John Micklethwait and Adrian Wooldridge, two analysts of the globalization process, underscore that the Washington demonstrators protesting the "cynical elite" merely repeated a "historical tradition." In the 1840s, demonstrators occupied the streets of London, then the economic metropolis of the world, to demand the liberalization of foreign trade. Today, the authors write, the street fighters demand the opposite.[16] The passion of the Anti–Corn Law League was no weaker than that of the current public citizen. The league's members refused to accept the policies of either the "complacent Whigs" or the "blood-stained Tories." The means of communication were more primitive. Letters to publications functioned in the capacity of today's Internet. And after the abolition of the Corn Laws in 1846, as imports of cheap wheat were made legal, the refusal to accept agroprotectionism remained a principle of the radical agenda. The *Labour Standard* decried ambiguous arguments like "We need fair trade" as a vehicle to "tsar-like despotism and a Cossack government." Why, then, the authors ask, was "free trade" so popular in those days? Because, they answer, the Victorians posed the liberalization of foreign trade as a "question of bread and butter." The "free breakfast table" became the battle cry of opponents of customs tariffs. Five years after the abolition of the Corn Laws, one-fourth of "the people's bread" was imported from abroad, and cheap food products were allowed. Millions of people left their villages to build a new life in the city. Today, the exact opposite is taking place. Globalization is now considered a problem because of fear that someone from the outside could steal one's job. But according to the authors, when "dangerous, inexpensive" steel comes to America, no one is prepared to admit that this leads to the production of inexpensive automobiles. No one points out that inexpensive imported food products aid poor Americans and that trade barriers hurt poor countries. IMF and World Bank economists and technocrats are usually the ones responsible for defending globalization. They normally do this by emphasizing the fact that the global economy is useful because of its efficiency. In Micklethwait and Wooldridge's opinion, globalization should be connected with the concept of freedom.

Former president George Bush tried to do this with the concept of a "New World Order." Clinton, however, did not make any similar efforts. Micklethwait and Wooldridge's conclusion will not receive a warm reception from current politicians. Sir Robert Peel, the landowner and prime minister who sacrificed his wealth by repealing the Corn Laws, was remembered as the man who made people's bread less expensive. Upon his death, they cried in the streets: "Who will do such a deed among today's politicians?" It is doubtful that the opponents of globalization would be convinced by such an argument. One thing, however, is certain: This "free-running system," with all of its advantages and disadvantages, cannot be stopped. Yet the voice of the protesters must be heard since several of their arguments are pertinent—especially their emphasis on the dangers and insecurity caused by the growing gap between rich and poor. The growth of prosperity in affluent countries is not enough to guarantee a general acceptance of globalization.

The discussion continues over the future role of the IMF in the globalizing world economy. But criticism surrounding its credit activities has muted. Voices decrying mistakes in the preparation of credit for financial crises in Southeast Asia, South America, and Russia have become less shrill. This was demonstrated at a meeting of the Kiel Institute for the World Economy on June 21–22, 2000. Several economists even praised the IMF for its speed in helping to overcome the most difficult financial crisis of the postwar era. William R. Cline, from the Institute of International Finance in Washington, praised the "massive financial boost that the IMF used to hinder a world financial crisis."[17] Cline emphasized that most of the IMF's past credit has been paid back, and former countries mired in crisis like Brazil and South Korea are once again on the path to healthy growth. Ricardo Hausmann, another participant and formerly an associate of the Inter-American Development Bank, also pointed to the effectiveness of the IMF's credit aid. The rest of the conference participants were less optimistic. But it was obvious that the discussion tended to move from fundamental criticism of the IMF to an overview of the national conditions of the financial market, thereby concentrating on ways to prevent future crises. According to Tommaso Padoa-Schioppa, an expert from the European Central Bank, nation-states have moved more quickly toward full capital market mobility than toward common financial market regulation. He further emphasized that regulations that focus on microeconomic solutions and individual banks and institutions are not enough to reduce the risks of the world financial market. Martin Hellwig (University of Mannheim) also underscored that recent economic crises were of a comprehensive nature, not simply the failure of individual banks. Hellwig added: "The IMF has an important role to play in this world of comprehensive economic risks." Harvard professor Jeffrey Sachs says, "With 60 programs underway, [the IMF] has no resources left to concentrate on the international financial system." Alan Greenspan, on the other hand, emphasizes the need to reduce government aid. He expressed this opinion at a meeting of the Council for

Foreign Relations (on July 13, 2000), claiming that during the march of globalization, which will undoubtedly bring unavoidable international financial crises, industrialized and developing countries should concentrate on creating a healthy, functioning bank system and an active capital market. This will ensure that when one financial source dries up, others can be tapped. Governments, Greenspan says, should not isolate investors from risk through bailouts in hard times.[18] He further maintains that "investors should not always be able to depend on states and international financial organizations to carry the whole burden of emergency actions during moments of new turbulence. . . . State financial boosts must be reduced to a minimum to prevent the irresponsible trade of investors in difficult times."

Robert Gilpin, an expert in the field of international economic policy, formulates some interesting answers to the questions raised by globalization.[19] He underscores Britain's first historical attempt to integrate the world's economy by repealing the protectionist Corn Laws in 1846. The result was a rapid increase in world trade, a dynamic flood of goods, capital, and tourists that led to a truly open world economy. Yet the growing political tensions that eventually led to World War I put an end to the globalization that began under the umbrella rule of Pax Britannica. Gilpin claims that we now have a new version of globalization to deal with, this time under the umbrella rule of the United States. The main question is whether this globalization will have a more secure future than Britain's. Gilpin is unsure since the political preconditions for economic openness have dramatically weakened in the last decades. Markets are neither autonomous nor self-regulating. The explosive growth of foreign trade and investment requires new rules and institutions. Yet the economic dimension of globalization is already overtaking the political preconditions necessary for such rules and institutions. Gilpin is convinced that the success of globalization will be ensured only if America uses the power of its strong, regulating hand. But although the United States is still the dominant superpower, it is not sure if it wants to play the role of leader in a global economic alliance. Gilpin also wonders if the expansion of regional integration communities promotes globalization. He comes to the conclusion that "economic regionalism has become an increasingly important threat to a unified global economy."[20] In his opinion, the problem of international financial relations is contradictory: "Whereas there is consensus among economists on the virtues of trade liberalization, no comparable agreement exists with respect to capital flows and whether or not they should be regulated."[21] It bears mentioning that there are few critics of the free flow of capital, though nation-states and international institutions are unable to control independent casino capital.

The IMF Is Optimistic About the Future of the World Economy

The IMF issued a report on the condition of the global economy just before its April 2000 meeting. It concluded that the emerging market economies had overcome the preliminary tensions and thus made it possible for the world economy to begin to experience unprecedented dynamic growth. The IMF predicted that the world economy would grow 4.2 percent in 2000, the highest rate since 1988, though it would experience a slight drop to 3.9 percent in 2001. Yet the IMF points to several things that could darken this rosy picture—for instance, inequality in growth dynamics from state to state, disharmony in currency relations, and overvalued prices on the capital markets, including the U.S. market. The report calls for the United States to initiate "a soft landing" for its overheated economy, and warns Europe not to cool its new, quick growth dynamics with higher interest rates. Japan should bring more movement into its "shaky" rehabilitation policy. According to IMF experts, the recovery will be quicker than expected. But insecurity reigns in individual countries over the continuation of growth. The report especially recommends careful observation of the situation in the United States. Although the prognosis for U.S. growth rates in 2000 (4.4 percent) was higher than that of other Western countries, certain factors could negatively affect growth and impact on other states. The overvalued capital market, the massive amount of borrowed money when savings are so low, and a giant discrepancy between U.S. investment abroad and much lower levels of foreign investment in the United States have created an imbalance that could turn the economic tide—an event that would have unforeseeable consequences. The best solution for the United States, the IMF claims, would be a soft landing. But if all these factors come together, a scenario could develop with an unexpected rise in inflation, a 25 percent drop on the capital market, or the devaluation of the dollar, which would result in a "hard landing" with negative effects on international development.

Will There Be a Successor to America in Its Role as Leader of the World Economy?

Martin Hüfner, chief economist at the Bayerische Vereinsbank in Munich, writes, "There is no candidate in sight far and wide who could be taken seriously."[22] In the United States, the powerful economic boom has not abated. Surprises, however, are always possible. In Hüfner's opinion, candidates for such a surprise would be China or Europe. But he feels that for China to be a real player, it must still undergo a fundamental transformation. That leaves Europe. The age of "Euro-sclerosis is over," and there are many signs that Europe could have a future similar to that of the United States. In 2000, the Euro region would have a growth rate of more than 3 percent, and 1.75 million new jobs would be created. Growth in Europe, Hüfner says, is based on a "solid foundation." The trade balance is positive, the savings of private households amount to 11 percent, and state debt has significantly decreased. While there are problems with the Euro and its entrance onto the foreign exchange market was disappointing, Hüfner is confident about future developments on the continent. He insists that "the first phase is dominated by negative elements. The positive elements first appear in the second phase." Europe's fixed-interest security market, Hüfner continues, is the world's second largest; its volume is 80 percent of that of the United States. "Europe has the largest futures market in the world. The European banks are among the largest and customer friendliest money institutions," Hüfner says. He concludes as follows: "Europe's renewed strength should cause Americans to return to the fundamentals of equality based upon fixed regulations."

Similar sentiments were expressed at the Davos Economic Forum in January 2000.[23] Europe could become a larger economic power than the United States as a result of future expansion to the east, but it will never achieve the integrity of its American partner, given all of its national minorities, immigrants, races, and religious variety. Europe has made significant advances in the integration of once warring enemy states. Germany, once described by Dwight Eisenhower as the "synthetic evil" of the world, has been integrated into Europe, and the German–French alliance has contributed much to the advancement of the EC. But the EU remains a grouping of independent states, and "decision making" will not equal the decisiveness of the United States in the foreseeable future. Moreover, the Euro will not be able to achieve the strength of the

U.S. dollar as a reserve currency, even if it turns the current trend of devaluation around. Four EU states have not yet entered the EMU, and the popularity of the common currency has dropped considerably. According to a poll taken in March 2000, only 35 percent of Swedes were prepared to vote for membership in the currency union in a national referendum; 41 percent said they would vote against.[24] Polls in Great Britain show similar trends. It is gratifying to see Western Europe on the verge of strengthening its economic power and increasing integration. Competition among economic giants could lead to improvements in the quality of goods and to a reduction in production costs. However, the positive developments in Europe will not necessarily challenge America's leading role in the global economy.

Transatlantic Mega-Concerns and Regional Integration Groups as the Backbone of the Global Economy

The global economy is already resting on a solid foundation. Five large technological branches, which have a deciding influence on the national economies of the entire planet, function as the motor of the global economy. Computers and telecommunications, the energy sector, and biotechnology and molecular technology are already active elements in every part of the world, and they are giving a powerful boost to the global economy, which could increase prosperity in the twenty-first century. Forty thousand transnational concerns have set up two hundred and fifty thousand sister concerns all over the planet. In China alone, there are forty thousand such branches; in Singapore eleven thousand; and in Eastern Europe fifty-five thousand. As discussed in chapter 4, ten players in the global economy will determine future developments around the globe (see Table 4.3).

Nation-states no longer determine the course of national economies; rather, it is the willingness of mega-concerns to invest capital or increase production in certain countries or to withdraw capital and reduce production in others. They increasingly determine the growth or decline of GDP, the amount of foreign trade, and the well-being of people on this planet. It bears mentioning that more than 30 percent of current world trade is conducted among the world's hundred largest industrial concerns. They influence the labor market more than the downward spiral of reeducation and investment programs of national economic policies. The U.S. aviation giant Boeing, which considers itself more of a global player than a U.S. concern, has already created sixty thousand jobs in Europe. Meanwhile, in the Unites States, fifty-six thousand people are employed by Airbus. As a result of transatlantic megafusions, economic alliances, and the like, the ever-growing multinational concerns no longer view themselves as national businesses but as members of the global economy. Their sphere of influence within the countries where they are active is constantly growing thanks to their expanding networks of raw materials, subcontractors for semifinished products, and local consumers of finished products. This network is increasingly removing itself from the control of national organizational structures and economic mechanisms and connecting itself directly to the global network.

Klaus Grubelnik, the globalization expert often quoted in this study, writes: "The future international division of labor is no longer dependent on the result of competition among nations, but rather on the result of competition between transnational concerns that function as leaders of the system and global players. Thus in place of Daimler/Chrysler's 'Made in Germany,' a 'Made by Mercedes-Benz' appears. . . . The economic giants are in the process of dividing the world among them. In the twenty-first century, a global oligopoly will dominate the most important economic branches."[25] National governments are increasingly unable to control global market powers. Globalization does not bring only advantages: Ruud Lubbers, the former Dutch head of government who now travels around the world as a globalization expert, has drawn attention to its dangers. The elimination of national borders could lead to a deficit in democratic and social responsibility, threaten the environment and security, and lead to social dumping and the overexploitation of natural resources. The Russian Mafia is spreading its activities throughout the world. According to the United Nations, global crime syndicates net an estimated gross income of over $1.5 billion.

Today's computer/Internet/casino capitalism is much different from the traditional capitalism of the nineteenth and early twentieth centuries. A large portion of national economies and an enormous amount of capital lie outside the control of nation-states. The globalizing economy requires a coordinated center that can avert imminent dangers. It must be able to control the movement of casino capital, bring more order to international economic relations, and help reduce poverty in the Third World.

Former German chancellor Willy Brandt's attempt to establish a "New World Order" failed. No one has repeated such an attempt since. Megacapitalists are increasingly worried about the future of capitalism. In

Davos in January 2000, speculator George Soros, who threw the Third World's capital markets into chaos, called for the establishment of "valid common rules" for the global economy and praised the "stabilizing role of the unions."[26] Though planned economies once played a role, capitalism has become the universal economic system. But it has many faces. A neoliberal system reigns in the United States, and the era of "big government," Bill Clinton emphasized, is over for good. The continuing boom, which has led to almost full employment and growing prosperity, proves that the economic system is appropriate for American conditions. In other countries, the government has the final say in many areas. In Sweden, for instance, the government has considerable influence over economic affairs, and, after a kill-or-cure remedy for its financial woes, the country is experiencing an unprecedented upswing under Social Democrat Göran Persson. Nonetheless, public spending is still incredibly high, at about 56 percent of total economic productivity; in the United States, public spending accounts for only 31 percent.[27] The socialist government in France, led by Lionel Jospin, also highly values the effective authority of the state to correct the invisible hand of the market, to fight unemployment, and to ensure a social balance. The Social Democratic governments of Britain and Germany, under Tony Blair and Gerhard Schröder respectively, place more value on business and the initiatives of management to create more economic efficiency. In Japan, on the other hand, traditional economic policies like life-long employment have lost their effectiveness; debt has grown to more than 7 percent of the GDP. This former economic giant is stuck in a recession it cannot escape. China, with one-fifth of the world's population, remains a developing country. Three-fourths of its people are concentrated in rural areas, making it impossible for China to create an adequate social order. The symbiosis of a socialist market economy and a dictatorial regime, which was conceived as a harmony of opposites (yin and yang), cannot indefinitely continue to function. Despite its higher growth rates, India, the world's second most populous country, still remains one of the poorest countries in the world because of its demographic explosion. Russia, governed by Vladimir Putin, is a country with ten thousand nuclear warheads and two-thirds of the population living below the poverty line. It has no hope of overcoming the current economic hardships, and the country's economic advisers are busy devising a system that is to resemble Augusto Pinochet's. And Africa sinks deeper into famine, plague, and civil war.

A technological revolution of gigantic proportions is in the process of changing the traditional social order. Robert Solow, Nobel Prize laureate, estimated that two-thirds of economic growth is a result of this unspecified technological progress, which is pushing globalization ahead. The nation-state is gradually losing control of a large part of its economy. Entire industrial branches, like computers, the automobile industry, and pharmacology, are joining together under the aegis of megafusions, alliances, and the like, into transatlantic multinationals that encircle the globe. Along with these mergers, which send economies of scale soaring to exorbitant heights, a growing share of world capital is leaving the spheres of production and trade, transforming itself into speculative casino capital that can jump from one capital market to the other at the speed of light and with the click of a button to seek out larger profits. This capital and the megamultis no longer have national borders. Their home is the global economy.

States located in a particular region are joining together in integrated communities in which national markets are transformed into a gigantic super-market without trade and customs barriers. These communities are then able to stand up to ever-increasing worldwide economic competition. The strongest such project, the EU, is in the process of expanding to twenty-five states through its inclusion of Central and East European countries. NAFTA operates in North America and Mercosur in South America, and the countries of the Pacific want to create a free trade zone of twenty-one member states by 2020. The United States, Japan, and China account for over 50 percent of world production. But a unified world order would be impossible. The deep and ever-growing gap between the poor South and the rich North makes it impossible. Whereas in the Southern countries 3 billion people (50 percent of the world's population) survive on but a few dollars a day, three multibillionaires in the rich North possess a fortune equal to that of the world's forty-eight poorest nations combined (a total population of 600 million). However, it is possible that the current and constantly expanding integration groups could cooperate with international institutions like the World Bank, IMF, and WTO to try to solve global economic problems and concentrate on the reduction of the gap between rich and poor. But Western aid and its use must be radically reformed. It must lead to self-help since progress in terms of civilization cannot be achieved through Western aid alone. Money should be provided for promising export-oriented investment projects that would prevent the corrupt bureaucracy from wasting it. If the world succeeds in reducing the discrepancy between its poor and rich nations, thereby allowing those poorer countries to participate in the growing prosperity and become equal economic partners, then the twenty-first century could be a time of stability, security, and peace throughout the world.

Conclusion: The Uncertain Future

Karl Marx predicted the evolution of capitalism into a highly concentrated system that would collapse under the pressure of the working class. He did not foresee that this class would steadily decline with the growth of modern technologies to 20 percent of the employed. His vision did not include the emergence of the service and information economies in the developed countries but was centered on a socialist system with collective property. The leader of Russian Bolsheviks, Vladimir Lenin thought the socioeconomic system existing at the time as "imperialism" would be "the last stage of capitalism" and would be resolved into a dictatorship of factory workers. This was to take place in Russia, where the industrial propletariat numbered no more than 5 percent of the employed. Both architects of socialism and communism wanted to do away with the state, which in the new system they envisaged would be redundant as a keeper of law and order. Lenin's utopia was realized during the troubles of World War I, six months after he was smuggled from Switzerland into Russia by German generals. The civil society that emerged under Alexander Kerensky, the single democracy in Russian history, was crushed without great effort by a small army led by Leon Trotsky. The casualties were no higher than during the French Revolution of 1789. There were many more victims of the subsequent civil war and foreign intervention. The casualties of hunger were greater. Productivity declined by half during the transition period from underdeveloped Russian capitalism to the never realized utopian socialism. The decline was similar to the one experienced in the 1990s on the way from collectivism to capitalism. The masses revolted in 1917—the sailors in Kronstadt, the peasants in Voronezh. Lenin tried to establish the New Economic Policy (NEP) just as Deng Xiaoping did in 1978 in China: private enterprise was allowed so long as the commanding heights of the economy remained in the hands of the state. The economy was restored.

Stalin wanted to conduct the revolution until the end. The NEP was reversed. Instead of withering away, Stalin's state became stronger than under the tsars. Stalin's goal was globalization via world revolution. But when the Soviet example, with massive terror and low living standards became less attractive to the Western Communist parties, Stalin was ready to realize his goal by conquest and setting in the Soviet steering model. He wished to act according to the principles of the Westphalian peace in 1648: *cuius regio eius religio.* The Hitler–Stalin pact opened the way to World War II. In advance, Stalin was allowed to occupy the eastern part of Poland and the Baltic countries. As a visitor in the war, he established the Soviet socioeconomic system in Central and Eastern Europe.

For fifty years, the Soviet bloc concentrated its economic attention on the military–industrial complex, which absorbed no less than 70 percent of the GNP. This took place while productivity levels were about one-third of those in the United States. Not much was left over for mass consumption. Collapse was unavoidable and took place when Mikhail Gorbachev initiated a radical reform with his *perestroika* and *glasnost* programs. This once again confirmed de Tocqueville's thesis that the real danger for unsuccessful government lies in starting to reform itself. The capitalist steering system won the contest. Indeed, Marx was right in saying that capitalism would concentrate production. At the time of the greatest boom, between 1972 and 1992, the number of multinationals rose from seven thousand to thirty-seven thousand. Their economic power became greater than that of many nation-states. Their annual sales reached $5.5 billion. Yet Marx erred in thinking that growing production would collide with capitalism's political and social systems. During the twenty-five years between 1970 and 1994, the annual income of capitalist countries rose from $10.1 trillion to $20 trillion. The increased income has gone in great part to increase the living standards of employees. The working class was no longer interested in an overthrow of a system that improved its working and living conditions. The Communist parties became negligible. Modern socialist leaders, such as Tony Blair and Gerhard Schröder, removed class struggle from their parties' programs, substituting for it entrepreneurship and innovation.

Did the collapse of the Soviet empire, with its globalization method via conquest and implantation of its political and economic systems, increase the chances of the traditional—and now universal—globalization method by expansion of national markets into a worldwide market? The political praxis of the Russian policymakers on their way to a market economy and pluralistic democracy has not as yet yielded an answer to this question. Vladimir Putin is striving to maintain a good relationship with the West, while also attempting to renew old Soviet friendships and restore old coalitions. Russian friendship with China was never as intense as now; old ties with Communist North Korea and Cuba, with India, Iran, and Iraq are being restored. The prospects for decreasing armaments, and most of all the nuclear arsenals, were never as bleak as they are today.

In mid-December 2000, a conference of prominent experts in Vienna discussed the issue of "Russia and Europe." The main speaker, Professor Andreas Kappeler, stressed without any hesitation that Russia is a European country, with Tolstoy, Dostoevsky, and Berdiaev having contributed greatly to European culture. The speaker went on to recommend that the Russian contribution be considered in the framework of the enlargement of the EU. The EU is not, however, ready to discuss this issue in the foreseeable future. Indeed, Russia's socioeconomic structure, the impact of the powerful oligarchs on the economy, the apparent kleptocracy—all of these while the majority of the population subsists at a bare minimum—are conditions without precedent in Europe. Russia wages a war of unprecedented ferocity against Chechnya without a real prospect for resolution in the near future. Russia participates in various conflicts among the former Soviet republics. Russia has not been able until now to comprehend that its imperial policy cannot be transferred to Europe and that the only way it can join Western civilization is by using civilized methods in its continuing transformation. For now, Russia remains a liability rather than an asset in the worldwide globalization process.

The success of globalization will depend above all on the opportunities for developing countries to participate in world trade and profits as a *conditio sine qua non* of diminishing the unbearable gap that separates these countries from the developed world. Violence, terrorism, and crime would be the consequences of a persisting separation between the two worlds. The Third World granted globalization real momentum by its decision in the 1960s to abolish protectionist policies in its foreign trade. Yet the gap has only widened since. The World Bank, the IMF, and the IIF have expressed their concern for the plight of the Third World. Funds have been provided. IIF credits to Third World countries have reached $166 billion. In January 2001, the World Bank passed a resolution to establish a "security web" to function as "a springboard for a secure future." Yet credits are granted without an effective concern for the proper use of the money. Much of it finds its way to havens for the benefit of the corrupt elites. Many developing countries are not poor for lack of qualified specialists—India is a case in point. The principal cause is the archaic social systems, with property concentrated in the hands of oligarchs with connections to government officials. Without a radical reform of these social systems, help from developed countries will not avail.

Notes

Notes to Introduction

1. *New York Times*, September 9, 2000.
2. *Wiener Zeitung*, November 8, 2000.
3. *Wall Street Journal*, September 25, 2000.
4. *New York Times*, September 27, 2000

Notes to Chapter 1

1. *Foreign Affairs*, September/October 1997.
2. *Der Spiegel* 2 (2000).
3. Ibid.
4. Ibid.
5. Ibid.
6. Ibid.
7. *The Economist*, September 11, 1999.
8. Ibid.
9. Daniel Bell, *The Coming of Post-Industrial Society* (New York: Basic Books, 1976).
10. Ibid.
11. Article service of the Austrian National Bank, January 1, 2000.
12. Cited in *Palm Beach Post*, February 3, 2000.
13. *Die Presse* (Vienna), November 19, 1999.
14. *The Economist*, November 27, 1999.
15. Ibid.
16. Francis Fukuyama, "The Left Should Love Globalization," *Wall Street Journal*, December 1, 1999.
17. *Wall Street Journal*, December 6, 1999.
18. *Die Presse*, November 25, 1999.
19. William Greider, *One World, Ready or Not: The Manic Logic of Global Capitalism* (New York: Simon and Schuster, 1997), p. 39.
20. Ibid., p. 228.

21. Ibid., p. 232.
22. Ibid., pp. 232 and 244.
23. *Newsweek*, October 11, 1997.
24. *Blick durch die Wirtschaft*, June 23, 1998.
25. Greider, p. 216.
26. *New York Times Magazine*, March 28, 1999, p. 61.
27. *The Economist*, November 27, 1999.
28. Roger Burbach, Orlando Nunez, and Boris Kagarlitsky, *Globalization and Its Discontents* (London: Pluto Press, 1997), p. 13.
29. Ibid., p. 75.
30. Cited in *Atlantic Monthly*, February 2, 1994, p. 46.
31. *Frankfurter Allgemeine Zeitung*, January 18, 2000.
32. Greider, p. 75.
33. Burbach et al, p. 14.
34. Michael Milken, "Prosperity and Social Capital," *Wall Street Journal*, June 23, 1999.
35. Cited in *Die Presse*, November 22, 1999.
36. Ibid.
37. Ibid.
38. *Wall Street Journal*, December 6, 1999.
39. Peter F. Drucker, "The Global Economy and the Nation State," *Foreign Affairs* 76, 5.
40. Cited in *Die Presse*, January 29, 2000.
41. Susan Strange, *The Retreat of the State* (New York: Cambridge University Press, 1996).
42. George Soros, *Open Society: Reforming Global Capitalism* (New York: Public Affairs, 2000), p. xi.
43. Ibid, p. xviii.
44. Drucker, p. 162.
45. Robert A. Pastor, ed., *A Century's Journey* (New York: Basic Books, 1999), p. 348.
46. Cited in *Die Presse*, January 29, 2000.
47. *Die Presse*, January 31, 2000.
48. Ibid.
49. Ibid., January 28, 2000.
50. *The World in 2000* (London: *The Economist*, 2000).
51. *Neue Zürcher Zeitung*, January 27, 2000.
52. *Frankfurter Allgemeine Zeitung*, November 16, 1999.
53. *The World in 2000*, p. 2.

Notes to Chapter 2

1. *Die Presse* (Vienna), January 13, 2000.
2. *Der Spiegel* 9 (2000).
3. Ibid., 8 (2000).
4. *Format* (Vienna), no. 48, November 29, 1999.
5. *The World in 2000* (London: *The Economist*, 2000), pp. 75–82.
6. In Saskia Sassen, *Globalization and Its Discontent* (New York: New Press, 1998), p. xiv.

7. William Greider, *One World, Ready or Not: The Manic Logic of Global Capitalism* (New York: Simon and Schuster, 1997), p. 11.
8. George Soros, "The Crisis of Global Capitalism," *Public Affairs*, 1998, p. xxi.
9. Karl Polanyi, *The Great Transformation* (Boston: Beacon Press, 1957), p. 29.
10. Brink Lindsey, "The Invisible Hand vs. the Dead Hand," in *Global Fortune*, ed. Ian Vásquez (Washington, D.C.: Cato Institute, 2001), p. 52.
11. Francis Fukuyama, "The Left Should Love Globalization," *Wall Street Journal*, December 1, 1999.
12. *The Economist*, November 27, 1999.
13. Stephen Moore and Julian Simon, "Twenty-Five Miraculous U.S. Trends of the Past 100 Years," in *Global Fortune*, p. 55.
14. W. Bowman Cutter, Joan Spero, and Laura D'Andrea Tyson, "New World, New Deal," *Foreign Affairs*, March/April 2000.
15. Cited in *Die Presse*, January 28, 2000.
16. Michael Milken in the *Wall Street Journal*, June 23, 1999.
17. Deutsche Bank research, *Ewu Monitor*, no. 82, February 10, 2000.
18. *Salzburger Nachrichten* 12 (2000).
19. Greider, p. 244.
20. Ibid., p. 245.
21. *Der Spiegel* 14 (2000).
22. Greider, p. 281.
23. Ibid., p. 282.
24. Cited in *Süddeutsche Zeitung*, March 21, 2000.
25. Cited in *Sun Sentinel*, April 16, 2000.
26. Daniel Yergin and Joseph Stanislaw, *The Commanding Heights* (New York: Simon and Schuster, 1998), p. 31.
27. Ibid. p. 28.
28. Robert A. Pastor, ed., *A Century's Journey* (New York: Basic Books, 1999), p. 54.
29. *The World in 2000*, pp. 75–79.
30. Josef Joffe, "Germany," in *A Century's Journey.*
31. *Der Spiegel* 15 (2000).
32. Ibid.
33. *The World in 2000*, p. 33.
34. *Der Spiegel* 15 (2000).
35. Ibid., 50 (2000).
36. Ibid., 24 (2000).
37. Thomas F. Remington, "Putin's Agenda," *Brown Journal of World Affairs*, Winter–Spring 2000, p. 136.
38. Cited in *Die Presse*, January 25, 2000.
39. Oleg Bogomolov, director of the Institute of International Economic and Political Studies, Russian Academy of Sciences, interview in *Der Speigel*, 30 (1999).
40. *Frankfurter Allgemeine Zeitung*, November 14, 2000.
41. *New York Times*, June 28, 2000.
42. *Die Presse*, May 29, 2000.
43. *Süddeutsche Zeitung*, May 17, 2000.
44. Sergei Khrushchev, "Economics and Elections in Russia's New Democracy," *Brown Journal of World Affairs*, Winter–Spring 2000, p. 177.

45. Andrei Illarionov, "Russia's Potemkin Capitalism," in *Global Fortune*, p. 193.

46. Ariel Cohen, "Corruption, Western Economic Assistance, and the Future of the Russian Economy," *Brown Journal of World Affairs*, Winter–Spring, p. 158.

47. Ibid., p. 159.

48. Cited in *New York Times*, November 24, 2000.

Notes to Chapter 3

1. *New York Times*, September 19, 1999.
2. According to the UN Population Division; cited in ibid.
3. *New York Times*, January 7, 2000.
4. Ibid., September 19, 1999.
5. Ibid.
6. *India Today 1990*.
7. Cited in *Handelsblatt*, October 29, 1999.
8. *Der Spiegel* 43 (1999).
9. *The Economist*, September 11, 1999.
10. William Greider, *One World, Ready or Not: The Manic Logic of Global Capitalism* (New York: Simon and Schuster, 1997), p. 12.
11. Heinz Kienzl, cited in *Arbeit und Wirtschaft* 4 (1998).
12. Greider, p. 17.
13. Paul Krugman "The Return of Depression Economics," *Foreign Affairs*, January/February 1999, p. 21.
14. Greider, p. 12.
15. *Der Spiegel* 44 (1999).
16. Greider, p. 27.
17. Cited in *Wall Street Journal*, September 27, 1999.
18. *Der Spiegel* 44 (1999).
19. Ralph Dahrendorf, "The Third Way and Liberty," *Foreign Affairs*, October 9, 1999.
20. Quoted in Isolde Charin, "Die Rückehr des Politischen," *Die Presse*, April 22, 1999.
21. *Der Spiegel* 44 (1999).
22. Ibid.
23. *Frankfurter Allgemeine Zeitung*, November 20, 1999.
24. *Der Spiegel* 43 (1999).
25. *The Economist*, December 5, 1998.
26. Ibid.
27. Cited in *Der Spiegel* 49 (1999).
28. *The Economist*, December 5, 1998, p. 200.
29. Ibid., November 13, 1999.
30. Jeffrey D. Sachs, "Life After Communism," *Wall Street Journal*, November 17, 1999.
31. Cited in *Wall Street Journal*, December 4, 1999.
32. *Süddeutsche Zeitung*, May 17, 2000.
33. *Die Presse* (Vienna), November 19, 1999.
34. *Neue Zürcher Zeitung*, November 19, 1999.

35. *Frankfurter Allgemeine Zeitung*, December 1, 1999.
36. Dow Jones News Wire, November 22, 1999.
37. Cited in *Die Presse* November 19, 1999.
38. Cited in *Der Spiegel* 45 (1999).
39. *Der Standard* (Vienna), December 7, 1999.
40. Cited in *Handlesblatt*, September 20, 2000.
41. According to the German Institute in Cologne, as cited in *Frankfurter Allgemeine Zeitung*, November 28, 2000.
42. *Die Presse*, November 22, 2000.

Notes to Chapter 4

1. Cited in *New York Times*, October 18, 1999.
2. Cited in *Wall Street Journal*, April 21, 1999.
3. Ibid., September 27, 1999.
4. Ezra F. Vogel, *The Four Little Dragons* (Cambridge, Mass.: Harvard University Press, 1991).
5. Daniel Yergin and Joseph Stanislaw, *Commanding Heights* (New York: Simon and Schuster, 1998), p. 221.
6. Ibid., p. 224.
7. *Wall Street Journal*, September 27, 1999.
8. William Greider, *One World Ready or Not: The Manic Logic of Global Capitalism* (New York: Simon and Schuster, 1997), pp. 282, 283.
9. Yergin and Stanislaw, p. 235.
10. Ibid.
11. Ibid., p.238.
12. Greider, p. 260.
13. *Der Spiegel* 2 (2000).
14. Klaus Grubelnik, "Vor uns das goldene Zeitalter," *Format* (Vienna), no. 119 (November 29, 1999).
15. Paul Kennedy, "Preparing for the Twenty-First Century," in *Globalization* (Bloomington: Indiana University Press, 2000), p. 324.
16. Cited in *Frankfurter Allegemeine Zeitung*, December 5, 2000.
17. *Neue Zürcher Zeitung*, January 11, 2001.
18. Cited by Kofi Annan, "The Politics of Globalization," in *Globalization*, p.130.
19. Cited in *Sun-Sentinel* (South Florida), January 21, 2001.
20. *New York Times*, January 7, 2001.
21. Ibid.
22. Ibid., January 14, 2001.

Notes to Chapter 5

1. Jeffrey Scott, "Whither U.S.–EU Trade Relations?" In *Transatlantic Economic Relations in the Post–Cold War Era*, ed. Barry Eichengreen. (New York: Council on Foreign Relations, 1998), pp. 36–68.
2. Stefan Collignon, *The World in 1999* (London: *The Economist*), p. 102.
3. *Der Spiegel* 21 (1999).
4. Ibid.

5. *The Economist*, January 2, 1998.
6. Cited in *Wall Street Journal*, June 18, 1999.
7. Cited in *Der Spiegel* 36 (1997).
8. Edward Luttwak, *Turbo-Capitalism* (New York: HarperCollins, 1999), p. 96.
9. Norman Birnbaum,"Meine Qual mit Amerika," *Der Spiegel* 46 (1998).
10. Cited in *Newsweek*, January 5, 1998.
11. Cited in *Foreign Affairs*, September/October 1997.
12. Cited in Daniel J. Boorstin, "A World of New Questions: From 'Why?' to 'How?'" *Wall Street Journal*, June 22, 1999.
13. *Wall Street Journal*, June 23, 1999.
14. Cited in *Foreign Affairs*, November 5, 1997, p. 76.
15. Isaiah Berlin, *Personal Impressions* (Harmondsworth: Penguin Books, 1980), p. 8.
16. Cited in *Foreign Affairs*, September/October 1997, p. 13.
17. Ibid.
18. Ibid., p. 30.
19. Ibid., September/October 1998, p. 63.
20. Cited in *Werkstattblätter* (Vienna: Dr. Karl-Renner Institute), no. 3 (May 1999), p. 43.
21. *Foreign Affairs*, November 18, 1997, p. 15.
22. Cited in *New York Times*, June 12, 1999.

Notes to Chapter 6

1. *Handelsblatt*, July 13, 1999.
2. *New York Times*, August 1, 1999.
3. Interview in *Der Spiegel* 31 (1999).
4. Cited in Susan Dunn, "Teddy Roosevelt Betrayed," *New York Times*, September 8, 1999.
5. *The Economist*, July 31, 1999.
6. Cited in *Frankfurter Allgemeine Zeitung*, June 14, 1999.
7. Ibid., June 8, 1999.
8. *The Economist*, January 2, 1999.
9. *Central Banking* 9, 4 (May 1999).
10. Cited in *New York Times*, July 7, 1999.
11. *Blaetter der Forschungsinstituts für Europafragen* (Vienna), 1999.
12. *Handelsblatt*, March 25, 1999.
13. *Süddeutsche Zeitung*, September 6, 1999.
14. Cited in *International Herald Tribune*, August 23, 1999.
15. *Frankfurter Allgemeine Zeitung*, June 8, 1999.
16. *Arbeit und Wirtschaft* 4 (1998).
17. *Trend* (Vienna) 5 (1998).
18. Cited in *Artikeldienst der Oesterreichischen Nationalbank*, July 29,1999.
19. Paul Krugman, "Who's Afraid of the Euro?" *Fortune*, April 7, 1998.
20. *Handelsblatt*, August 2, 1999.
21. *Wall Street Journal*, September 13, 1999.
22. Cited in *Handelsblatt*, August 28–29, 1999.
23. *The Banker*, August 1999, and *Artikeldienst der Österreichischen Nationalbank*, September 3, 1999.
24. *The Banker*, August 1999.

Notes to Chapter 7

1. Melitta Aschauer, "Erweiterung und Vertiefung der EU," *Zukunftswerkstätte* (Vienna), May 1999.
2. *Wirtschaftsblatt* (Vienna), September 2, 1998.
3. *Die Presse* (Vienna), June 25, 1999.
4. Ibid.
5. *Wall Street Journal for Europe*, January 1998
6. *New York Times*, *Global Review*, April 20, 1999.
7. *New York Times*, April 20, 1999.
8. *Wall Street Journal for Europe*, January 1998.
9. *Wprost* (Warsaw), 1998.
10. *Der Spiegel* 30 (2000).
11. *The Economist*, March 13, 1999.
12. Ibid., August 1, 1999.
13. *Wall Street Journal*, September 27, 1998.
14. *Handelsblatt*, September 20, 1999.
15. *Der Standard* (Vienna), September 22, 1999.

Notes to Chapter 8

1. Cited in *Foreign Affairs*, September/October 1997, p. 65.
2. Cited in *New York Review of Books*, August 12, 1999.
3. *The Economist*, November 21, 1999.
4. Paul Kubicek, "End of the Line for the Commonwealth of Independent States," *Problems of Post-Communism* 46, 3/4.
5. *Handelsblatt*, September 27,1999.
6. Economic Commission for Europe, *Economic Survey of Europe 1995 and 1996.*
7. *Economic Bulletin for Europe* 49.
8. Martha Brill Olcott, "Central Asia: The Calculus of Independence," *Current History*, October 1995, pp. 337–342.
9. Kubicek, p. 21.
10. Cited in *Die Presse*, May 22, 2000.
11. Kubicek, p. 22.
12. *Der Spiegel*, September 20, 1999.
13. *The Economist*, November 21, 1999.
14. Cited in *Foreign Affairs*, September/October 1999.
15. Cited in *The Economist*, November 21, 1998.
16. Cited in *Die Presse*, June 20, 2000.
17. Ibid., June 21, 2000.

Notes to Chapter 9

1. *Frankfurter Allgemeine Zeitung*, December 15, 1999.
2. Cited in ibid.
3. *Handelsblatt*, March 23, 2000.
4. *New York Times*, April 16, 2000.

5. Cited in ibid.

6. "Reform of the IMF—Conservative and Cautions," *Frankfurter Allgemeine Zeitung*, April 10, 2000.

7. *Frankfurter Allgemeine Zeitung*, April 14, 2000.

8. Ibid.

9. *Handelsblatt*, April 18, 2000.

10. Ibid.

11. Ibid.

12. Cited in *Der Spiegel* 14 (2000).

13. Cited in *Die Presse* (Vienna), April 14, 2000.

14. Cited in *Sun-Sentinel* (South Florida) April 19, 2000.

15. *Wall Street Journal*, April 14, 2000.

16. Ibid., April 17, 2000.

17. Cited in *Handelsblatt*, June 21, 2000.

18. *New York Times*, July 3, 2000.

19. Robert Gilpin, *The Challenge of Global Capitalism* (Princeton: Princeton University Press, 2000).

20. Ibid., p. 336.

21. Ibid., p. 160.

22. "The European Decade," *Der Spiegel* 18 (2000).

23. See *Die Presse*, January 29, 2000.

24. *Financial Times*, March 29, 2000.

25. Klaus Grubelnik, "Vor uns das goldene Zeitalter," *Format* (Vienna), no. 119 (November 29, 1999), p. 93.

26. Cited in *Die Presse*, January 29, 2000.

27. *Der Spiegel* 19 (2000).

Index

F

G

H

M

N

O

P

About the Author

Adam Zwass (1913–2001) for many years held senior positions in the central banking systems of Poland and the USSR. From 1963 to 1968 he was Councillor in the Secretariat of the Council of Mutual Economic Assistance (CMEA) in Moscow, where he was responsible for financial settlements and the work of the International Bank for Economic Cooperation.

After his emigration to Vienna, Austria, Dr. Zwass was affiliated for over twenty years with Austrian and German research institutes and served as an adviser to the Austrian National Bank and major private banks. He published his analyses of socioeconomic developments in the globalizing world in several European journals and newspapers.

Dr. Zwass was the author of ten previous books, translated into several languages, and of hundreds of articles published in Europe and the United States. His most recent books in English are *Incomplete Revolutions: The Successes and Failures of Capitalist Transition Strategies in Post-Communist Economies* (1999), *From Failed Communism to Underdeveloped Capitalism* (1995), and *Council for Mutual Economic Assistance* (1989).